The Charmed Kitchen

Cooking with
Herbs & Spices

by
Judi Strauss

The Charmed Kitchen
Cooking with Herbs & Spices

Second Edition

by
Judi Strauss

ISBN - 9781626130456
Library of Congress Control Number - 2014959348

Published by ATBOSH Media ltd.
Cleveland, Ohio, USA

www.atbosh.com

Table of Contents

1 Getting Started: How to Use This Book   5

2 An Alphabetical Listing of Herbs and Spices   7

3 Which Herbs and Spices Do I Use With?   27

4 Herb Blends   33

5 Appetizers and Snacks   47

6 Soups   73

7 Salads and Dressings   99

8 Main Dishes   141

9 Vegetables, Pasta & Other Side Dishes   255

10 Breads   303

11 Beverages and Teas   337

12 Desserts and Sweets   355

13 Sauces, Condiments, and Etc.   371

14 Herb Vinegars   401

15 Buying and Storing Herbs and Spices   405

16 Preservation   409

About the Author   419

Chapter 1
Getting Started:
How to Use This Book

If your idea of cooking with herbs and spices has been to use a sprinkling of parsley now and then, or maybe a dash of seasoned salt now is the time to expand your horizons. Cooking.... really cooking.... with herbs and spices makes an ordinary dish extraordinary. I am a person who grows herbs and cooks with them and I am always trying new combinations to add interest to my dishes. Through the years I have found few limits to the ways I can use herbs and spices in the kitchen. As an added bonus I find that, without sacrificing taste, I don't need to use as much salt.

So if herbs and spices are so useful, why don't people use more of them when they cook? In my classes many of my students have expressed a certain "fear" of herbs. They find using herbs as intimidating as choosing the right wine to go with dinner.

I hope that if I accomplish one thing with this book it is to change that fear into action and use. In order to overcome this fear all you need a sense of adventure and some fresh, frozen or dried herbs and spices. There are "use charts" in this book to assist you in choosing which herbs to use with which foods but don't be limited by what any chart says, including mine. If you discover an herb whose flavor you prefer I urge you to try it on different dishes. Experiment! Live dangerously!

Begin with herbs you are familiar with and then branch out to unfamiliar herbs. After some practice you'll find that using herbs and spices is as natural as adding salt and pepper. Once you learn the taste of different herbs and spices you will discover your likes and dislikes. Along the way you are sure to find some new favorites.

An experienced cook knows how to use a light hand with herbs. You don't want to overpower your food. You are trying to enhance taste through the addition of new flavors, a layering of flavors. Vary recipes to your preferences and don't limit yourself. One of the hardest parts of writing this book was measuring as I cooked so I could write my recipes to standards that anyone could follow. Truth be known I rarely follow recipes exactly. That is just the way I cook. As you work with this book open yourself up to new and creative tastes and have a good time!

Chapter 2
An Alphabetical Listing of Herbs and Spices

This listing is meant to serve as a guide to using specific herbs and spices when you cook. This does not mean that you should feel limited to only what is listed here. Over centuries of use certain herbs and spices just seem to pair up well with certain foods.

Allspice This is one of the most popular spices used in American kitchens today in baking, particularly in apple and pumpkin pies. Allspice tastes like a combination of cinnamon, cloves and nutmeg. It goes well with beef dishes, particularly stews, and is sometimes used in vegetable dishes. Allspice is great with tomato dishes and in pickling. It is also used widely in the cuisines of the Middle East, North Africa and Asia.

Anise Anise has the taste of licorice. It is used in baking, mostly for cookies. Anise seeds can also be used in place of fennel seeds in dishes such as Italian sausages and spaghetti sauce. Anise seeds are used to flavor the liqueur Anisette. A few anise seeds can be ground up with coffee beans or added to ground coffee to make licorice-flavored coffee.

Basil Just about any main dish is improved with the addition of basil. It is the essential ingredient in classic pesto sauce. Basil is a sweet-flavored herb used widely in Italian cuisine. It complements the flavor of tomato dishes and well as other vegetables. It goes well with beef and chicken dishes and in soups and salad dressings.

The large-leaf variety can be used almost like a lettuce wrap, delicately wrapped around a filling. Basil comes in a wide assortment of varieties and flavors. There is lemon basil, which is great with chicken and seafood and even in tea. Cinnamon basil works well with Indian and other Asian cuisines. Cinnamon basil is wonderful with meat dishes. Thai basil, as expected is used with Asian dishes-but can be used in everything from salad dressing to red sauces.

Bay Leaf Also called Sweet Bay. The flavor of bay leaf is a combination of both sweet and a little spicy. It is most often added to soup, especially chicken soup. It goes well with a wide array of foods including meats, fishes and vegetables. Bay is often used in pickles. It also goes well with recipes using dried beans, like baked beans or bean soups. When you toss that bay leaf into the pot be sure to fish it out later! Bay leaf stays tough and someone could choke on it. Bay leaves can also be tied into cheesecloth or put in a tea ball with other herbs and spices for easier removal later.

Bergamot Also known as bee balm and Monarda, this member of the mint family has a light orange flavor and is used in herb teas and fruit salads. Petals of the flowers are also edible and make a decorative addition to salads, dips and pasta dishes.

Borage Leaves taste like cucumber and can be eaten in salads. Older leaves get tough, so use young leaves. Borage flowers are blue, pink or lavender and are edible. They make a pretty addition to salads, soups or most any food.

Caraway Probably best known as an addition to rye bread. Caraway seeds can also be used on crackers, blended into cheeses, with sauerkraut and with carrots and potatoes. The seeds are also used to flavor the liqueur Akavit. According to tradition, it is drunk, ice cold, at midnight on New Year's Eve for good luck in the New Year.

Cardamom Seeds are ground into a powder used to flavor breads, cakes cookies and other baked goods. Cardamom has a rich sweet flavor and fragrance used by Scandinavians. Cardamom is more expensive than most other spices. To keep it longer store in the fridge or freezer. As with other spices, buying the seed pods and grinding your own will result in stronger flavor than pre-ground. Cardamom also adds a nice flavor to frostings and glazes. Also used to flavor coffee.

Cayenne Pepper Cayenne, commonly referred to as red pepper, is not a peppercorn in the way that black pepper is a peppercorn "bud". Cayenne is the dried seeds and fruit of a variety of vegetable pepper. This is a very hot seasoning used in many cuisines. It is essential in Cajun and Creole cooking. It is hotter than black pepper so use with caution. It also used widely in Italian and Mexican cooking. Like other red spices cayenne pepper should be stored in the refrigerator to retain its flavor.

Celery Leaves Dried or fresh celery leaves add a

wonderful flavor to soups stocks and stews. Also makes a nice addition to salad dressings and vegetable dips. Add to marinades for meat or fish. Fresh leaves can be chopped and added to salads. (See also Lovage)

Celery Seeds Pungent tasty seeds are used to flavor salads, salad dressings, vegetable dishes, fish, dips, soups and stews. These seeds taste particularly good with tomatoes and in cabbage dishes. They make a nice addition to coleslaw or sweet and sour cabbage. (See also Lovage)

Chamomile Flowers from this herb are used to make a soothing herbal teas. They can be used fresh or dried. Flowers can also be used to decorate a salad plate, dips or fruit plates.

Chervil Chervil is sometimes called French parsley. Used like parsley, but chervil is more pungent. The spicier flavor is very appealing. Chervil does not hold its flavor when dried, however, and is best used fresh or frozen. It does not require a lot of sunlight, so you can grow a pot on most any windowsill. Chervil definitely deserves more attention in our kitchens. Use in soups, stews and salad dressings. Goes very well with poultry.

Chili Powder Most chili powder is spicy but not really hot. There is a wide assortment of chili powders out there and some do pack some heat. Generally though, you should think of it as warm rather than hot. Chili powder is simply ground up chili peppers mixed with small amounts of other seasonings. These can include cumin, garlic and even a little oregano. It is used to flavor the dish of the same name. It tastes good in meat and chicken dishes and is added to barbecue sauces. It also adds zip to dry beans. Chili powder is also used in Mexican dishes. It is a red seasoning and should be kept refrigerated.

Chives Chives have a mild onion flavor and can be used in vegetable dishes, with meats, poultry, soups and salads. Chives are also used in egg dishes and they make a pretty and tasty garnish to most any dish. Blossoms can be steeped in vinegar to flavor. Blossoms are also edible and can dress up a salad plate or a party tray of vegetables.

Cilantro Pungent leaves are used in Hispanic and Asian cuisines. While the leaves look like parsley the flavor is quite different. Excellent with poultry dishes, sauces, seafood and meats. Some people find the odor of cilantro when cooking unpleasant. It does taste different than the way it smells. Cilantro is a great garnish for soups and salads. It also adds a zip to casseroles and stews. Cilantro does not hold its flavor when dried, use it fresh or frozen. See also Coriander.

Cinnamon A versatile spice, cinnamon is actually tree bark. It can be purchased already ground or in stick form for grinding as needed. The flavor is best when freshly ground. Cinnamon goes with many flavors although in western culture it is used mainly in apple dishes, baked goods, pumpkin dishes and in cider. Much of the world uses cinnamon in meat dishes routinely. The taste of cinnamon is complimentary to meat and poultry dishes as well as rice and bean dishes. It is good with fruits, salads dressings and sauces. I always add a little cinnamon to my chili.

Cloves This spice is used in both main dishes and desserts. Sometimes used to stud ham and pork roasts, it is also used in pickling, especially fruits, in baked goods, and in Indian cuisine. Sometimes whole cloves are stuck in an onion to add flavor to soup stocks and stews. Also adds good flavor to bean dishes and gravies. Cloves can also spice up a mug of cider and it makes a tasty addition to herb tea. Whole cloves are sometimes stuck in oranges, apples, pears, and other citrus fruit, then rolled in ground cinnamon and allowed to dry. These pomanders make a fragrant addition to a holiday centerpiece, or can be strung as ornaments or hung in closets.

Coriander Coriander is the seed from cilantro. Used in many Asian cultures, the taste is a little like lemon and sage. The seeds are usually ground before use. The seeds are used in poultry dishes, soups, sauces and sometimes in baked goods. Also makes a nice touch in dressings and pickles.

Cumin Cumin is the seed of a relative of parsley. It has a strong fragrance that is used widely in Hispanic cooking. Wonderful in chili, cumin is also tasty with poultry and meat dishes. It goes well in soups and stews and is also used in pickles and sausages. Cumin can also be used with vegetable dishes and makes a flavorful addition to cornbread. Seeds can be used whole or ground.

Curry Powder Curry powder is actually a combination of several herbs and spices. As personal tastes differ, so do curries. They can be fairly mild to fiery hot. When using curry powder for the first time use a light hand until you determine the heat of the curry powder you are using. Curry powder may contain all or most of the following: cumin, coriander, cinnamon, cayenne pepper, black pepper, nutmeg, turmeric, salt and allspice. Curry powder is used in sauces, meat and poultry, vegetable dishes, seafood and for curried eggs.

Dill Seed These flavorful seeds are used in pickles and with salad dressings. It also tastes good with potato dishes and with cabbage. They can also be used in salads and pasta dishes. Also is used in soups and in egg dishes.

Dill Weed Dill weed refers to the fresh or dried leaves of the dill plant. Dill goes well with vegetables, particularly carrots, cucumbers, cabbage and potatoes. It adds a good flavor to salad dressings and dips, especially spinach dip. Dill weed also goes well with chicken and fish. It can be used in marinades or placed directly on the coals when grilling fish or chicken. Dill can also be used with meats and, of course, in pickles.

Fennel Seeds Fennel seeds have a licorice flavor

and are essential to Italian sausage. The seeds are also good in tomato sauces and pasta dishes. They can be used as a substitute for anise seeds or for caraway seeds in rye bread. They also add a nice taste to pizza sauce. Fennel seeds can be used in other breads and are sometimes used in pickles. They are also used in apple pie. Seeds can be used whole or ground, but should be ground as used to retain flavor. The leaves of fennel go well with fish dishes and can be used in marinades, or like fresh dill weed, can be thrown directly on the coals when grilling. This plant should not be confused with Florence fennel, which is grown for its swollen stems. The stems are used as a vegetable eaten raw in salads or cooked in soups and stews. Both plants produce edible leaves and seeds, but fennel will come back each year and Florence fennel dies after the stem is harvested.

Fenugreek This seed has a flavor similar to maple syrup. Fenugreek is used in curries and other Indian dishes. The seeds can be crushed or used whole. They go well with meat dishes, poultry, rice dishes and soups. Seeds can also be boiled in sugar syrup for a mock maple syrup.

Garlic Whole books have been written to extol the virtues of this lovely herb. Garlic is used in sauces, soups, meats, poultry and fish dishes. Also used with vegetables, butter and in pickles. Garlic also tastes good in bean dishes. Garlic cloves can be roasted whole and then the squeezed out of their skins and spread on Italian bread. It can be used fresh, dried, diced and powdered. How garlic in prepared affects its flavor. Roasted whole cloves have a sweet, mellow flavor, where sautéed garlic and raw garlic will have a stronger flavor. When sautéing garlic be careful not to let it burn. Garlic that burns will take on a bitter flavor. If you grow your own garlic, do try the greens. The tender leaves of the garlic plant add a wonderful taste to salad dressings, sauces and marinades. Garlic is also reported to repel vampires!

Garlic Chives The spicy leaves of this herb can be used anywhere you would use garlic. The tender greens can be used raw or cooked. Use with meats, poultry, seafood, sauces, dips and salad dressings. Can be chopped and sprinkled on food as you would chives; however the flavor is stronger than chives.

Ginger, or Ginger root Ginger is sometimes called ginger root because it is the part of the plant that we use. Ginger can be used fresh or dried and powdered. Fresh ginger tastes much better and should be used whenever possible. The problem is that fresh ginger root may spoil before you can use it. The easy solution is to store the root in the freezer. When you want to use it, just take it out of the freezer, remove peel from the portion you'll need and grate what you need for your recipe. Don't let it thaw out, though. That will make it turn to mush and be pretty much useless. Ginger is used in Asian dishes, fruit spreads and chutneys. It is used in baking, notably gingerbread and in pumpkin and apple pies. Ginger is sometimes used in pickles and in pot roasts. Ginger is what gives sauerbraten its distinctive flavor. Ginger has a flavor that is both spicy and sweet making it a very versatile seasoning. Ginger is said to aid in digestion so it goes well with spicy foods and of course is used to make real ginger ale.

Lavender Blossoms and leaves of English lavender can be added to marinades for lamb, chicken or pork. It has a distinctive spicy taste and has to be used with a light hand. Try using lavender to dress up a salad and in baked goods. Lavender also can be added to beef dishes, sauces and soups. It is also used in the French seasoning Herbs de Provence. I use the blossoms to flavor vinegar.

Lemon Balm / Lemon Mint These close
relatives (both mints) share a light, lemony fragrance and flavor. They make wonderful tea herbs and can also be used with chicken and fish dishes. They work well in salad dressings and marinades. Lemon balm loses most of its flavor when dried so always use fresh or frozen. Lemon mint holds up somewhat better to drying. Both can also be boiled in sugar syrup and then strained to make a light flavored sweetener for tea.

Lemon Grass This herb is native to the Far East and
is used largely is Asian cuisine. The outer parts are very tough but can be stripped away to reveal the more tender inner stems. The stems of this grass are added to soup stocks for flavor and are chopped and added to stir-fries. Like lemon balm and lemon mint, the stems of this plant can be boiled in a sugar syrup to make a lemon flavored syrup. The syrup can also be mixed with club soda and poured over ice for a light summer beverage. Stems can also be used fresh or dried as a tea herb.

Lemon Peel Lemon peel is used in sauces, desserts
and fish dishes. It can also be used with chicken in marinades and glazes. Sometimes also referred to as lemon zest, only the yellow part of the peel is used. The white part of the peel tastes bitter. A zester can be used to remove the peel from a fresh lemon, or you can use a sharp knife. The zest can be used fresh or allowed to air dry. Dry pieces can easily be powdered in a blender, processor or coffee mill. Although it can be stored at room temperature, the powdered lemon peel will hold its flavor much longer if refrigerated or frozen. The same thing can be done with other citrus peel like oranges, limes and tangerines. You can also freeze fresh zest for use later on.

Lemon Thyme As the name implies this thyme plant has a light, lemony flavor. It can be used with chicken and fish dishes and makes a nice addition to salad dressings and marinades. This herb also takes great in vegetables dishes and soups. This aromatic flavoring also pairs up well with any shellfish, especially shrimp and clams.

Mace This spice is pungent and sweet. Often used with nutmeg. Mace is used in spice cakes, pies and other sweets. Mace is actually the outer shell of nutmeg, ground into a fine powder. Mace goes well with apples and pears. (See Nutmeg)

Marjoram Widely useful herb closely related to oregano. Marjoram is used in meat and poultry dishes and in soups and stews. Marjoram also goes well with all vegetables, but particularly with beans including green beans, limas and dry beans. It is also used in stuffings, sausages and compliments lamb. Marjoram also goes well in egg dishes.

Mint There is a wide assortment of mints to choose from when cooking. Mints are used for herb teas, but also go well with vegetable dishes, especially peas. Mint also goes well with lamb and chicken dishes and in salad dressings, sauces and marinades. Used to make mint jelly it is a must in Middle East cuisine including the wheat dish, tabbouleh. Mint leaves are also a vital ingredient in mint juleps.

Nasturtium Leaves of this plant are peppery tasting and can be used as a substitute for watercress. They can be chopped fine and added to salads, sandwiches and dips. The flowers are edible and can be used to decorate salads, soups, fruit plates and vegetable platters.

Mustard, Dry Sometimes called ground mustard, it can improve the flavor of meat and poultry dishes. Also goes well with fish dishes and in salad dressings. Add to deviled eggs or egg salad for some extra tang. Mustard can also be added to cheese sauces and baked beans. It is also used to make homemade mustard.

Mustard Seeds Can be ground and used as dry mustard. These seeds have some bite. Used whole in meat and poultry dishes, they can also be sprinkled in potato or pasta salads. Used also in salad dressings and in many pickles. Mustard seeds are also used in mayonnaise and with seafood.

Nutmeg Sweet, aromatic and versatile, nutmeg is used widely in baking. The taste works well in quick breads, custards and pies. Nutmeg really goes well with either apples or pumpkin. Nutmeg is also grated into beverages like eggnog and hot chocolate. Nutmeg goes with many vegetables and is also used in some meat dishes. Although available ground, nutmeg should really be bought whole and ground or grated as needed. The flavor of freshly ground nutmeg is light years ahead of already ground. You can get a nutmeg grater as most cookware stores. Or you can grate it on the smallest size holes of a cheese grater.

Orange Peel Orange peel or orange zest can be added to cakes, cookies, breads, and other baked goods. It can also be added to beef, chicken, and duck recipes. Orange peel adds a nice taste to barbecue sauces, fruit sauces, and salad dressings. When added to sweet and sour sauce, it makes a nice accompaniment for roast duck. Using the peel in dishes with orange juice will intensify the flavor of the juice. As with lemon peel, use only the colored part of the orange peel. The white part of the peel will make your food bitter. The peel can be used fresh or dried in strips or grated. Air-dried peel can be powdered in a blender or grinder. The powdered peel can be stored at room temperature. For a longer shelf life, store orange or other citrus peel in the refrigerator or freezer.

Oregano Oregano is a spicy herb used in many Italian dishes and sauces. It is also used in many Mexican dishes. Its strong flavor needs a light hand. Oregano goes well with any tomato-based dish. It also enhances the flavor of meat dishes, poultry, soups and stews. Oregano is a must for pizza sauce or Italian salad dressing.

Paprika Paprika is dried and powdered red peppers. Paprika peppers are not usually hot, but they can be! The mild bite and rich, sweet flavor of paprika is used in vegetable dishes and pasta salads. Paprika is also used in potato salads or deviled eggs. Paprika goes well with chicken and meat dishes, and of course is used for Chicken Paprikash. Paprika can be decorative, or flavorful, in soups and stews, egg dishes, or dusted over fish. Paprika is also a common ingredient in pork and beans, in salad dressings and marinades. Like all red spices, paprika should be stored in the refrigerator to retain freshness.

Parsley Parsley is almost certainly the most widely used herb in America. Its mild flavor enhances most food. Parsley is used in meat dishes, with poultry, fish, in soups and stews, with vegetables, and in dressings. Fresh parsley is certainly preferred, but it does hold flavor well when dried. There are several types of parsley. When buying it fresh, the flat-leaved variety produces a stronger flavor. There is also a specific variety of parsley that is grown for the large taproot it produces. The root is used to flavor soup stocks. Not only high in Vitamin C, parsley is high in chlorophyll, and chewing it will freshen your breath. That is where the tradition of placing a sprig of parsley on a dinner plate to freshen one's breath after eating got started.

Pepper, Black, White, or Green Pepper is very spicy, with white more mild in flavor than black. All true peppercorns are the flower bud from a tropical plant. Black pepper bears the husk intact. Green peppercorns are immature buds. The husk is removed from white peppercorns. Pepper is adaptable to most any food. Peppercorns can be mixed, and ground fresh in a pepper mill for better flavor. Use pepper with meats, poultry, fish, vegetables and dressings. Pepper also adds spice to beans, pasta dishes and to pickles. Pepper, Red (see Cayenne)

Peppercorn, Pink Not really a peppercorn at all, pink peppercorns are a sweet plant bud from Madagascar. Their mild flavor is palatable enough to be consumed whole. Pink peppercorns are softer than white, black, red, or green peppercorns ... too soft to be ground alone in a pepper mill ... and thus they are usually mixed with other peppercorns for use in grinders. Pink peppercorns are much more expensive than the other peppers.

Pineapple Sage Mild, pineapple-flavored sage leaves are used in herb teas and in fruit salads. Use pineapple sage in lemonade, iced tea, and fruit juices. Pineapple sage is tasty in marinades, especially for pork, chicken and seafood. Also use pineapple sage in salad dressings and sauce.

Poppy Seed This nutty-flavored seed is used widely in baking. Sprinkled on top of breads and rolls, poppy seed is also used in some cakes and muffins. The crushed, cooked seeds become a popular filling in assorted pastries.

Rosemary Rosemary is sweet, pungent, and spicy. This strong-flavored herb should be used sparingly to avoid overpowering a dish. Rosemary is really great with lamb, pork, or chicken. It can also be used on roasts, in soups, stews, and potato dishes. Rosemary stands up well to strong vegetable flavors, like turnip, cauliflower, and kale. Rosemary can be used to flavor jellies or infused to flavor tea.

Saffron Saffron holds the distinction of being the most expensive herb in the world. Harvesting saffron from the flowers of a fall-blooming crocus is a time consuming task, and keeps this flavorful seasoning highly prized and high-priced. Aromatic saffron adds rich flavor to chicken dishes, soups, rice dishes, and some curries. Saffron in rolls and breads colors food a bright, telltale yellow. To lower preparation costs, sometimes turmeric is substituted for saffron as a yellowing agent. However, the flavor is not the same. An economical solution for your kitchen might be to add a little turmeric when using saffron just to heighten the color. Edible marigold petals are also sometimes used to give foods saffron yellow color. And there is an herb, marketed as "American saffron", that is not saffron at all, but dried petals from the safflower. While it looks like saffron, the flavor is inferior.

Sage Like rosemary, sage has strong flavor, and can overpower a dish if used too liberally. Traditionally used in poultry stuffing, sage is also used with meats, stews, and soups. It is also used with shellfish and other seafood. Sage is also sometimes used with cottage cheese, and in dips, in poultry seasoning, sausages, and with any wild game, especially venison.

Salad Burnet Salad burnet leaves are used in salads, dressings, and dips. With a taste similar to cucumber, salad burnet can also be used to decorate a plate as a garnish.

Savory Sometimes called "the bean herb" because it goes very well with dry beans, savory also adds a sweet and mellow flavor to chicken and beef dishes. It goes with almost any meat or fish. Savory tastes good in salad dressings and sauces. The flavor compliments soups and stews, and adds a wonderful richness to tomato dishes. The flavor is similar to thyme.

Sorrel Sorrel leaves have a lemony taste. Used raw, young sorrel leaves can be added to soups and sauces, egg or pasta dishes. Because sorrel leaves are high in oxalic acid, they should be eaten in moderation. Or, the leaves can be blanched and rinsed to reduce the oxalic acid.

Tarragon Tarragon has a sweet, almost anise flavor. It is used a lot in French cuisine. It goes well with chicken dishes, and in soups or salads. Tarragon is used in sauces, or with vegetables or fish and to flavor vinegar.

Thyme Thyme is very versatile. It goes well with everything from beef and chicken, to clams and tomatoes. Use a pinch of thyme in salad dressings, vegetable dishes, soups, and stews. Though fresh thyme is certainly preferred, thyme does hold up well to drying.

Turmeric Turmeric tastes a little like mustard. Turmeric adds yellow color, and is sometimes used as a substitute for saffron. Turmeric is added to curries, rice dishes, and breads, and sometimes is used to prepare pickles and relishes. It is used widely in Asian cuisine.

Vanilla The vanilla "bean" is actually the seedpod of an orchid. The extract is used to flavor sweets, cakes, cookies, and syrups. You can make your own vanilla extract by steeping a vanilla bean in vodka or bourbon for several weeks.

Chapter 2: Herbs & Spices

Chapter 3
Which Herbs and Spices Do I Use With....?

I think it is helpful to look at a situation from both sides. To ease your selection, in this book I have provided a listing of herbs and spices, and their common uses. Now I am also including the following list of foods, followed by the herbs and spices that are commonly used with each food. This way, when you are sitting in your kitchen with a piece of chicken, rather than searching the fine print in the herb and spice chapter to find where chicken might be listed, in the listing below you can easily look up chicken. As I cautioned in Chapter 2, this is not a complete list because there are no absolutes. If you prefer a certain combination of herbs and foods, it is sensible to please your own taste.

Beans (dried) Basil; cumin; cayenne; chili powder; garam masala; onion; oregano; sage; savory; thyme; vegetable herb blends.

Beef Basil; bay; chili powder; cilantro; cumin; garlic; ginger; marjoram; mustard; oregano; parsley; pepper; rosemary; sage; savory; tarragon; thyme.

Breads Anise; basil; caraway seed; cardamom; cinnamon; coriander; cumin; dill; garlic; lemon peel; marjoram; onion; orange peel; oregano; poppy seed; rosemary; saffron; sage; sesame seed; thyme.

Cheese and Dairy Basil; caraway seed;

celery seed; chervil; chili peppers; chives; coriander; cumin; curry; dill; garlic; lemon peel; marjoram; mint; mustard; nutmeg; paprika; parsley; pepper; sage; tarragon; thyme.

Chicken and Poultry
Allspice; basil; bay; celery leaves; cinnamon; curry; dill; garlic; ginger; lavender; lemongrass; lemon peel; lovage; orange peel; paprika; parsley; pepper; pineapple sage; rosemary; saffron; sage; tarragon.

Eggs
Basil; celery seeds; chervil; chili peppers; chili powder; chives; curry; dill; fennel; ginger; lemon peel; lovage; marjoram; oregano; paprika; parsley; pepper; sage; tarragon; thyme.

Fish and Seafood
Basil; bay; chives; curry; dill; fennel; garlic; ginger; mustard; oregano; parsley; savory; tarragon.

Fruit
Allspice; anise; cardamom; celery seed; cinnamon; cloves; coriander; ginger; lavender; mint; nutmeg; pineapple sage.

Lamb
Basil; bay; chervil; cinnamon; coriander; cumin; curry; dill; garlic; mint; parsley; pepper; rosemary; savory; tarragon; thyme.

Pork
Caraway seed; cilantro; cloves; cumin; fennel; garam masala; ginger; oregano; paprika; parsley; pepper; pineapple sage; rosemary; sage; savory.

Salad Dressings
Basil; celery seed; chives;

cilantro; dill; fennel; garlic; lovage; marjoram; mustard; oregano; paprika; pepper; rosemary; saffron; tarragon; thyme.

Soups Basil; bay; chervil; chili peppers; chili powder; chives; cumin; dill; fennel; garlic; marjoram; oregano; parsley; pepper; rosemary; sage; savory; thyme.

Sweets and Desserts Allspice; anise; cardamom; cinnamon; cloves; fennel; lavender; lemon peel; ginger; mace; mint; nutmeg; orange peel; pineapple sage; rosemary.

Vegetables

Asparagus-Dill; mint; mustard seed; parsley; rosemary; sesame seed; tarragon.

Beans, Lima-Basil; cilantro; marjoram; oregano; sage; savory; tarragon; thyme.

Beans, snap-Basil; chili powder; cilantro; cumin; dill; marjoram; mint; mustard seed; oregano; parsley; savory; tarragon; thyme.

Beets-Allspice; bay leaves; caraway seed; chives; cloves; dill; ginger; mustard seed; savory; thyme.

Broccoli-Basil; chives; cumin; dill; marjoram; mustard seed; oregano; tarragon; thyme.

Brussels sprouts-Basil; caraway seed; chervil; chives; dill; mustard seed; parsley; oregano; sage; thyme.

Cabbage-Allspice; caraway seed; celery leaves; celery seed; chervil; chives; dill; lovage; mint; marjoram; mustard seed; nutmeg; oregano; parsley; savory; tarragon.

Carrots-Allspice; basil; bay leaves; caraway seed; chervil; chives; cilantro; dill; fennel; ginger; mace; marjoram; mint; oregano; parsley; savory; thyme.

Cauliflower-Caraway seed; celery seed; chives; dill; mace; marjoram; parsley; oregano; tarragon; thyme.

Collards-Chives; dill; marjoram; oregano; paprika; parsley; sage; savory; thyme.

Corn-Basil; chili powder; chives; cilantro; cumin; dill; lovage; marjoram; oregano; paprika; parsley; rosemary; savory; thyme.

Cucumbers-Basil; chives; dill; lovage; mint; parsley; tarragon; thyme.

Eggplant-Basil; chervil; chives; cilantro; cumin; curry; fennel; lovage; marjoram; oregano; parsley; rosemary; savory; thyme.

Kale-Basil; chervil; chives; cumin; dill; parsley; oregano; sage; thyme.

Leeks-Basil; chervil; chives; cilantro; cumin; dill; fennel; marjoram; oregano; parsley; rosemary; sage; tarragon; thyme.

Mustard greens-Basil; chives; cilantro; cumin; marjoram; mint; oregano; parsley; savory; thyme.

Okra-Basil; chervil; chives; chili powder; cilantro; cumin; dill; parsley; sage; tarragon; thyme.

Onions-Basil; caraway seed; celery seed; celery leaves; dill; mustard seed; nutmeg; oregano; parsley; sage; savory; thyme.

Peas-Basil; chervil; chives; cilantro; dill; ginger; marjoram; mint; oregano; parsley; rosemary; savory; thyme.

Peppers-Basil; chives; cumin; fennel; marjoram; oregano; parsley; savory; thyme.

Potatoes-Basil; bay leaves; caraway seed; celery leaves; celery seed; chervil; chili powder; chives; cumin; dill; lovage; mustard seed; marjoram; oregano; parsley; rosemary; sage; tarragon; thyme.

Spinach-Basil; chives; dill; marjoram; oregano; parsley; thyme.

Squash, summer-Basil; chives; chervil; dill; fennel; lovage; marjoram; oregano; parsley; savory; thyme.

Squash, winter-Allspice; chives; cinnamon; cloves; cumin; fennel; ginger; nutmeg; parsley; rosemary; sage; savory; tarragon; thyme.

Sweet Potatoes-Allspice; cardamom; caraway seed; chives; cinnamon; cloves; fennel; ginger; mace; marjoram; nutmeg; parsley; savory; thyme.

Tomatoes-Basil; bay leaf; celery leaves; celery seed; chervil; chili powder; chives; cilantro; cumin; dill; fennel; lovage; marjoram; oregano; parsley; rosemary; sage; savory; tarragon; thyme.

Chapter 4
Herb Blends

Apple Pie Spice
Bouquet Garni
Cajun Seasoning
Garam Masala
Chili Powder
Creole Seasoning
Creole Seafood Seasoning
Curry Powder 1
Curry Powder 2
Everyday Herb Blend 1
Everyday Herb Blend 2
Five Spice Powder
Fines Herbs
Herbes de Provence
Italian Seasoning
Pickling Spice
Pizza Seasoning
Poultry Seasoning
Pumpkin Pie Spice
Salad & Vegetable Seasoning
Seafood Seasoning
Tuscan Seasoning

Sometimes it's more convenient to use premixed blends to save time when cooking. You can buy herb and spice combinations already mixed; however, many store bought blends contain a lot of salt. The advantage of making your own is that you can change the proportions to suit your own taste, adding and deleting ingredients. If the herbs have been combined in a blender they will hold their flavor better if refrigerated.

Apple Pie Spice

½ c. cinnamon
2 T. nutmeg
1 T. ground allspice
1 ½ t. ground cloves
1 t. ground ginger
½ t. ground mace (optional)

Combine all ingredients in a blender. Store in a cool, dry place.

Bouquet Garni

Basil Leaves
Bay
Oregano
Parsley

Bouquet Garni is a mix of four or sometimes more herbs, usually fresh, that are tied together or put in a cheesecloth bag and used to flavor soups and stews. In addition to the herbs listed above, any of the herbs in the Fines Herbes blend can be used, as there are several versions of Bouquet Garni. You can sometimes find Bouquet Garni for specific foods, such as fish or poultry.

Cajun Seasoning

2 T. paprika
2 T. dried thyme
1 T. garlic powder
1 T. dried celery leaves, or dried parsley or lovage
1 T. celery seed
1 T. salt
2 t. cayenne pepper
2 t. freshly ground black pepper
2 t. ground white pepper

Combine all ingredients in a blender. Store in a cool, dry place.

Chili Powder

1 c. dried chili peppers (medium hot)
3 T. cumin
3 T. dried minced garlic
2 T. dried oregano
2 t. cayenne pepper (or to taste)

Combine all ingredients in a blender. Store in refrigerator to maintain freshness.

Creole Seasoning

3 T. paprika
3 T. salt
3 T. dried minced garlic
1½ T. fresh ground black pepper
1½ T. onion powder
1 T. dried oregano
2 t. cayenne
2 t. dried thyme

Combine all ingredients in a blender. Store in a cool, dry place.

Creole Seafood Seasoning

3 T. paprika
3 T. dried minced onion
2 T. salt
2 T. dried minced garlic
1 T. freshly ground black pepper
1 T. cayenne pepper
1 T. dried thyme

Combine all ingredients in a blender. Store in a cool, dry place.

Curry Powder 1

1 T. cumin
1 T. ground coriander
2 t. ground turmeric
2 t. ground nutmeg
2 t. salt
1 t. cinnamon
½ t. cayenne pepper
¼ t. freshly ground black pepper

Combine all ingredients in a spice mill until powdered. Store in a cool, dry place.

Curry Powder 2

3 T. coriander seed
3 T. cumin seed
2 T. turmeric
1½ T. mustard seed
1 T. fennel seed
1 T. salt
2 t. ground ginger
2 t. ground nutmeg
2 t. peppercorns
½ t. cayenne pepper
8 whole cloves
5 cardamom pods

Combine all ingredients in a spice grinder or blender until powdered. Store in a cool, dry place.

Everyday Herb Blend 1

1 T. paprika
1 T. dried parsley
2 t. dried oregano
2 t. dried thyme
2 t. dried minced onion
1½ t. dried mustard
1 t. dried dill
1 t. dried minced garlic
1 t. celery seed
½ t. freshly ground pepper

Combine all ingredients in a blender. Store in a cool, dry place. Use this blend in chicken and meat dishes. It is also good in dips and salad dressings, or it can be added to ground meat for meatloaf. This makes a nice herb shake to reduce salt use.

Everyday Herb Blend 2

1 T. dried minced garlic
2 t. dried basil
2 t. dried marjoram
2 t. onion powder
2 t. dried parsley
1 t. dried sage
1 t. dried savory
1 t. dried thyme
½ t. freshly ground black pepper
½ t. cayenne pepper
½ t. dried oregano

Combine all ingredients in a blender. Store in a cool, dry place. Inspired by a recipe from the American Heart Association, this herb mixture goes with most foods. It adds a nice flavor to vegetables, soups, salads, chicken, fish, or beef.

Five Spice Powder

1 t. cinnamon
½ t. fennel seed
¼ t. freshly ground pepper
¼ t. cloves
1 star anise

Combine all ingredients in a small food processor or in a spice mill. Grind until smooth. Five Spice Powder is used in Asian cooking, primarily in meat or chicken dishes. As it is strong-flavored, use with a light hand.

Fines Herbes

¼ c. parsley
2 T. chervil
2 T. chives
2 T. tarragon

When possible, mix small amounts of fresh herbs and use as needed. Dried substitutions can be made, though chervil does not retain its flavor when dried. You can also combine fresh herbs and store them in the freezer until you need them. If you are combining fresh and dried herbs in the same recipe, remember that dried herbs are more concentrated in flavor. Therefore, measure less of the amounts indicated for fresh herbs, and add more to taste, if needed. Fines Herbes are used in egg dishes, and with fish or chicken.

Garam Masala

20 cardamom seeds, pods removed (or 2 t. ground cardamom)
1 T. ground cinnamon
2 t. dried minced garlic
1 t. cumin
1 t. whole cloves
1 t. peppercorns
½ t. grated nutmeg

Combine spices in a small food processor or in a spice grinder. Blend until smooth and store in a cool, dry place. This spice blend is used in Indian cooking, and adds spicy flavor to chicken, pork, or lamb dishes. Garam Masala is also good combined with rice, or in soups.

Herbes de Provence

1 T. thyme
1 T. rosemary
1 T. savory
2 t. basil
1 t. lavender (optional)
2 bay leaves

Blend fresh or dried herbs until bay leaves are powdered. Rub this mixture on grilled meats, roasts, chicken, or fish. If using fresh herbs, make small amounts and freeze what is unused.

Italian Seasoning

½ c. dried basil
½ c. dried oregano
2 T. onion powder
2 T. garlic powder
2 T. marjoram
1 T. dried rosemary
1 T. dried parsley
1 t. crushed red pepper flakes

Use this blend in Italian dishes, or add to vinegar and oil for a quick Italian dressing.

Pickling Spice

2 T. dill seed
2 T. mustard seed
2 T. whole coriander
2 T. celery seed
1 T. whole allspice
1 T. peppercorns
2 t. whole cloves
1 t. ground ginger
1 (2") cinnamon stick, broken into pieces
3 bay leaves, crumbled
3 whole red hot peppers, crumbled, or 2 t. dried red pepper flakes

While this spice blend is used most often in pickles, it can also be tied in a cheesecloth bag and added to pot roast, pork dishes, or sauerkraut. Also used in beet relishes and corned beef.

Pizza Seasoning

½ c. dried basil
3 T. dried oregano
¼ c. dried onion
1 T. red pepper flakes
1 T. fennel seed
1 T. dried minced garlic or 2 t. garlic powder

Combine ingredients in blender. Store in a cool, dry place.

Poultry Seasoning

¼ c. dried parsley
3 T. dried marjoram
3 T. dried rosemary
3 T. dried thyme
2 T. dried savory
1 T. celery seed
1 T. dried sage
2 t. dried oregano
2 t. dried basil
1 t. ground allspice
1 t. fresh ground pepper

Combine all ingredients in a blender. Store in the fridge to maintain freshness.

Pumpkin Pie Spice

½ c. cinnamon
3 T. ground ginger
2 T. ground nutmeg
1 T. ground cloves

Combine all ingredients. Use 1½ tablespoons for every 2 cups of cooked pumpkin.

Salad and Vegetable Seasoning

½ c. dried parsley
½ c. dried onion
2 T. dried thyme
1 T. celery seed
1 T. dried savory
2 t. dried basil
2 t. dried dill weed
2 t. dried oregano
2 t. dried marjoram
1 t. dried minced garlic
1 t. dried tarragon

Combine all ingredients in blender and store in a cool, dry place.

Seafood Seasoning

3 T. parsley flakes
3 T. dried minced onion
1 T. dill weed
1 T. savory or thyme
2 t. basil
2 t. oregano
2 t. celery seed
1 t. dill seed
1 t. dried minced garlic

Combine all ingredients and store in a cool, dry place. Use in marinades for fish, seafood soups, stews and chowders

Tuscan Seasoning

½ c. dried basil
½ c. dried oregano
½ c. dried marjoram
3 T. dried minced onion
2 T. dried minced garlic
2 T. dried rosemary
2 T. dried parsley
1 t. crushed red pepper

Use this blend in tomato sauce or other Italian dishes. Also, you can add to vinegar and oil with a little salt, if desired, to make a salad dressing.

Chapter 5
Appetizers and Snacks

Herbed Nuts
Quick Herb Spread
Easy Cottage Cheese Dip
Brie with Pesto & Sun-dried Tomatoes
Herb Cheese Ball
Pizza Cheese Ball
Herbed Cheese Puffs
Marinated Vegetables
Yogurt Cheese Dip
Tomato Sorbet
Spiced Olives
Chicken Pâté with Herbs
Mushroom Appetizer
Caponata
Butternut Squash Spread
Herbed Fried Pasta
Bruschetta
Herbed Scallop Kabobs
Stuffed Cherry Tomatoes
Cucumber with Herbed Cheese
Spinach Dip
Oysters & Herbs
Island Meatballs
Bean Dip

Herbed Nuts

2 T. oil
1 T. fresh rosemary, minced, or 1 teaspoon dried, crumbled
1 T. fresh mint, minced, or 1 teaspoon dried, crumbled
1 t. hot pepper sauce, optional
2 c. nuts (walnuts, pecans, Brazil nuts, or cashews)

Toss all ingredients together. Bake herbed nuts on a cookie sheet for 10-15 minutes at 350 degrees. Store in an airtight container in a cool place. Makes about 2 cups.

Quick Herb Spread

1 (8 oz.) package cream cheese, softened
1 T. balsamic vinegar
2 T. fresh chopped parsley, chervil or cilantro
1 T. chopped chives
1 T. minced dates
1 T. minced walnuts

Combine all ingredients and serve as a spread for crackers, or as a topper for bagels and quick breads.

Easy Cottage Cheese Dip

1 c. cottage cheese
2 T. milk
2 T. fresh lemon juice
3 T. mayonnaise
½ c. fresh chopped parsley
2 green onions, wash, trimmed and chopped
1 t. fresh thyme, minced or ½ t. dried
½ t. cayenne pepper

In blender or food processor, combine the cheese, milk, juice and mayonnaise. When smooth, add remaining ingredients and continue blending until well mixed. Serve with raw veggies or use as a topper for baked potatoes. Makes about 1½ cups.

Variations

Pesto Cottage Cheese Dip: Combine the cottage cheese, milk, lemon juice, and mayonnaise. Then add 1 cup firmly packed fresh basil leaves, 2 cloves garlic, ¼ cup olive oil, ¼ cup freshly grated Parmesan cheese, and ¼ cup pine nuts.

Summertime Cottage Cheese Dip: Combine the cottage cheese, milk, lemon juice, and mayonnaise. Then add ¼ cup fresh dill, 1 cup tightly-packed, cooked and drained spinach and 2 green onions, trimmed and chopped. Blend until smooth and stir in 1 (6 oz.) can of water chestnuts, drained and chopped.

Brie with Pesto and Sun-dried Tomatoes

2 c. basil leaves
3 T. pine nuts
2 T. olive oil
2 cloves garlic, minced
½ c. sun-dried tomatoes, soaked in water and refrigerated overnight
1 t. oregano
salt and pepper to taste
2 lb. wheel of Brie

Combine basil, pine nuts, 1 T. of the oil and the garlic in a blender or food processor until smooth. Add salt and pepper. Set aside. Drain tomatoes and chop coarsely. Sprinkle with remaining oil and oregano. Salt and pepper to taste. Set aside. Cut Brie into thirds horizontally.

To stack Brie: Place bottom third on platter or serving plate and cover with the pesto mixture. Place middle third on top and spread with the tomato mixture. Top with remaining Brie layer. Wrap and refrigerate overnight. Serve at room temperature, or warmed slightly in an oven. Serve with crackers or a good quality French bread, or other crusty bread. Serves 30.

Herb Cheese Ball

1 (8 oz.) package cream cheese, softened (low-fat is fine)
1 T. mayonnaise
2-3 T. chopped green onion
2 t. Salad and Vegetable Seasoning (see Chapter 4)
1 t. Dijon style mustard
Cayenne pepper to taste

Combine all ingredients either by hand or in a processor. Form into a ball and chill. Before serving, you can roll the cheese ball in chopped nuts, chopped parsley or paprika, or serve plain. Serve with crackers or with pita bread slices.

Pizza Cheese Ball

1 (8 oz.) package cream cheese, softened (low-fat works fine)
1 T. mayonnaise
2 T. chopped pimento
2 t. Pizza Seasoning (see Chapter 4)
2 T. chopped green onion
3-4 slices crisp bacon or turkey bacon, crumbled, optional

Combine all ingredients either by hand or in a processor. Form into a ball and chill. Cheese ball can be rolled in chopped nuts, parsley or paprika, or can be left plain. Serve with crackers or pita bread slices.

Serving suggestion: Cover the cheese ball in sliced pepperoni.

Herbed Cheese Puffs

1 Ib. cheddar cheese, grated
½ c. butter
½ t. cayenne pepper
2 t. dried parsley
2 t. dried thyme
1 t. dried oregano
1 t. dried marjoram
1¾ c. flour

Cream together cheese and butter. Stir in remaining ingredients. Mix well. Roll on floured surface to ¼-inch thickness. Cut dough into 1-inch squares, or use tiny cookie cutters to make assorted shapes. You can also cut the dough into narrow strips, but handle carefully. Place cheese puffs on ungreased baking sheet and bake in a 350-degree oven for 12-15 minutes, or until lightly browned. Don't over-bake. Cheese puffs can be stored in an airtight container for about 2 weeks, or they can be frozen and thawed as needed.

Marinated Vegetables

Vegetables:
1 or 2 bunches broccoli, washed and trimmed
1 small cauliflower, washed and cut up
1 zucchini, washed and cut into sticks
12 oz. mushrooms, washed and stems trimmed
2 or 3 sweet peppers, any color, cut into long strips

Marinade:
½ c. olive oil (or other vegetable oil)
1 c. cider vinegar (an Herb Vinegar can be used, see Chapter 14)
⅓ c. sugar
¼ c. water
1 t. salt
2 cloves garlic, minced
1 T. Salad and Vegetable Seasoning or Tuscan Seasoning (see Chapter 4)

The vegetables are similar to pickles. Mix or match vegetables according to what is in season. Cherry tomatoes are great if you can get homegrown. Certain veggies, (mushrooms, cauliflower, and broccoli), are better after being marinated for at least a couple of days, while more tender vegetables, such as tomatoes and peppers, are ready after 1 day.

Combine prepped veggies in a bowl that has a tight-fitting lid. Pour the marinade over the veggies. The marinade does not need to cover the veggies. Cover the bowl, and shake or turn to coat the veggies with marinade. Refrigerate. Shake or stir the veggies from time to time. The vegetables will soften in the marinade, and moisture will be drawn out of them. By the next morning, you will notice more liquid in the bowl, usually enough to cover the vegetables. Add more veggies as needed.

To serve, remove the veggies from the marinade with a slotted spoon, and arrange on a tray. Marinated vegetables can be served alone, or they can be accompanied by cheeses, olives, other pickled vegetables, pâtés, and crusty breads. Marinated veggies can also serve as a first course, and are great at parties and picnics.

Yogurt Cheese Dip

1 (16 oz.) carton plain yogurt, or 8 oz. Greek yogurt
¼ c. diced cucumber
2 green onions, washed, trimmed and minced
2 T. diced pimento
2 T. minced fresh parsley
2 T. fresh cilantro, minced
assorted fresh veggies and crackers

To make yogurt cheese, line a fine strainer with cheesecloth, or insert a coffee filter. Spoon the plain yogurt into the strainer, and mount the strainer over a bowl to collect the water that will drain off the yogurt. Cover and refrigerate overnight, pouring off water as needed. By the next day, you will discover that the yogurt has thickened into a soft, spreadable cheese. This cheese can be substituted for sour cream, or even cream cheese in baking. Yogurt cheese is also a good base for dips, as we use it here. Or, you can add yogurt cheese to main dishes for instant sauces, as in stroganoff. You do not have to strain the Greek yogurt.

To make the yogurt cheese dip, combine the yogurt cheese with cucumber, green onions, pimento, parsley, and pimento. Stir to blend. Chill at least a couple of hours, to allow the flavors to blend. Serve with crudités, or on crackers. Makes about 2 cups.

Variations

Pesto Yogurt Cheese Dip: To the yogurt cheese, add: 2/3 cup Pesto Sauce (see Chapter 12). Sprinkle the top of the dip with extra Parmesan cheese.

Italian Yogurt Dip: To the yogurt cheese, add: 1 T. Italian Seasoning (see Chapter 4). 2 T. Parmesan cheese, 2 green onions, minced, and 1 sweet pepper (red, green, or yellow), seeded and minced.

Refried Bean Dip: To the yogurt cheese, add: 1 cup of refried beans, 2 green chilies, minced, 2 t. cumin, and ¼ cup fresh cilantro, minced.

Taco Yogurt Dip: To the yogurt cheese, add: 2 t. cumin, 2 t. chili powder, 1 t. turmeric, 1 small onion, minced, 4 sun-dried tomatoes, soaked in warm water for 2 hours, then drained and chopped (or soaked in water in the fridge overnight), 1 cup of shredded cheddar cheese and ½ cup of sliced black olives.

I could go on and on, but you get the idea. Yogurt cheese gives you a tangy base for lots of dips, or it can become a low-fat addition to your favorite recipes, as a substitute for higher-fat dairy products.

Tomato Sorbet

2 c. tomato juice or tomato juice blend
2 t. sugar
2 t. fresh lemon juice
1 t. Worcestershire sauce
¼ t. fresh ground pepper
⅓ c. fresh basil leaves or 2 T. fresh chopped dill weed

Combine all ingredients in a blender until smooth. Freeze in a covered container. Soften slightly so you can break out in pieces. Process frozen mixture in a small food processor and serve immediately. Decorate with cucumber slices or with basil leaves. Serves 4.

Spiced Olives

Marinade:
¼ c. vinegar
2 T. olive oil
2 T. balsamic vinegar
1 T. fresh lemon juice
1 t. orange zest
1 t. dried thyme, crumbled or 1 T. fresh
4 bay leaves, crumbled coarsely
2 sprigs fresh rosemary, or 1 t. dried
2 garlic cloves, peeled
1 small red hot pepper
1½ c. brine-cured olives

Combine all ingredients and refrigerate for a couple of days before serving. Drain marinade to serve. The olives go well with cheeses and pâté.

Chicken Pâté with Herbs

2 lbs. skinless, boneless chicken, cubed
½ c. butter
½ c. minced onion
2 eggs
½ c. fresh parsley
½ c. fresh basil
1 t. salt
¼ t. hot pepper sauce
¼ t. fresh ground nutmeg
2 c. light cream

Preheat oven to 350. Line a 9x5 loaf pan with foil, and butter the foil. In a food processor, combine the raw chicken, eggs, and seasonings. Process until smooth, then chill.

Note: You will probably have to process the chicken in two batches.

While the chicken is chilling in the refrigerator, melt the butter in a skillet, and sauté the onion until tender. When the onion is cooked, retrieve your processed chicken. Combine the chicken mixture with the onions, blending until very smooth. While the processor is running, add the cream. Again, this procedure will be split into two batches of chicken purée, to account for limited space in the processor food bowl. Pour your creamy chicken purée into the loaf pan with the buttered foil, folding the sides of the foil over the purée to cover the chicken. Cover this loaf pan tightly with additional foil. Put the loaf pan in a larger roasting pan, and fill the roasting pan with enough water to rise up sides of the loaf pan about 2 inches. Carefully place the roasting pan in the oven, and bake the pate for about

1½ hours. After baking, remove the loaf pan from the roaster. When the loaf pan is cool, refrigerate it overnight. To make the chicken pâté more solid, place a weight on the top of the loaf pan during refrigeration. To serve the chicken pâté, unwrap the foil, carefully unmold it from the loaf pan, and transfer it to a serving platter. Garnish with basil leaves and fruit.

Mushroom Appetizer

2 lb. fresh mushrooms, washed and stems trimmed
1 stick butter
2 T. balsamic vinegar
1 T. Italian Seasoning, (see Chapter 4)
1 T. dried minced onion
1 t. dried minced garlic
1 t. salt

Heat butter in skillet and add mushrooms. Cook over medium heat until most of the liquid has evaporated, about 30 minutes. Add remaining ingredients and simmer for 30 minutes longer. Makes 3 cups.

Caponata

This tasty eggplant spread is great served on crusty breads, pita, or crackers.

2 eggplants, peeled and cut into 1-inch cubes
salt
olive oil for frying
2 onions, chopped
3 cloves garlic, minced
½ c. green or black pitted olives, sliced
½ c. bottled capers, drained
1 c. tomato sauce or 2 cups chopped tomatoes
¼ c. red wine vinegar
¼ c. balsamic vinegar
2 T. Tuscan Seasoning (see Chapter 4)
1 T. sugar
⅓ c. pine nuts

Sprinkle eggplant slices with salt and allow to stand in a bowl for 1 hour. Meanwhile, heat a little oil in a skillet and sauté the onions until they begin to brown. Stir in the garlic, olives, and capers, and sauté until heated through.

Place onion mixture in a large bowl and stir in the tomato sauce, vinegars, Tuscan Seasoning and sugar. Stir well to blend. Drain and rinse eggplant cubes. Drain again and pat dry with paper toweling. Heat oil in skillet. Fry the eggplant cubes in oil until tender and browned around the edges. Place eggplant in bowl with onion mixture, and stir well to combine. Cover and chill several hours or overnight. Serve with breads or crackers. Makes enough for 8-10 servings as a first course.

Butternut Squash Spread

1 large butternut squash, or 2 small acorn squash,
halved and seeded
1 c. sour cream, strained yogurt or Greek yogurt
½ c. diced sweet onion
⅓ c. mayonnaise
2 T. honey
1 T. fresh chopped parsley
2 t. dried oregano
1 t. chili powder
1 t. ground cumin
1 t. dried minced garlic
½ t. paprika
dash of hot pepper sauce
salt to taste
Crusty breads and sliced smoked sausage

Bake the squash, covered, in a conventional oven, at
350 for 45 minutes, or in a microwave oven on High
power for 15 minutes, until squash is tender. Allow the
squash to cool enough to handle. Spoon the flesh of the
squash into a medium bowl, and mash it to break up
any big lumps. Add remaining ingredients, except
breads and sausage. Stir to blend well. Before serving,
place the sausage slices under the broiler to brown
lightly. Serve the spread either warm or at room
temperature, with the breads and sausage. Makes 4
cups.

Herbed Fried Pasta

If you've never cooked pasta this way before, stand back once your family gets a taste!

1 lb. uncooked pasta (I use bow ties, rotini, multi-colored shells, or other fun shapes)
oil for frying
⅓ c. grated Parmesan cheese
1½ T. Italian Seasoning (see Chapter 4)
¼ t. cayenne pepper

Cook pasta according to package directions.

Note: It is important to drain the cooked pasta well and pat it dry because water on the pasta will cause the frying oil to splatter.

Heat a couple of inches of oil in a skillet and fry the pasta, a handful at a time, until it is golden brown. Drain off excess oil from fried pasta, and set aside. Repeat with remaining pasta until all the pasta is fried. Combine the remaining ingredients in a bag, and shake to blend seasonings. Add the fried pasta to the bag, a few handfuls at a time, shaking to coat the pasta with seasoning. Makes about 6 cups.

Bruschetta

Bruschetta is a term used for toasted bread slices topped with assorted mixtures, generally containing cheese, herbs, tomatoes, and onions, although there are countless variations. This is a fun and easy starter to make, and will certainly be a hit at parties or family get-togethers.

1 loaf Italian or French bread
¼ c. olive oil
3 cloves garlic, minced
1 T. oil
1 medium onion, chopped
salt and pepper to taste
12 oz. mushrooms, washed, trimmed and chopped
2 c. shredded provolone
2 medium tomatoes, sliced thin
1-2 T. Tuscan or Pizza Seasoning (see Chapter 4)
1 c. ripe pitted olives, sliced

Slice the bread on the diagonal, 1-2 inches thick. If the slices are too large you can cut them in half. Arrange the sliced bread on a baking sheet. Combine the olive oil and garlic and brush on the top of the slices. Bake the slices in a preheated 350-degree oven until the bread is toasted and golden, about 10-15 minutes. Alternately, you can toast the slices over the open flame of a grill, for that 'flame-broiled' look.

Heat the 1-tablespoon of oil in a skillet, and cook the onions and mushrooms until tender. Season with salt and pepper. Divide the onion mixture among the bread slices. Divide the cheese among the slices as well. Place 1 slice of tomato on each piece of bread. If the tomatoes are too large, cut them in half. Sprinkle the seasonings among the bread slices, and top off with the olives. Place bread in a preheated 400-degree oven and bake until the bruschetta is heated through. Makes about 24 appetizers.

Topping variations for bruschetta could include: sautéed eggplant, diced sweet peppers or pepper rings, pepperoni, artichoke hearts, olives, Parmesan cheese, or even pesto sauce brushed on the bread to replace the garlic and oil.

Herbed Scallop Kabobs

1 Ib. fresh sea scallops
36 fresh mushrooms, washed and stems trimmed
1 can (20 oz.) pineapple chunks
2 sweet red peppers, seeded and cut into chunks
¼ c. white wine
2 T. white wine vinegar
juice of a fresh lemon or lime
¾ c. fresh basil leaves
2 T. fresh chopped dill
3 cloves garlic
salt and fresh ground pepper to taste

Soak short wooden skewers in water for 30 minutes before using. Place 1 each of the scallop, mushrooms, pineapple, and pepper chunks on the skewers. Combine the remaining ingredients in a blender until smooth. Place kabobs in a shallow dish and cover with the marinade. Place in the fridge, covered, for 1 hour. Place kabobs on a broiler pan and cook under the broiler, turning once until evenly browned, about 3-5 minutes per side. Brush kabobs with the marinade when turning. Discard any unused marinade. Makes 36 appetizers.

Stuffed Cherry Tomatoes

40 cherry tomatoes (a mix of red, yellow, and pink if available)
1 (8 oz.) package cream cheese, softened
1 (6 oz.) can crab meat, drained and picked over
½ c. sour cream
½ c. minced shallots
1 T. fresh or 1 t. dried oregano
1 T. fresh or 1 t. dried thyme
1 t. garlic powder
1 t. onion powder
dash cayenne pepper

Cut the tops off the tomatoes, and scoop out the insides. Invert the tomatoes on paper toweling to drain. Combine the remaining ingredients in a food processor and pulse a few times to combine well. Chill filling 1 hour. Spoon the filling into tomatoes, or pipe in the filling with a large decorating star tip. Garnish with snipped fresh herbs, if desired. Makes 40 appetizers.

Cucumber with Herbed Cheese

½ of a large gourmet cucumber, sliced thin
2 (8 oz.) packages cream cheese, softened
4 green onions, trimmed and chopped
½ c. fresh cilantro or parsley
2 T. fresh chopped dill
dash cayenne pepper
Additional snipped dill and diced red sweet pepper for
garnish
50 cracker rounds

Place cucumber slices between paper towels to remove
excess moisture. Combine the cream cheese, onions,
herbs, and seasonings in a food processor and combine
until smooth. Place cheese mixture in a pastry bag with
a star tip, and pipe a little onto a cracker. Top with a
cucumber slice, and pipe on an additional dollop of
cheese. Garnish with dill and red pepper. Repeat with
remaining cucumber slices and crackers. Makes about
50.

Spinach and Artichoke Dip

1 10 oz. package of frozen spinach (thawed and drained)
1 can (about 14 oz.) artichoke hearts, drained and chopped
1 c. mayonnaise
1 c. sour cream or Greek yogurt
1 c. fresh cilantro or parsley, chopped
2 T. lemon juice
3 green onions, trimmed and chopped
3 T. fresh-snipped dill weed, or 1 T. dried
2 T. dried minced onion
1 T. dried basil
1 t. garlic powder
½ t. dried tarragon
½ t. dried thyme
½ t. cumin
¼ t. chili powder
2 t. salt
1 can water chestnuts, drained and chopped
2 c. shredded cheddar cheese

Combine all ingredients in a medium bowl. Stir to blend well. Cover and chill well before using. Makes 3 cups.

Oysters and Herbs

2 dozen oysters, shucked
1 T. butter or margarine
½ c. minced sweet onion
⅓ c. minced sweet red pepper
¼ c. diced celery
1 T. chopped parsley
1 T. chopped cilantro
2 t. chopped basil
1 t. chopped dill
1 t. chopped mint
juice of ½ a lime
salt to taste
dash of hot pepper sauce
2 T. breadcrumbs
2 T. Parmesan cheese

Place 4 oysters each in 6 individual ovenproof dishes. Heat butter in a skillet, and sauté the vegetables until tender. Remove from heat and stir in the seasonings, lime juice, salt, if needed, and hot sauce. Toss to mix well. In small bowl, combine the breadcrumbs and the cheese. Place about 1 rounded tablespoonful of the vegetable mixture in each dish of oysters. Top with a sprinkle of 2 teaspoons of the cheese mixture. Bake in a 450-degree oven for 10-12 minutes or until bubbly. Makes 6 appetizer servings.

Island Meatballs

1 lb. lean ground beef or turkey
1 egg
⅓ c. breadcrumbs
1 small onion, diced
½ c. minced sweet pepper
2 T. peanut butter
2 T. chopped cilantro
1 T. chopped cinnamon basil, or regular basil
2 t. grated ginger
1 t. salt
½ t. allspice
¼ t. red pepper flakes, or to taste
1 20 oz. can pineapple chunks, drained
Sweet and Sour Sauce (see Chapter 13)

Combine meat with egg, breadcrumbs, onion, pepper, peanut butter, and seasonings. Mix until well blended then chill. Form this chilled mixture into 1½-inch meatballs. Bake in a preheated 350-degree oven for 45 minutes. Remove from oven and skewer a meatball on a toothpick, along with a chunk of pineapple. Brush with sauce, and broil the meatballs for 3-4 minutes, to lightly brown. Serve with extra sauce. Makes about 30 meatballs.

Bean Dip

2 c. cooked beans such as black, pinto, great
northern, kidney, garbanzo, black-eyed, cranberry, etc.
*However, if you use canned beans, additional
salt may not be necessary.*

½ c. fresh chopped cilantro
3 cloves garlic
2 T. dried minced onion
2 T. olive oil
juice of 1 lime
1 t. cumin
1 t. chili powder
1 t. oregano
½ t. paprika
½ t. red pepper flakes, or to taste
salt to taste
1 T. red wine or cider vinegar, optional

Place beans in food processor, and purée. Add
remaining ingredients, blending until smooth. If dip is
too dry, add extra vinegar or oil. Reduce or omit vinegar
if dip is soupy. Makes 2½ cups.

Chapter 6
Soups

Zucchini Soup with Herbs
Italian Bean & Herb Soup
Pam's Lettuce Soup
Cauliflower & Sweet Potato Soup
Vegetarian Vegetable Soup
Garden Vegetable Soup
Sorrel Soup
Springtime Asparagus Soup
Seafood Bisque
Easy Corn & Clam Chowder
Spinach Soup
Spicy Chicken Soup
Creamy Vegetable Soup
Spicy Black Bean Soup
Winter Squash Soup
Cream of Broccoli Soup
Zesty Fish Soup
Lamb & Lentil Soup
Pumpkin Soup
Turkey Vegetable Soup
Chinese Noodle Soup
Avocado Soup
Dilled Cucumber Soup
Fresh Tomato Soup
Spicy Gazpacho
Fresh Pea Soup

Zucchini Soup with Herbs

2 medium onions, chopped
2 T. oil or butter
2 qts. chicken or vegetable stock
6 cups cubed zucchini
¼ c. raw brown or white rice
2 T. flour
1 T. oil
¼ c. fresh chopped parsley
2 T. fresh basil, chopped
1 t. oregano
½ t. thyme
salt and pepper to taste

Sauté onion in 2 T. oil or butter until slightly browned. Add stock, zucchini, and rice. Simmer until rice is cooked, about 40 minutes for brown, or 15-20 minutes for white rice. In small bowl combine flour with remaining oil and blend until smooth. Add a little hot soup and whisk until smooth. Pour flour mixture into the soup then add herbs and other seasonings. Simmer for 3-4 minutes and serve. Serves 6-8.

Italian Bean and Herb Soup

2 cans, (about 15 oz.) kidney beans, drained and rinsed
1 (15 oz.) can garbanzo beans, drained and rinsed
1 (28 oz.) can diced tomatoes
1 large onion, chopped
1 qt. stock, beef, chicken, or vegetable
2-3 cloves garlic, minced
2-3 small zucchini, diced
I T. Italian Seasoning (see Chapter 4)
Fresh basil sprigs for garnish

In saucepan, combine all ingredients except herbs. Bring to a boil, reduce heat, and simmer until vegetables are tender, about 20 minutes. Stir in Italian Seasoning and add salt and pepper, as needed. Cook an additional 5-10 minutes. Ladle into bowls and garnish with the fresh basil. Serves 6-8.

Pam's Lettuce Soup

4 T. butter
4 T. flour
6 c. chicken stock
1 head lettuce, coarsely chopped (I like romaine)
½ c. thinly sliced celery
1 T. fresh chopped parsley
1 t. chopped tarragon
salt and pepper to taste

Melt butter in saucepan, stir in flour. Cook until bubbly. Gradually add the stock and bring to a boil. Boil 1 minute. Stir in remaining ingredients and simmer 5 minutes. Serves 4-6.

Cauliflower and Sweet Potato Soup

2 T. oil
2 medium onions, chopped
1 large head cauliflower, cut into florets
6 c. vegetable or chicken stock
1 large sweet potato, peeled and cubed
1 c. milk
3 T. fresh parsley, chopped
2 T. fresh chives, snipped
¼ t. fresh ground nutmeg
salt and pepper to taste

In saucepan sauté onions until transparent. Add remaining ingredients-except herbs-and simmer until the potatoes are cooked. Remove from heat and purée the soup in a food processor or blender, in small batches, until smooth. Return to heat and add the herbs and salt and pepper if desired. Simmer 5 minutes. Serves 8.

Vegetarian Vegetable Soup

2 T. oil
2 medium onions, chopped
2 cloves garlic, minced
3 carrots, peeled and diced
2 c. chopped cabbage
2 c. peeled and diced potatoes
2 ribs celery, diced
½ c. uncooked barley
1 (15 or 16 oz.) can kidney beans, drained and rinsed
1 (28 oz.) can tomatoes, chopped
8 oz. sliced mushrooms
Water or vegetable stock
1 lb. fresh spinach, washed and cut into strips (or 1
(10 oz.) package frozen chopped spinach, thawed)
2 T. fresh parsley
1 T. fresh thyme
1 T. fresh marjoram
1 t. fresh tarragon
1 t. fresh savory
Paste-type vegetable soup base to taste-if using water
salt and pepper to taste

In saucepan, sauté onions in oil until lightly browned. Add garlic and sauté 1 minute more, being careful not to burn the garlic. Add the carrots, cabbage, potatoes, celery, barley, kidney beans, tomatoes (including liquid), mushrooms and enough water to cover vegetables by 1-2 inches over the top of the vegetables. Or use vegetable stock if you prefer. Cover and simmer until the vegetables are cooked, about 25 minutes. Add remaining ingredients and cook about 5 minutes more. Adjust seasonings if needed. Makes 10-12 servings.

Garden Vegetable Soup

¼ c. butter
3 leeks trimmed of dark green leaves and roots, halved
lengthwise, and rinsed well to remove sand
2 c. diced carrots
2 medium parsnips, peeled and diced
2 turnips, peeled and diced
2 c. peeled and diced potatoes
6 c. cubed fresh tomatoes
2 c. green beans, trimmed and cut into 1-inch pieces
6 c. chicken stock
¼ c. chopped parsley
¼ c. chopped basil
2 t. tarragon, crumbled
2 t. mint, crumbled, or 2 T. fresh mint, minced
salt and pepper to taste

Cut leeks crosswise into 12-inch slices. Rinse and drain
again to remove any sand. Heat butter in a saucepan
and add all ingredients-except the green beans and the
herbs. Simmer until the vegetables are tender, about 25
minutes. Add beans and herbs and simmer until beans
are just tender, about 5-7 minutes. Serves 6-8.

Sorrel Soup

2 medium onions, chopped
2 T. oil
2 lbs. potatoes, peeled and cubed
1 rib celery, sliced
1 medium carrot, peeled and diced
1 qt. chicken or vegetable stock
1 qt. milk
⅓ c. flour
1 lb. sorrel leaves, washed and spun dry
salt and pepper to taste

In saucepan, sauté onions in oil until tender. Add potatoes, celery, carrots, stock, and 3 cups of the milk. Simmer until potatoes are very tender, about 20 minutes. Mash the vegetables in the soup several times to break up a little. In a container with a tight-fitting lid, combine the remaining milk and the flour. Secure lid and shake vigorously to combine. There should be no lumps in the flour. Pour the flour mixture into the hot soup and cook 3-4 minutes. Toss in sorrel leaves, adjust seasonings, and serve. Garnish with fresh-snipped chives, if desired. Serves 6-8.

Springtime Asparagus Soup

2 T. oil
3 green onions, washed, trimmed, and sliced
1½ lbs. asparagus, washed, trimmed, and cut into ¾-inch pieces
6 c. chicken or vegetable stock
1 c. cooked rice
1 c. sour cream or yogurt
½ c. fresh dill, snipped
salt and pepper to taste

In saucepan, sauté onions in oil until tender. Add asparagus and stock, and simmer 5-8 minutes. Remove about half the soup and purée in a blender until smooth. Return to pan. You can also use an immersion blender to purée the soup a little. Add rice. Ladle a small amount of hot soup into the sour cream and stir until smooth. Pour warmed sour cream mixture into soup. Add the dill and adjust seasonings. Cook at just under simmer for 1 minute to wilt dill, then serve. Serves 4-6.

Seafood Bisque

3 c. fish, vegetable, or chicken stock
2 c. clam juice
½ lb. raw shrimp, peeled and deveined
¼ lb. scallops
6 oz. can crabmeat, picked over
3 green onions (washed, trimmed, and chopped)
3 ribs celery, diced
1 carrot, peeled and diced
½ c. tomato sauce
¼ c. diced fresh red pepper
2 bay leaves
2 T. butter or oil
⅓ c. flour
½ c. white wine
2 c. milk (part half and half, if desired)
2 lbs. mussels in their shells, rinsed and scrubbed
well
3 T. fresh parsley
1 T. fresh thyme
2 t. fresh dill
1 t. fresh tarragon
½ t. fresh ground pepper
salt to taste

In large saucepan, combine the stock, clam juice, shrimp, scallops, crabmeat, vegetables, tomato sauce, and bay leaves. Simmer 15 minutes. In a separate pan, combine butter and flour. Cook until bubbly. Stir in wine and milk, and simmer until mixture thickens, stirring constantly. Add mussels to the seafood mixture, then stir in the thickened sauce. Add the herbs, pepper and salt to taste. Cover and simmer for 5 minutes, or until mussels open. Remove bay leaves, and serve.

Easy Corn and Clam Chowder

1 (14-16 oz.) can cream style corn
1 (10 oz.) can clams, undrained
2 c. milk
1 T. butter (optional)
2 T. fresh parsley
1 t. dried dill
1 t. dried savory
salt and pepper to taste
fresh chopped chives for garnish (optional)

In medium saucepan combine all ingredients-except chives-and heat over low to medium heat, stirring occasionally, until heated through. Serves 3-4.

As a variation of this recipe, you can omit the clams, and add cooked chicken.

Spinach Soup

1 lb. fresh, or 1(10 oz.) package frozen spinach
2 c. chicken stock
2 T. butter
1 large leek
1 (12 oz.) can evaporated skim milk
salt and pepper to taste
1 T. fresh-snipped dill
1 T. fresh-snipped mint

If using fresh spinach, wash, trim, and chop spinach coarsely. Simmer the spinach in hot chicken stock until tender. If using frozen spinach, simmer in broth until thawed. Set aside. In a separate pan, heat the butter. Trim the end and the dark green parts off the leek. Split the leek lengthwise and rinse under running water. Cut the leek crosswise into ½-inch slices. Sauté the leek in the butter until tender. Add to the spinach mixture, then stir in the remaining ingredients. Heat through until steaming, but do not boil. Garnish with a dill or mint sprig. Serves 2-3.

Spicy Chicken Soup

2 T. oil
3 medium onions, chopped
2 ribs celery, diced
2 carrots, peeled and diced
½ c. flour
½ c. white wine
3 c. chicken stock
2 c. milk
¾ lb. skinless chicken, diced
1 t. chili powder
1 t. cumin
½ t. curry powder
1 t. dried marjoram
½ t. parsley
fresh ground pepper
salt to taste

In medium saucepan heat oil and sauté onions until tender. Add celery and carrots and cook, stirring often, until carrots are crisp tender. Add flour, and toss with vegetables to coat. Stir in wine and stock, and stir until smooth. Add remaining ingredients and simmer until chicken is cooked, about 10 minutes. Serves 6-8.

Creamy Vegetable Soup

3 T. oil
2 c. chopped onion
4 ribs celery, diced
2-3 medium carrots, peeled and diced
2 cloves garlic, minced
6 cups chicken stock
1 c. fresh corn, or frozen
1 c. sliced zucchini
1 (14-16 oz.) can tomatoes, chopped
2 c. fresh or frozen green beans, cut into 1-inch pieces
2 T. fresh parsley, chopped
2 t. dried thyme, crumbled
2 t. dried marjoram, crumbled
2 t. dried basil, crumbled
¼ c. flour
3 T. oil
salt and pepper to taste

In saucepan, sauté the onion in oil until translucent. Add celery, carrots, and garlic. Sauté about 5 minutes more, being careful not to burn the garlic. Add the chicken stock and cook until the veggies are tender, about 15 minutes. Add remaining vegetables and cook until beans are tender, about 7 minutes. Meanwhile in small pan or bowl combine the flour and oil and whisk until smooth. Ladle a little of the hot soup into the flour mix and whisk until smooth and thick. Add flour mixture and herbs to the soup, and simmer 2-3 minutes to thicken slightly. Add salt and pepper, if needed. Serves 6-8.

Spicy Black Bean Soup

12 oz. dried black beans
3 T. olive oil
2 cups chopped onions
6 cloves garlic, minced
3 sweet peppers, seeded and chopped
1 c. apple cider or juice
⅓ c. chopped parsley
3 T. lime juice
3 T. soy sauce
3 bay leaves
2 t. cumin
1 t. curry powder
1 t. chili powder
1 t. fresh ground ginger
½ t. ground cloves
½ t. hot pepper sauce
2 small apples, peeled and chopped
¼ c. raisins
1 c. hulled pumpkin seeds, toasted

Rinse beans and place in pot. Cover with water and bring to a boil. Simmer 5 minutes. Turn off heat and let stand 1 hour. Drain beans and rinse again. Put in soup pot and add about 6-7 cups cold water. Simmer over low heat until tender. In skillet heat the oil and sauté the onions until lightly browned. Add the peppers and garlic and sauté about 3 minutes more. Add vegetable mixture and remaining ingredients, except the apples, raisins and seeds. Simmer soup about 1 hour more. Add the raisins and apples, and cook 10 minutes more. Ladle soup into bowls and sprinkle with pumpkin seeds. Serves 6-8.

Winter Squash Soup

2 large onions, chopped
2 T. oil
8-10 cups peeled and cubed winter squash
4 c. chicken stock
1 T. fresh grated ginger
1 t. ground allspice
½ t. cinnamon
½ t. cumin
½ t. cayenne pepper to taste
salt to taste
1½ c. evaporated milk
¼ c. fresh chopped parsley
Hulled pumpkin seeds

Heat oil in skillet and sauté onions until tender. Add squash, stock, and spices. Bring to a boil, then cover pan and simmer until squash is tender, about 25 minutes. While soup is cooking, toast the pumpkin seeds. Place the seeds in a small skillet over medium heat. As the seeds toast they will pop and jump in the pan. They will be toasted in about 5-10 minutes. When soup is ready, remove from heat and purée in batches in a food processor or blender until smooth. Return soup to the saucepan, and stir in condensed milk and parsley. Heat until almost simmering, and cook 5 minutes longer. Sprinkle toasted pumpkin seeds on top of the soup after serving. Makes 6-8 servings.

Cream of Broccoli Soup

1 c. chicken broth
4 c. broccoli florets
3 c. milk
2 T. fresh chopped parsley
2 T. snipped fresh chives
1 T. fresh tarragon leaves
salt and pepper to taste
¼ c. flour
fresh ground nutmeg

In medium saucepan, cook chicken broth and broccoli, covered about 10 minutes until broccoli is tender. Add 2½ cups of the milk and seasonings. Combine remaining ½ cup milk with flour and stir until smooth. Pour into soup and heat until bubbly and thickened. Ladle into bowls and sprinkle with a little nutmeg. 4 servings.

Zesty Fish Soup

2 T. oil or butter
1 medium onion, chopped
2 ribs celery, diced
2 medium carrots, peeled and diced
2 small zucchini, diced
1 (28 oz.) can of tomatoes, chopped and undrained
1 c. clam juice
1 lb. mild fish, such as cod or haddock, cut into cubes
salt to taste
2 T. fresh chopped cilantro
1 T. fresh thyme, or 1 t. dried
½ t. cumin
½ t. fresh ground pepper

Heat oil or butter in a saucepan. Add onion and sauté until onion is wilted. Add celery, carrots, and zucchini. Sauté for 10 more minutes. Add tomatoes and clam juice, and bring to a simmer. Cover and simmer 10 minutes. Add fish and seasonings and simmer for another 10 minutes, uncovered, until fish is cooked. Serves 4.

Lamb and Lentil Soup

2 c. lentils
water
3 T. oil
1-1 ½ lbs. lamb stew meat, cut into cubes
3 large onions, diced
4 cloves garlic, minced
3 ribs celery, diced
4 carrots, peeled and diced
1 (28 oz.) can tomatoes, cut-up, undrained
8 cups chicken or vegetable stock
3 bay leaves
1 T. fresh thyme
1 t. cumin
½ t. coriander
¼ t. pepper
¼ t. allspice
¼ c. fresh chopped cilantro
¼ c. fresh chopped mint leaves

Rinse lentils and place them in a medium saucepan, covering with water and cooking until tender, about 30 minutes. Drain lentils.

While lentils are cooking, prepare the rest of the soup. Heat oil in large saucepan, and add lamb chunks. Cook, stirring, until well browned, and no pink is visible. Add onions and sauté 10 minutes more. Add remaining vegetables, tomatoes with liquid, broth, bay leaves, thyme, cumin, coriander, pepper and allspice. Cover and simmer 45 minutes, or until lamb is tender. Add lentils and simmer, covered, 20 minutes more. Sprinkle soup with cilantro and mint before serving. Makes 8 servings.

Pumpkin Soup

2 T. butter or oil
2 large onions, chopped
1 T. flour
2 c. chicken stock
2 c. cooked pumpkin
2 c. milk
½ c. evaporated milk
salt and pepper to taste
1 t. fresh ground ginger
½ t. allspice
½ t. cardamom
¼ t. cumin
¼ t. thyme leaves
fresh ground nutmeg

Heat butter or oil in saucepan and add onions, cooking until lightly browned. Stir in flour until onions are evenly coated. Stir in stock slowly to prevent lumps. Bring to a simmer. Stir in remaining ingredients-except nutmeg-and heat through. Cook 5 minutes longer to blend flavors. This soup can be served in a hollowed-out fresh pumpkin. Sprinkle fresh nutmeg on the top before serving. Serves 6.

Turkey Vegetable Soup

2 T. oil
1 large onion, chopped
3 ribs celery, diced
3 medium carrots, peeled and diced
1 small potato, diced
1 c. chopped cabbage
1 medium tomato, diced
8 c. turkey or chicken stock
2-3 c. diced cooked turkey
½ c. fresh chopped parsley
1 T. fresh chopped marjoram, or 1 t. dried
1 T. fresh thyme, or 1 t. dried
1 t. fresh savory or a pinch of dried savory
salt and pepper to taste
2 T. oil
2 T. flour
fresh-snipped chives

Heat oil in large saucepan, and sauté onion until tender. Add remaining vegetables and sauté 5 minutes. Add stock and simmer, covered, until vegetables are tender, about 20 minutes. Stir in turkey and herbs, and cook 5 minutes more. While turkey is cooking, combine the flour and oil in small bowl. Ladle some of the hot soup into the flour mixture, whisking to avoid lumps. Add about 1 cup of stock in all. Pour the mixture into the soup, and simmer 3 minutes to thicken and cook the flour. Sprinkle individual servings with chives, if desired. Makes 8 servings.

Chinese Noodle Soup

4 oz. cellophane noodles, also called bean threads, or use vermicelli
2 T. oil
1 c. chopped onion
1 large carrot, peeled and cut into matchstick pieces
1 clove garlic, minced
4 oz. sliced mushrooms
1 c. thinly sliced Chinese cabbage
½ c. diced sweet red pepper
6 c. chicken stock
1 T. soy sauce, or to taste
2 t. fresh grated ginger
1 t. crushed coriander
½ t. red pepper flakes, or to taste
2 c. cooked, cubed chicken
1 c. finely sliced bok choy greens, or spinach
1 c. bean sprouts
3 green onions, trimmed and chopped

Place noodles in a big bowl and cover with boiling water. Let stand 5 minutes, then drain and set aside. In large saucepan or Dutch oven (or use a wok if you prefer) heat the oil and sauté the onions until tender. Add carrot, garlic, and mushrooms. Sauté about 4 minutes. Add the Chinese cabbage and the red pepper, and sauté 2 minutes longer.

Add stock, soy, ginger, coriander, and pepper flakes. Bring to a boil and stir in chicken, bok choy, sprouts, and noodles. Simmer, covered, 5 minutes. Ladle into bowls and sprinkle with green onion. Serves 4-6.

Avocado Soup

4 c. chicken stock
2 c. milk
2 t. chili powder
1 t. cumin
1 t. garlic powder
hot pepper sauce to taste
salt to taste
3 ripe avocados
¼ c. fresh cilantro leaves, chopped
1 c. sour cream or yogurt
snipped fresh mint

Heat stock and milk together until just beginning to bubble around edges. Stir in seasonings and keep warm. Peel and seed avocados, and place them in a food processor or blender with the stock mixture (place only what will comfortably fit, and blend in two batches if need be).

Stir in the cilantro. Stir a little of the warm soup into the yogurt, whisking to prevent lumps. Return warmed yogurt to the pan and heat through but do not boil. Ladle into bowls and garnish with snipped mint. Serves 4-6.

Dilled Cucumber Soup

This is a refreshing dish for a hot summer day.

2 cucumbers, peeled and seeded
2 c. Greek yogurt or sour cream
salt to taste
cayenne pepper to taste
¼-⅓ c. fresh-snipped dill
1 T. fresh chopped cilantro or parsley
1½ c. milk
2 ribs celery, diced
1 sweet red pepper, seeded and diced
lemon wedges and dill sprigs for garnish

Place the two cucumbers on a cutting surface. Finely chop one cucumber into a large bowl. Cut the other cucumber into chunks, and place it in the bowl of a food processor or blender. Add yogurt and seasonings, and blend until smooth. Add the puréed cucumber to the other cucumber, then add remaining ingredients-except the lemons and dill sprigs. Chill soup, covered, for several hours or overnight. To serve, ladle soup into chilled bowls, and garnish with lemon wedges and extra dill sprigs. Serves 4.

Fresh Tomato Soup

This wonderful soup is a great way to use a summer's bounty of tomatoes. You could add rice and serve it warm, but I prefer it cold. I've been known to eat it right out of the fridge for breakfast. Use only vine-ripened tomatoes. If you must substitute, use canned tomatoes over hot house-grown. In summer, I grow a lot of yellow tomatoes, and sometimes make this dish with them. It's really pretty.

3 lbs. fresh tomatoes, peeled and chopped
1 c. beef stock, chicken stock or clam juice
1 sweet pepper, seeded and diced
½ c. fresh chopped basil, minced
2 T. fresh chopped parsley
juice of 1 lemon or lime
2 t. brown sugar
½ t. cumin
salt to taste
hot pepper sauce to taste
dash Worcestershire sauce
Greek yogurt and snipped chives as a garnish

Place half of the tomatoes in a blender and mix until smooth. Place tomato purée with all other ingredients-except the yogurt and chives-and whisk to blend well. Cover and chill several hours or overnight. Ladle soup into chilled bowls. Garnish with a drizzle of yogurt across the top, and a sprinkling of snipped chives. A few longer pieces of chives can also be used as a garnish. Serves 6-8.

Spicy Gazpacho

3 lbs. ripe tomatoes, peeled
2 cucumbers, peeled and seeded
½ c. chopped sweet onion
1 sweet red pepper, seeded and chopped
1 sweet green pepper, seeded and chopped
2 ribs celery, chopped
3-4 cloves garlic
¼ c. chopped cilantro
2 T. chopped parsley
juice of 2 limes
2 T. balsamic vinegar
2 t. chili powder
2 t. cumin
2 t. red pepper flakes
salt to taste
1 yellow sweet pepper, seeded and cut into matchsticks
2-3 green chilies, seeded and sliced into rings.
1 c. sour cream

Purée all ingredients together-except the yellow sweet pepper and green chilies. You will most probably do this in several batches. Pour the purée into a large bowl. Cover and chill overnight. To serve, ladle soup into chilled bowls, and garnish with yellow peppers, chilies, and sour cream, if desired. Serves 8.

Fresh Pea Soup with Dill

This delightful recipe comes from Anna Welker. It is a great springtime soup and has become a favorite of mine. I make it with English peas. It can also be made with green beans.

2 T. butter or oil
1 medium onion, chopped
2 c. fresh English peas, pea pods (sliced), or sugar snaps (sliced)
¼-½ c. fresh chopped dill
4 c. chicken stock
salt and pepper to taste
3 T. flour
1 c. sour cream

Heat butter or oil in medium saucepan. Sauté onion until tender. Add peas, dill, stock and salt and pepper. Cook until peas are the desired tenderness, about 3-7 minutes. Combine the flour and sour cream in a small bowl. Ladle 1 cup of hot soup into the sour cream mixture, and stir to smooth. Pour this mixture into the soup and cook, barely simmering, until soup thickens, about 4 minutes. You can use less flour if you like a thinner soup, or dilute with milk if too thick. To serve, ladle into bowls and garnish with dill sprigs. Serves 3-4.

Chapter 7
Salads & Dressings

Salads

Chick Pea Salad
Cucumbers & Sour Cream
Spiced Chick Pea Salad
Polynesian Cole Slaw
Tabbouleh
Pesto Potato Salad
Italian Bread Salad
Overnight Slaw
Easy Italian Pasta Salad
Just in Thyme Potato Salad
Warm Pasta Salad
Red Pasta Salad
Herbed Wild Rice Salad
Wild Green Salad
Tangy Tomato Salad
Lettuce & Nasturtium Salad
Wilted Green Salad
Spring Pea Salad
Pea Pod Salad
Herb & Mustard Potato Salad
Springtime Rice Salad
Herb Crab Salad
Rosemary, Potato & Bean Salad
Spicy Three Bean Salad
Pasta Salad with Herbs & Cucumbers
Mom's Best Tossed Salad
Fruited Chicken Salad
Layered Mexican Salad
Couscous Salad

Dressings

Italian Vinaigrette Dressing
Tangy Curry Dressing
Lemon Dill Dressing
Pesto Vinaigrette
Fruit Salad Dressing
Gingered Fruit Salad Dressing
Greek Style Dressing
Dill Dressing
Sesame Dressing
Lime Vinaigrette
Herb Vinaigrette
Fresh Herb Vinaigrette
Apple Vinaigrette
Tomato & Herb Dressing
Orange Vinaigrette
French Tarragon Dressing
Raspberry-Chive Vinaigrette
Parsley Dressing

Chick Pea Salad

1 (15 oz.) can chick peas, drained and rinsed
1 onion, minced
1 rib celery, diced
½ c. fresh chopped parsley
2 T. fresh basil or 2 t. dried
1 T. fresh savory or 1 t. dried
salt to taste
¼ c. olive oil
2 T. vinegar
1 T. balsamic vinegar

Combine all ingredients and chill several hours or overnight. Serve on a bed of lettuce or mixed greens. Serves 2-3.

Cucumbers and Sour Cream

2-3 medium cucumbers, peeled and sliced
1 c. dairy sour cream
¼ c. vinegar
¼ c. sugar
2 green onions, trimmed and sliced
2 T. fresh-snipped dill or 2 t. dried
1 T. fresh-snipped chives (optional)

Combine all ingredients and cover. Chill for at least 30 minutes before serving. Can be served alone, on a bed of greens, or in pita bread. Serves 4-6.

Spiced Chick Pea Salad

3 (15 oz.) cans chick peas, drained and rinsed
1 sweet red pepper, seeded and chopped
1 sweet green or yellow pepper, seeded and chopped
3-4 green onions (washed, trimmed, and chopped)
¼ c. olive oil
2 T. red wine vinegar
2 T. balsamic vinegar
1 clove garlic, minced
1 t. fresh ginger, grated
1 t. ground cumin
½ t. ground coriander
½ c. fresh parsley, chopped
¼ c. fresh cilantro chopped
¼ t. cayenne pepper
Salt to taste

Combine peas and veggies in medium bowl. In smaller bowl combine oil, vinegars, herbs and spices. Adjust seasonings to your taste. Pour dressing over pea mixture and toss to coat. Chill before serving. Serves 4-6.

Polynesian Cole Slaw

This recipe comes from my friend Malikah. It has become a favorite summer salad of mine.

4 c. shredded cabbage
1 (11 oz.) can mandarin oranges, drained
1 (8 oz.) can pineapple tidbits, drained, reserving 2 T. juice
¼ c. mayonnaise
½ t. fresh grated ginger
¼ t. white pepper
¼ t. nutmeg

Combine cabbage, oranges, and pineapple. Combine in a separate bowl the mayo, reserved juice, and seasonings. Pour over cabbage mix and toss gently to coat. Chill for several hours or overnight before serving. Serves 8.

Tabbouleh

2 c. cracked wheat, fine size or bulgur wheat
(uncooked)
4 green onions (washed, trimmed, and minced)
2 c. fresh parsley, minced
1½ c. fresh mint leaves, minced
1 t. salt
½ t. fresh ground pepper
juice of 2 lemons, about ¼ cup
¼ c. olive oil
2 large tomatoes, seeded and diced
1 medium cucumber, peeled and chopped, optional

Rinse wheat in cold water, drain, and chill several hours or overnight to soften. Combine remaining ingredients and toss with wheat. Tabbouleh can be eaten on a bed of greens, or stuffed into pita bread for a light summer meal. Serves 6-8.

Note: This recipe really needs fresh herbs for best results.

Pesto Potato Salad

2 lbs. boiling potatoes, cut into bite-sized pieces
1 c. basil leaves
3 T. pine nuts
3 T. olive oil
2 garlic cloves, minced
⅓ c. Parmesan cheese

Boil or steam potatoes until tender. Cool. In blender, combine remaining ingredients, reserving 1 T. pine nuts. Blend until smooth, and toss with potatoes. Sprinkle reserved nuts on top. Chill. Serves 6-8.

Italian Bread Salad

1 lb. day old crusty bread, cut into 1-inch cubes,
about 8 cups, preferably whole wheat
5-6 plum tomatoes, washed and sliced
½ English cucumber, sliced
1 c. sliced sweet onion
⅔ c. olive oil
⅓ c. red wine vinegar
3 T. balsamic vinegar
¼ c. fresh basil leaves cut into narrow strips
2 t. Italian Seasoning (see Chapter 4)

In large bowl mix together the bread and veggies. In
separate bowl mix remaining ingredients and toss over
bread mixture. Make sure that all the bread is coated.
Makes 6-8 servings.

Overnight Slaw

½ c. sugar
¼ c. cider vinegar
1 t. mustard seed
1 t. celery seed
1 t. salt
½ t. dill seed
½ small head cabbage, shredded
1 sweet pepper. minced
1 small onion, minced
3 or 4 ribs celery, minced
1 small carrot, grated

Combine all ingredients and cover. Chill overnight.
Serves 6-8.

Easy Italian Pasta Salad

6 oz. angel hair pasta
1 (6 oz.) jar marinated artichoke hearts, drained and chopped (reserve ½ c. marinade liquid)
1 small zucchini, diced
1 sweet red or green pepper, diced
1 carrot, cut into matchstick-sized pieces
4 oz. mozzarella cheese, shredded
¼ c. olive oil
3 T. red wine vinegar
1 T. balsamic vinegar
2 t. Tuscan Seasoning (see Chapter 4)

Cook pasta according to package directions. Drain and cool. Add vegetables and cheese. Combine remaining ingredients in blender and process until well mixed. Toss over pasta, cover, and chill several hours before serving. Makes 4-6 servings.

Just in Thyme Potato Salad

2 lbs. boiling potatoes, cut into bite-sized pieces
½ c. olive oil
¼ c. red wine vinegar
1 T. fresh lemon juice
2 t. fresh thyme leaves
salt and pepper to taste

Boil or steam potatoes until tender. Drain, and toss with the rest of the ingredients. Serve immediately, or chill several hours and serve cold. Serves 6-8.

Warm Pasta Salad

1 lb. plum tomatoes, chopped
1 medium onion, chopped
4 oz. sliced mushrooms, uncooked
2 cloves garlic, minced
¼ c. fresh parsley, chopped
¼ c. fresh basil, chopped
2 T. fresh chives, minced
1 T. fresh mint leaves, minced
1 t. dried oregano, or 1 T. fresh minced
½ c. olive oil
¼ c. red wine vinegar
3 T. balsamic vinegar
Dash of hot pepper flakes
salt to taste
1 lb. rotini, shells or other pasta, uncooked

Combine all ingredients-except pasta, and chill, covered, in fridge overnight. Cook the pasta according to package directions, and drain. Immediately toss hot pasta with cold sauce and serve. You can also serve pasta salad with Parmesan cheese on the side. Serves 6.

Red Pasta Salad

1 lb. rotini, shells or other pasta, cooked, drained and cooled
1 c. finely shredded cabbage
1 c. fresh bean sprouts
2 c. cherry tomatoes, washed and halved
4 green onions, washed, trimmed and chopped
1 green pepper, seeded and chopped
1 red pepper, seeded and chopped
1 small zucchini, diced
1 small carrot, peeled and sliced thin

Dressing:
¾ c. olive oil
2 T. fresh lime juice
2 T. red wine vinegar
1 T. balsamic vinegar
2 cloves garlic, minced
2 T. basil leaves, chopped, or 2 t. dried
2 T. fresh parsley, chopped, or 2 t. dried
1 t. fresh rosemary, chopped, or ⅓ t. dried
1 t. fresh thyme, chopped, or ⅓ t. dried
1 t. fresh orange zest or 1 t. dried orange peel
1 c. whole berry cranberry sauce, puréed

Add vegetables to pasta. In a separate bowl, whisk together the dressing ingredients and pour over pasta. Stir to coat. Cover, and chill before serving. Serves 6-8.

Herbed Wild Rice Salad

2 c. cooked wild rice
3 green onions, washed, trimmed and sliced
1 sweet red pepper, chopped
2 ribs celery, chopped
¼ c. oil
2 T. white wine vinegar
2 T. fresh lemon juice
1 T. fresh-snipped chives or 1 t. dried
1 T. fresh cilantro, chopped
1 T. fresh parsley, chopped, or 1 t. dried
¼ t. fresh rosemary or a pinch of dried
salt and pepper to taste

Combine all ingredients in a medium bowl. Chill several hours or overnight to blend flavors. Serves 4-6.

Wild Green Salad

8-10 cups assorted wild salad greens such as: dandelion greens, French sorrel, lamb's quarters and/or mixed baby greens, including: spinach and assorted lettuces
¼ c. olive oil
2 T. red wine vinegar
1 T. balsamic vinegar
2 t. sugar
2 t. fresh dill leaves
2 t. fresh tarragon
salt and fresh ground pepper to taste

Wash and dry the greens. Combine remaining ingredients in a small bowl and whisk. Toss over greens and serve. Serves 8.

Tangy Tomato Salad

½ c. olive oil
2 green onions, washed, trimmed, and chopped
2 T. red wine vinegar
1 T. fresh lemon juice
¼ c. fresh lovage leaves, chopped (celery leaves can be substituted)
2 T. fresh cilantro, minced
¼ t. coriander seed, ground
¼ t. celery seed or lovage seed
salt and fresh ground pepper to taste
4 lbs. of assorted fresh tomatoes, chopped coarsely
red, yellow, orange, or pink
Assorted cherry and pear-shaped tomatoes for garnish
Fresh cilantro

Combine all ingredients-except tomatoes-in a small bowl. Whisk lightly to blend. In a medium bowl, combine chopped tomatoes with dressing. Chill about 1 hour before serving. Garnish with whole cherry tomatoes and sprigs of cilantro. Serves 6-8.

Lettuce and Nasturtium Salad

8 cups assorted salad greens, preferably red and green
leaf lettuce, and romaine
½ c. nasturtium leaves, chopped
½ c. nasturtium blossoms, rinsed and spun dry
½ c. olive oil
¼ c. red wine vinegar
1 T. sugar
1 c. fresh mint leaves, washed and spun dry
2 T. minced fresh chives

Rinse and spin dry greens, and tear into bite-sized
pieces. Combine in bowl with nasturtium leaves. Set
blossoms aside. Place the oil in a blender and, while
blender is running, add remaining ingredients until
dressing is smooth. Pour dressing over lettuce and
nasturtium greens, and toss well to coat. Sprinkle
blossoms on individual servings of salad. Serves 8.

Wilted Greens Salad

8 c. washed romaine lettuce leaves, torn into bite-sized pieces
2 c. washed dandelion greens, torn into bite-sized pieces
4 c. washed spinach leaves, torn into bite-sized pieces
⅓ c. olive oil
½ c. chopped green onion
⅓ c. balsamic vinegar
½ c. pitted and chopped green olives
salt and pepper to taste
2 T. chopped chives
2 T. chopped dill
1 T. chopped parsley
½ t. dried tarragon
4 oz. turkey ham, diced
4 oz. shredded mozzarella

Combine greens in a large bowl. In skillet, heat oil and sauté green onion 3-4 minutes. Add vinegar, olives, salt and pepper and herbs. Cook until mixture starts to boil. Pour this mixture over the greens and toss to coat evenly. Greens will wilt somewhat Toss in the ham and cheese, and serve. Makes 6-8 servings

Spring Pea Salad

4 c. sugar snap peas, pea pods, or fresh-shelled peas
3 green onions (trimmed, washed, and chopped)
1 (6 oz.) can water chestnuts, drained and chopped
¼ c. olive oil
2 T. rice vinegar
½ c. fresh mint leaves
2 T. fresh dill weed
Salt and pepper to taste

Note: If using sugar snap peas or pea pods, wash, trim, and steam them for about 5 minutes.

Rinse them under cold water to stop cooking. For shelled peas, steam for about 3 minutes, then rinse under cold water. Add green onions and water chestnuts to cooked peas, and set aside. Combine dressing ingredients in a blender or food processor and blend until smooth. Toss over pea mixture to coat. Chill several hours before serving. Makes 6-8 servings.

Pea Pod Salad

4 oz. pea pods, trimmed and washed
2 green onions, trimmed and chopped
8 oz. mushrooms, washed, trimmed, and sliced
½ c. shredded Chinese cabbage
½ c. sweet red pepper, cut into matchstick slices
⅓ c. rice vinegar or white wine vinegar
2 T. Thai basil or regular basil
2 T. chopped parsley
1 clove garlic
1 t. grated ginger
½ t. coriander
salt and pepper to taste
½ c. oil

Blanch the pea pods in boiling water for 3 minutes. Drain and refresh under cold water. Toss pea pods with remaining vegetables. Combine the vinegar and seasonings in a blender until smooth. Add the oil in a slow stream, with the machine running. Dressing will thicken. Pour this dressing over the pea pod mixture, and toss to coat well. Cover and refrigerate 1 hour before serving. Serves 4.

Herb and Mustard Potato Salad

4 lbs. boiling potatoes
4 eggs, hard-boiled
4-5 green onions, washed, trimmed, and chopped
3 ribs celery, chopped
1 sweet red pepper, seeded and chopped
1 c. mayonnaise
½ c. plain yogurt
2 T. Dijon-style mustard
¼ c. fresh parsley, chopped
2 T. fresh basil, chopped
1 T. fresh thyme
2 T. fresh lemon juice
1 t. paprika
Dash of cayenne
Salt to taste

Peel potatoes if desired. Cut into bite-sized pieces. Boil potatoes until tender. Drain. Peel and chop eggs. Combine all ingredients with warm potatoes, and serve immediately. You can chill several hours or overnight and serve cold. Makes 6-8 servings.

Springtime Rice Salad

3-4 c. cooked white or brown rice, at room
temperature
1 can (6 oz.) mandarin oranges, drained-reserving 2 T.
of the liquid
1 c. pea pods blanched 3 minutes, rinsed, and cut into
1-inch pieces
¼ c. olive oil
¼ c. rice vinegar
¼ c. fresh chopped mint
2 T. fresh chopped chives
2 T. orange juice
1 t. orange peel
salt and pepper to taste

In medium bowl combine the rice, oranges, and peas.
In a separate bowl, whisk together the oil, vinegar,
herbs, juice, liquid from the oranges, peel, and salt and
pepper. Pour this dressing over the rice and toss gently
to combine, without breaking up orange pieces. Chill
before serving. Makes 8-10 servings.

Herb Crab Salad

2 cups crabmeat (imitation crab can be substituted)
¾ c. halved cherry tomatoes, mixed-red and yellow, if available
½ c. chopped English cucumbers
1 rib celery, diced
½ c. pitted black olives, sliced
3 T. mayonnaise
2 T. sour cream or yogurt
1 T. fresh lime juice
1 T. fresh cilantro, chopped
1 T. fresh chives, minced
¼ t. dried tarragon
Fresh ground pepper, to taste
2-3 c. Bibb lettuce leaves, washed and spun dry

In a small bowl combine the crabmeat, tomatoes, cucumbers, celery and olives. In a separate bowl, combine the remaining ingredients-except the lettuce-and pour dressing over the crabmeat mixture. Chill at least 2 hours before serving. To serve, line plates with Bibb lettuce leaves, and top with crabmeat salad. Garnish with additional tomatoes, if desired. Serves 2.

Rosemary Potato and Bean Salad

2-3 lbs. boiling potatoes
2 lbs. fresh green beans washed, trimmed, and cut
into 1-inch pieces
1 sweet onion, chopped
½ c. chopped sweet pepper
⅔ c. olive oil
1 clove garlic
⅓ c. red wine vinegar
1 T. fresh rosemary leaves or 1 t. dried leaves
1 T. fresh parsley

Peel potatoes, if desired. Cut into bite-sized pieces. Boil potatoes until tender. Drain and cool. Cook the green beans until just tender, about 8 minutes. Drain and cool. Combine the potatoes, beans, onion, and pepper. Combine remaining ingredients in a blender, and mix until smooth. Pour over potato mixture, and toss to coat. Chill before serving. Makes 8-10 servings

Spicy Three-Bean Salad

1 (15-17 oz.) can kidney beans, drained
1 (19 oz.) can chick peas, drained
1 lb. green beans washed, trimmed and cut into 1-inch pieces
1 red onion, sliced very thin
⅔ c. olive oil
⅓ c. red wine vinegar
2 T. balsamic vinegar
1 T. fresh lime juice
2 cloves garlic
1 t. red pepper flakes
1 c. fresh cilantro, rinsed and spun dry
1 t. salt
1 t. cumin
1 t. chili powder

Boil green beans for 7-9 minutes, or just until tender. Drain and rinse under cool water. In a medium bowl, combine the green beans with the kidney beans, chick peas, and onion. Combine the remaining ingredients in a blender until smooth, and pour over the bean mixture. Chill overnight before serving. Makes 8-10 servings.

Pasta Salad
with Herbs and Cucumbers

1 lb. pasta (rotini, macaroni, penne, or broken spaghetti)
1 English cucumber, cubed
5 hard-cooked eggs
3-4 green onions, washed, trimmed, and chopped
⅔ c. olive oil
½ c. rice vinegar
2 T. sugar
1 T. mustard
½ c. fresh parsley leaves, chopped
½ c. fresh basil, chopped
½ c. fresh dill, chopped
¼ c. fresh mint leaves, chopped
Salt and pepper to taste

Cook pasta according to package directions, and rinse under cool water. Drain well. Combine prepared pasta with vegetables. Peel and chop eggs and add to pasta mixture. In a blender, combine the oil with the remaining ingredients until well mixed. Pour over pasta and toss to coat well. Chill at least 2 hours or overnight. Makes 8-10 servings.

Mom's Best Tossed Salad

I grew up in a home where salads were a big event. It was always a special treat when Mom made a big salad. Still miss salads at Mom's. Prepared carefully, and always tossed, they are a treat I still enjoy. The greens are a mix of red and green leaf lettuce, and a bit of romaine or some spinach.

Anchovy paste, optional
Assorted greens
Carrots
Chinese cabbage
Cucumber
Fresh mushrooms
Garden fresh tomatoes, in season
Green onions
Herbs
Oil-Salad oil, olive oil, or add a little walnut oil for a special treat.
Salt & Pepper
Sugar (optional)
Vinegar, cider or red wine and/or balsamic

Prep the greens early in the day, washing and spinning them dry. Then bag them up and put them in the fridge for at least several hours to crisp. You can prepare the other veggies closer to serving time: cutting tomatoes into chunks, chopping green onions and thinly slicing cucumbers, peeling them if needed. Mushrooms are cleaned and sliced thin. Chinese cabbage, or nappa, is sliced into very thin strips. Carrots are sliced thin or shredded, and other seasonal vegetables may be added. Finally, the wooden salad bowl is prepped by being rubbed with a little anchovy paste.

Tear the greens into bite-sized pieces and put them into the salad bowl, allowing about 2 cups per person. Add the other vegetables. Sprinkle lightly with salt and pepper, then a light drizzle of oil. Toss until the leaves are coated. It will take a lot less oil than you think. Next, chop whatever fresh herbs you have on hand. I always enjoy basil, parsley, cilantro, dill, or the mints. You can use dry herbs in a pinch, adding them to the vinegar a couple of minutes ahead to soften.

Sprinkle the fresh herbs into the salad bowl, and pour small amount of the vinegars over the salad. Like the oil, a little vinegar goes a long way. You won't need too much. Use about equal amounts of regular vinegar and balsamic vinegar. If you prefer a less tangy dressing, add sugar. Toss the dressing into the salad until the greens are well coated.

Add homemade or good quality boxed croutons if you like. Serve the salad immediately after tossing. Serve as a first course when possible. Stand back, people will want seconds.

Fruited Chicken Salad

4 c. cooked chicken, cubed
2 ribs celery, diced
2 c. seedless grapes, washed and stemmed
4 oz. Swiss cheese, cubed
2-3 c. cooked pasta
½ c. oil
⅓ c. orange juice concentrate, thawed
2 T. honey
2 T. vinegar
1 T. balsamic vinegar
2 T. lovage leaves or celery leaves, minced
1 T. fresh chives, minced
1 t. poppy seed
1 t. celery seed
Salt and pepper to taste

In a medium bowl, combine chicken, celery, grapes, cheese, and pasta. In a small bowl, whisk together the remaining ingredients until well blended, and pour over the chicken mixture. Toss well to coat, and chill before serving. Serves 4-6

Layered Mexican Salad

1 c. dry black beans
2 T. olive oil
2 T. white wine vinegar
½ t. salt
2 c. sliced lettuce (I like romaine)
1½ c. fresh corn, cooked 2 minutes or frozen corn, thawed
½ c. chopped green pepper
½ c. chopped sweet red or yellow pepper
2 c. tomato, chopped and seeded red and yellow, if available
1 c. grated Monterey Jack cheese
½ avocado (save till the end of preparation to slice)
½ c. chopped red onion
½ c. chopped pitted black olives

Dressing:
3-5 fresh or canned green chilies
½ c. white wine vinegar
2 T. balsamic vinegar
1 t. salt
⅔ c. olive oil
⅓ c. fresh packed cilantro

Prepare beans: Rinse and pick over beans. Place beans in a saucepan, and cover with 2 inches of water. Boil for 2 minutes, turn off the heat, and soak beans for 1 hour. Drain off the water, rinse beans, and cover with 2 inches of water again. Simmer until tender, 1-2 hours. Drain and rinse with cold water to refresh. Drain cooked beans.

Toss beans with the oil, white wine vinegar, and salt. Place the lettuce in the bottom of a glass bowl. Cover with the beans. Combine the corn and peppers, and layer on top of the beans. Place the tomatoes over the corn layer and the cheese over the tomatoes. Cover the salad, and chill for 8 hours.

Before serving, slice the avocado into thin slices, and arrange the slices like the spokes of a wheel on top of the salad. Garnish with the onion and olives. Process the dressing ingredients in a blender until smooth. Serve the dressing on the side, with the salad. Serves 8-10.

Couscous Salad

1 c. couscous
3 green onions, trimmed and chopped
1 red or yellow sweet pepper, seeded and chopped
2 ribs celery, chopped
½ c. fresh peas-cooked 1 minute or ½ frozen peas, thawed
¼ c. sliced black olives
¼ c. white wine vinegar
1 T. balsamic vinegar
½ c. chopped cilantro leaves
¼ c. chopped parsley leaves
1 T. celery seed
½ t. cumin
½ t. chili powder
salt and pepper to taste
2 T. oil

Cook couscous according to package directions. Drain and cool. Combine couscous with vegetables and olives. In a blender, combine the vinegars. Add the seasonings, and blend until the herbs are minced. Pour in the oil in a slow stream, with the machine running. Pour this dressing over the salad, and toss to coat well. Makes 4 servings.

Dressings
Italian Vinaigrette Dressing

¾ c. olive oil
⅓ c. red wine vinegar
1 T. water
1 T. sugar
1 clove garlic, minced
salt and pepper to taste
2 t. Italian Seasoning (see Chapter 4)

Make several hours ahead to blend flavors. Put all ingredients in a jar and shake well to blend. For a creamier texture, combine all *but* the oil in a blender. Mix well and, with blender running, pour oil into blender bowl in a slow stream. Dressing will emulsify and thicken.

Variations

Use the Herb Blends in Chapter 4 to vary the dressing

Cajun or Creole Vinaigrette: 1 t. either Cajun or Creole herb blend. Mix well.

Curry Vinaigrette: 1 t. of Curry Powder and add 2 tablespoons lemon juice

Herb Vinaigrette: Add 1-2 t. Everyday Herb Blend, Fines Herbes, Herbes de Provence, or Salad and Vegetable Seasoning to other ingredients.

Chinese 5 Spice Vinaigrette: Use ½ t. Five Spice Powder, and add 1 T. sesame oil.

Tuscan: Add 2 t. Tuscan Seasoning

Pizza Vinaigrette: Use 2 t. Pizza Seasoning. You can add 2-3 T. Parmesan cheese and a few slices of pepperoni, cut into thin strips. After tossing greens with dressing, you might want to sprinkle a little mozzarella cheese on the salad.

Tangy Curry Dressing

⅔ c. sugar
¼ c. olive oil
½ c. red wine vinegar
1 T. balsamic vinegar
1 T. fresh lemon or lime juice
1 T. chili sauce
1 t. Dijon mustard
1 t. Worcestershire sauce
½ t. curry powder
½ t. cumin
1 clove garlic, minced cayenne to taste

Whisk all ingredients together until sugar is dissolved. Store in fridge until ready to use. Can be used on chicken, seafood or fruit salads. Makes 1 cup of dressing.

Lemon Dill Dressing

¾ c. olive oil
½ c. fresh lemon juice
1 T. Dijon mustard
1 T. dill, minced
3 cloves garlic
½ t. salt
½ t. tarragon, crushed
½ t. rosemary, crushed
¼ t. cumin
¼ t. paprika
Pepper to taste

Combine all ingredients in blender until smooth. Use on vegetable salads, especially tomato and cucumber salads, or mixed greens. Also makes a nice dressing for canned tuna or fish, and chicken. Makes 1 cup of dressing.

Pesto Vinaigrette

1 c. fresh basil leaves
½ c. olive oil
2 cloves garlic
½ c. red wine vinegar or Basil Vinegar (See Chapter 14 on Herb Vinegars)
2 T. Parmesan cheese
Salt and pepper to taste
2 T. pine nuts (optional)

In blender or processor combine oil, basil, and garlic until well blended. Add vinegar and cheese and blend a few moments longer. Add salt and pepper to taste. Makes 1½ cups of dressing.

Note: Although you can add the pine nuts to the dressing at this point, I really like to sprinkle them on the salad when served.

This dressing is great on a mixed green salad, including romaine lettuce and fresh garden tomatoes. Being especially fond of sweet multicolored peppers, I also pour this dressing over a plate of peppers cut into thin strips. Pesto Vinaigrette can also be used as a marinade for veggies or chicken.

Fruit Salad Dressing

½ c. sugar
½ c. orange juice
⅓ c. fresh lime juice
¼ c. water
1 T. cornstarch
1 t. orange zest
3 T. fresh mint leaves, chopped
2 T. pineapple sage leaves, chopped (optional)
½ t. celery seed
Assorted fresh fruits

In a small saucepan, combine all ingredients-except fruit. Heat over medium heat, stirring constantly, until dressing starts to bubble and thicken. Remove from heat and allow to cool down before using. Toss with fresh fruits or serve on the side for dipping. Makes 1½ cups of dressing.

Gingered Fruit Salad Dressing

⅓ c. orange juice
¼ c. honey
1 T. lemon or lime juice
1 t. freshly grated ginger

Mix all ingredients and pour over assorted fruits. Works really well with pineapple, citrus fruit, or pears. Makes ¾ cup of dressing.

Greek Style Dressing

¾ c. olive oil
¼ c. vinegar
2 T. fresh lemon juice
1 T. fresh oregano or 1 t. dried
2 cloves garlic
¼ c. Greek or black olives, pitted and cut up
4-6 anchovies, cut up
½ c. feta cheese
salt and pepper to taste

In a blender, combine all ingredients--except anchovies and cheese. Process briefly to mix well. The anchovies and cheese can be stirred in before serving. Tastes great on a bed of mixed greens, or in chef's salads, especially with tomatoes and cucumbers. Makes 1 cup of dressing.

Dill Dressing

1 c. buttermilk
2 T. balsamic vinegar
1 T. lemon juice
1 T. sugar
2 T. fresh dill, minced, or 2 t. dried and crumbled
1 t. pepper
¼ t. cumin

Mix all ingredients together and chill well before using on mixed greens and vegetables salads. Great on cucumbers! Makes 1 cup of dressing.

Sesame Dressing

One of my favorite flavors is sesame. I love tahini, a paste made from sesame seed. To me the final touch of any good stir-fry is a drizzle of sesame oil. Its sweet and nutty flavor is unique but overpowering if you add too much, so be gentle. This dressing is great over a bed of baby greens, with perhaps a few pea pods, green onions, and pea shoots tossed in. Sesame Dressing is also great on spinach greens, or for just dipping sweet peppers in as a light and casual side dish.

½ c. rice vinegar, (available in Asian markets, and some supermarkets)
2 T. sherry (not cooking sherry)
2 T. brown sugar
1 T. tahini (sesame seed paste available in many grocery stores)
1 T. tamari sauce or soy sauce
2 t. fresh grated ginger
2 cloves garlic, minced
1 t. ground coriander
½ t. chili powder
½ t. red pepper flakes
½ c. olive oil
¼ c. sesame oil
2 T. sesame seed, toasted

Combine all ingredients-except the oils and sesame seeds in a blender. Blend until smooth. While blender is running, slowly add the oils. The dressing will emulsify and thicken. Stir in the sesame seeds and chill. Makes 1½ cups of dressing.

Lime Vinaigrette

¼ c. fresh lime juice
1 green onion, trimmed and chopped
2 T. fresh chopped parsley
1 T. fresh chopped basil
1 T. fresh chopped mint
½ t. salt
¼ t. cayenne pepper, or to taste
½ c. safflower oil
¼ c. walnut oil

Mix in a blender or food processor until well blended.
Makes 1 cup of dressing

Herb Vinaigrette

¼ c. red wine vinegar
2 T. Everyday Herb Blend 2, (see Chapter 4)
2 t. sugar
1 t. salt
½ c. olive oil

Shake together in container with tight fitting lid. Makes
¾ cup of dressing.

Fresh Herb Vinaigrette

¼ c. red wine vinegar
1 T. fresh chopped parsley
1 T. fresh chopped chervil
1 T. fresh thyme leaves
1 t. fresh tarragon leaves
½ t. salt
½ t. pepper
½ t. celery seed
½ c. olive oil
2 T. walnut oil

Combine all ingredients in blender and mix on low speed for 15 seconds. Makes about 1 cup of dressing.

Apple Vinaigrette

½ c. apple cider
¼ c. cider vinegar
1 T. fresh rosemary leaves
½ t. salt
¼ t. red pepper flakes
¾ c. olive oil

Combine all ingredients in a blender-except the oil. Mix until smooth. Add the oil in a slow stream, while blending. Dressing will thicken. Makes 1½ cups of dressing.

Tomato and Herb Dressing

1 c. tomatoes peeled, seeded, and chopped (fresh is
preferred, but canned are O.K.)
½ c. loosely-packed basil leaves
2 green onions, trimmed and chopped
2 T. fresh chopped celery or lovage leaves, or 2 t. dried
1 T. fresh chopped oregano or 1 t. dried
½ t. salt
½ t. garlic powder
½ c. olive oil
dash hot red pepper sauce

Combine all ingredients in a blender until smooth.
Makes 1½ cups of dressing.

Orange Vinaigrette

⅓ c. fresh squeezed orange juice
½ t. ground coriander
½ t. cumin
½ t. salt
pepper to taste
⅔ c. olive oil

Shake all ingredients together until well blended. Makes
1 cup of dressing.

French Tarragon Dressing

½ c. tarragon vinegar
1 T. Dijon-style mustard
2 T. fresh chopped tarragon or 2 t. dried
1 T. fresh chopped chervil or parsley
1 clove garlic
½ t. salt
pepper to taste
¾ c. olive oil

Combine all ingredients in a blender, except oil. While blending, add oil slowly until well incorporated. Chill before serving. Makes 1 cup of dressing.

Raspberry-Chive Vinaigrette

½ c. raspberry vinegar
3 T. minced chives
1 T. minced parsley
1 T. lime juice
1 T. honey
salt and pepper to taste
¼ c. olive oil
¼ c. walnut oil

Combine all ingredients in a small bowl-except the oils. Pour the oils into the vinegar mixture in a slow stream, whisking as you go to emulsify the mixture. You can do this in a blender, for a smoother end product. Makes 1 cup of dressing.

Parsley Dressing

1 T. cornstarch
1 T. honey
1 c. water
¼ c. red wine vinegar
2 T. balsamic vinegar
2 T. catsup
1 t. onion powder
1 t. garlic powder
1 t. Worcestershire sauce
½ t. salt
¼ t. pepper
½ c. fresh parsley leaves

In a small saucepan, combine the cornstarch, honey, and water. Mix until no lumps are visible. Heat until mixture starts to bubble. Cook, just simmering, for a few minutes more. Cool mixture and place in a blender with the remaining ingredients. Blend until the parsley is chopped fine. Makes about 1½ cups of dressing.

Variation: Use whatever herb you like in a salad. The following herbs will all work well in place of the parsley: cilantro, basil, tarragon (use 2 tablespoons only), dill, mint, lemon balm, chive, or pineapple sage.

Chapter 7: Salads and Dressings

Chapter 8
Main Dishes

Beef, Pork and Lamb
Herbed Lamb Chops
Braised Lamb Shanks
Spinach and Sorrel Roulade
Osso Buco
Herbed Lamb Kebobs
Pork Chops Piccata
Thai Steak with Pea Pods
Curried Lamb Riblets with Cucumber Yogurt Sauce
Roast Leg of Lamb with Herbs
Pork Loin with Herbs
Stuffed Pork Chops
Taco Casserole
Pizza Burgers
Herb Stuffed Veal Breast
Mexican Meatballs
Spicy Beef Ribs
Korean Beef Stir Fry
Sauerbraten
Curried Steak
Hearty Oxtail and Herb Stew
Cassoulet

Sausages
Lamb Sausage
Breakfast Sausage
Chorizo
Italian Sausage

Poultry
Herbed Chicken and Dumplings
Chicken Marsala
Asian Chicken and Shrimp
Chicken with Tomato Dressing
Herb Roasted Chicken
Pacific Rim Chicken
Four Seasons Chicken Salad
Easy Cacciatore
Curried Chicken
Pesto Chicken
Rosemary Chicken with Oranges
Spicy Pineapple Chicken
Chicken with Cucumbers
Savory Chicken with Mushrooms
Saté Chicken
Rock Cornish Hens with Herbs
Ethiopian Chicken
Chicken with Chutney
Company Duck
Mulled Duck
English Poached Goose
Tarragon Chicken

Seafood
Gumbo
Mussels Steamed with Herbs
Kabobs with Herbs
Marinated Shrimp
Creole Jambalaya
Grilled Swordfish
Tune and Pasta Pesto
Angel Hair Pasta with Herbed Clam Sauce
Crab Cakes with Basil Sauce

Vegetarian
Vegetarian Tacos
Vegetarian Burritos
Lentil Chili
Vegetarian Chili
Mushroom Quiche with Herbs
Spicy Beans and Rice
Chili Bean Spoon Bread
Curried Vegetables with Rice Noodles
No Pigs in These Blankets
Stuffed Peppers
Black-eyed Pea Casserole
Multi-Grain Pizza
Italian Pinto Bean Casserole
Eggplant Parmesan
Veggie Burgers
Veggies Burgers 2

Beef, Pork and Lamb
Herbed Lamb Chops

8 small rib lamb chops or 4 blade-cut chops
2 T. olive oil
2 cloves garlic, minced
2 medium onions, chopped
1 t. dried tarragon
1 t. dried thyme
1 t. fresh rosemary or ½ t. dried
⅓ c. Madeira wine
salt and pepper to taste

Heat oil in skillet and cook chops, turning to cook evenly on both sides until desired doneness is achieved. Remove chops from pan, set aside and keep warm. Meanwhile add garlic, onions, and herbs to skillet and cook, stirring frequently, until onions are translucent and tender. Pour wine over onions to deglaze pan and to make a sauce for the lamb chops. Cook until the wine is reduced by about half. This will take 5 minutes or so. Return the chops to the skillet and spoon sauce over them to flavor, adding salt and pepper as desired. Serves 4.

Braised Lamb Shanks

4 lamb shanks
flour for dredging the shanks
¼ c. olive oil
4 medium onions cut into thin slices
4 large carrots, peeled and cut into chunks
8 cloves garlic, minced
1 c. Marsala wine (not cooking wine)
1 c. stock (lamb, chicken, or vegetable)
1½-2 lbs. new potatoes
2 T. fresh parsley or 2 t. dried
1 T. fresh mint, or 1 t. dried
1 t. fresh rosemary, or ½ t. dried
1 t. fresh thyme, or ½ t. dried
½ t. paprika
salt and pepper to taste

Dredge shanks in flour and set aside. Heat oil in a large kettle or skillet, and brown the shanks, turning to brown on all sides. Set browned shanks aside and place onions in skillet with remaining oil. Cook over medium heat until lightly browned. Add carrots and garlic and cook 5 minutes more, being careful not to burn the garlic. Return the shanks to the pan, and add wine and stock. Cover and simmer until the shanks are almost tender, about 3 hours. Add the potatoes and cook until they are tender, about 20 minutes. Remove potatoes from the pan, cut them in half, and place in an ovenproof dish. Place potatoes at 400 degrees until the potatoes are lightly browned, about 20 minutes. Meanwhile, add the herbs to the shanks, stir to blend, and add salt and pepper to taste. Serve shanks with the potatoes. Makes 4 servings.

Spinach and Sorrel Roulade

2-2½ lbs. flank steak, trimmed of excess fat
salt and pepper to taste
¼ c. oil
2 c. beef stock
bay leaf

Stuffing:
¼ c. butter
1 lb. fresh spinach, rinsed, drained, and chopped
or one (10 oz.) package frozen spinach, thawed and
drained
2 cups fresh sorrel leaves, rinsed and chopped
1 medium carrot, peeled and diced
1 medium onion, chopped
2 t. each dried thyme and marjoram
1 package (6 oz.) corn bread stuffing mix or any
stuffing mix

Start by preparing stuffing. Melt butter in skillet and
add vegetables, sautéing until vegetables are just
tender, about 4 minutes. Add the stuffing mix, herbs,
and whatever water stuffing mix requires. Cover skillet
and simmer for about 8 minutes. Set aside. Place the
steak on a cutting board and, using a very sharp knife,
butterfly the meat. To butterfly the steak, hold the knife
parallel to the meat and cut all the way through--except
for a 1-inch strip along 1 side. Open the steak and place
the meat between 2 pieces of waxed paper. Pound it flat,
using a kitchen mallet. Salt and pepper the meat, and
cover it with the stuffing, leaving ½-inch around the
border. Roll up the meat with the grain, jellyroll style.
When rolled, secure with string about every 2-3 inches.
Heat oil in Dutch oven. Add the meat and brown on all
sides. Add broth and bay leaf and simmer, covered,

until meat is tender, about 1½ hours. To serve, remove from broth, cut off and discard strings, and slice into 1-inch slices. Makes 6-8 servings. Goes well with rice.

Osso Buco

This dish is traditionally made with veal shanks, but you can defy tradition and use beef shanks, lamb shanks, or even chicken thighs! The only rule for making Osso Buco is that you must make a vat of it. The flavors blend better that way.

4-5 lbs. veal shanks
Flour
½ stick butter
¼ c. olive oil
2 large onions, chopped
4 large carrots, peeled and chopped
4 ribs celery, chopped
2 lbs. fresh or canned tomatoes, peeled and chopped
4-5 cloves garlic, minced
1 c. white wine
1 qt. stock (chicken, beef, or veal)
salt and fresh ground pepper to taste
3 bay leaves
1 T. dried parsley
1 T. dried thyme
1 t. dried savory
½ t. dried rosemary
fresh chopped parsley

Dredge the shanks in the flour, and brown them in the butter and oil. Sauté until well browned, then place in a roasting pan. Sauté the onions in the same pan until tender. Add the carrots and celery, and sauté until the vegetables are getting tender. Add the vegetables to the roasting pan and the rest of the ingredients-except the herbs. Cover the roasting pan and bake at 350 degrees until the shanks are tender, about 1½ hours. Remove lid and add the herbs. Cook, uncovered, 45 minutes

148

more. Remove the shanks and keep them warm. Strain the pan juices. Skim off any visible fat and boil until the juices reduce to 2-3 cups. Pour this over the shanks, and garnish with the parsley. Serves 8-10.

Herbed Lamb Kabobs

Marinade:
½ c. fresh lime juice
½ c. red wine
2 T. fresh parsley
2 T. Fine Herbs or Herbes de Provence (see Chapter 4)
3 cloves garlic, minced
1 t. hot red pepper sauce
1 t. salt
½ t. fresh ground pepper
½ c. olive oil

Kabobs:
4 lbs. boneless lamb, cut into 1-inch cubes
8 oz. mushrooms, wiped clean and trimmed
2 red sweet peppers, seeded and cut into eighths
2 yellow sweet peppers, seeded and cut into eighths
4 medium onions, peeled and cut into quarters
16 cherry tomatoes
2 small zucchini, cut into chunks

Combine the marinade ingredients and add the lamb cubes. Place in a bowl, cover and refrigerate for at least 8 hours. Soak 16 wooden skewers in water for 1 hour. Then skewer the kabob ingredients, rotating them as best you can. Reserve the remaining marinade and place in saucepan and bring to a boil. Grill the kabobs until done, about 20 minutes for medium. While grilling, occasionally brush the kabobs with the remaining marinade. Serves 8.

Pork Chops Piccata

4 rib pork chops, 1-inch thick, trimmed of excess fat
salt and pepper to taste
flour for dredging the chops
¼ c. olive oil
½ c. red wine
¼ c. fresh lemon juice
2 T. orange juice concentrate
1 T. lime juice
2 T. fresh chopped parsley leaves
2 T. fresh chopped cilantro
1 t. dried basil
1 t. dried marjoram
1 t. dried savory
½ t. paprika

Season chops with salt and pepper, then dredge in flour. Heat the olive oil in a skillet and cook the chops, turning to brown evenly. After chops have browned. Turn down heat and continue cooking until juices run clear when chop is pierced with a fork. Remove the pork and keep warm. Add the wine to the pan to deglaze it. Stir to loosen any brown bits stuck in the bottom of the pan. Add juices and seasonings and cook over high heat until sauce is reduced by half. Strain the sauce and pour over the pork to serve. Chops are good served with oven roasted new potatoes or hot pasta. Serves 4.

Thai Steak with Pea Pods

1¼ lb. boneless steak
2 t. freshly grated ginger
2 T. oil
2 garlic cloves, minced
½ c. chopped shallots
1 lb. pea pods, washed and trimmed or 1 lb. sugar snap peas
½ lb. fresh bean sprouts
2 green onions, trimmed and chopped
2 T. sesame seed, toasted, optional

Dressing:
1 t. minced garlic cloves
¼ c. fresh lime juice
¼ c. rice vinegar
¼ c. soy sauce
2 T. honey
2 T. dried mint leaves
2 t. hot red pepper sauce
⅛ t. ground cloves
½ c. olive oil

Rub the steak with the ginger and brush with a little of the oil. Allow to stand for 10 minutes. Meanwhile, heat remaining oil in skillet and sauté garlic, shallots, and pea pods until pods are just heated through. Remove from heat.

Grill or broil the steak, and while it is cooking mix the dressing ingredients and set aside. When the steak is done, remove from heat and allow to stand 10 minutes before cutting into ½-inch strips. Place pea pod mixture and bean sprouts in bowl and toss with dressing. Toss in steak strips and divide salad among 4 serving plates.

Garnish with green onions and toasted sesame seed, if desired. Serves 4.

Curried Lamb Riblets with Cucumber Yogurt Sauce

Lamb riblets are generally inexpensive, as well as a fun meal. If you haven't tried them, this may be a fine time.

3-4 lbs. lamb riblets
oil
salt and pepper to taste
garlic powder
onion powder
cumin
curry powder (see Chapter 4)
dried mint leaves, crumbled

Sauce:
2 c. plain yogurt
1 medium cucumbers, peeled, seeded, and chopped
½ c. fresh chopped mint leaves
¼ c. fresh-snipped dill weed
2 t. celery seed

Rub oil over the riblets. Season the ribs with the salt and pepper. Sprinkle with the other seasonings, according to your own taste.

Note: Curry powders can vary in heat, so better a light hand to begin! Add more to taste after they are cooked, if you feel that they need it.

Bake the riblets on a rack in a baking dish at 350 degrees for about 1 hour and 30 minutes, turning now and then. They should brown nicely in this time. If you like them crisper, just put them under the broiler for 5-10 minutes at the end of the cooking time.

Note: They can also be grilled. Plan on an hour and 45 minutes on the grill.

While the riblets are cooking, combine and chill the sauce. Serve it on the side. Serves 4.

Roast Leg of Lamb with Herbs

Marinade:
½ c. Dijon mustard
⅓ c. minced shallots
3 cloves garlic, minced
2 T. fresh chervil, or 2 T. fresh parsley
1 T. fresh rosemary, or 1 t. dried
1 T. fresh savory, or 1 t. dried
1 T. fresh lovage or 1 t. dried or 2 T. fresh chopped
celery leaves
1 T. salt
1 T. coarse ground pepper
½ c. apple cider
¼ c. olive oil
1 (7-8) lb. leg of lamb, deboned if desired
3 cups beef or lamb stock
½ c. milk
3-4 T. flour
2 T. apple butter, optional

In blender or food processor combine all marinade ingredients except the oil. Pulse a few times to combine well. Add the oil in a slow stream while the processor is running. Place leg of lamb in a large pan and rub it with the marinade, pressing the herbs into the flesh to facilitate sticking. Cover lamb and refrigerate for at least 5 hours or preferably overnight. Several times during this marinating process turn the roast and rub the marinade in again. Preheat oven to 450 degrees. Place lamb in a roasting pan with a rack in the bottom. Roast at 450 for 20 minutes, then turn down the oven to 350 and continue roasting until the lamb is done. It will take at least 1½ hours, but use a meat thermometer if you are unsure.

During the first hour of roasting brush the lamb once with remaining marinade, then discard remaining marinade. When lamb is done to your liking remove it from the oven and let it stand at least 15 minutes before carving. While roast is standing you can make the gravy. Place roasting pan on stove burner and turn on heat under it to medium high. Pour in the stock and stir it around, loosening any of the brown bits from the bottom of the pan. With some assistance, pour this mixture through a strainer into a medium saucepan, using a spatula to loosen any remaining bits from the roasting pan. Heat the stock and in a small container with a tight fitting lid combine the milk and flour, using more flour for a thicker gravy, according to your taste. Place lid on container and shake vigorously so no lumps are observed. Pour this mixture into the saucepan, straining it through the sieve used earlier, if desired. Add apple butter if desired and stir over medium high heat until thickened and smooth. As you carve the leg of lamb pour any platter juices into the gravy. Serve with rice or mashed potatoes, if desired. Makes 8 servings.

Pork Loin with Herbs

1 T. olive oil
1 T. dried parsley
1 t. dried thyme
1 t. caraway seed
1 t. dried basil
½ t. dried oregano
½ t. fennel seed
¼ t. cayenne pepper
¼ t. salt
2 cloves garlic, minced
1 (4-5) lb. boneless pork loin, tied into a roll

Gravy:
¼ c. applejack or apple brandy (apple cider may be substituted)
2 cups pork, chicken or veal stock
1 T. olive oil
2-3 T. flour
2 large sweet onions, sliced into thin slices
salt and pepper to taste
1 t. freshly grated ginger, optional

Brush roast with the oil. Mix seasonings well in a small bowl.

Note: For a finer texture you can pulse the herbs a few times in a small food processor or in a blender.

Actually, what I find works well is to use the old mortar and pestle to crush the herbs, especially the seeds, releasing their flavors without making them into a fine powder.

Prepare the herbs and rub them all over the pork. Then place the pork in a pan, cover and refrigerate overnight or at least for 6 hours.

Preheat the oven to 375 and roast the herbed pork on a pan with a rack until it registers 155 on a meat thermometer or until the juices run clear when pierced. The "juices running clear" method only works if you pierce the thickest part of the roast with a large fork to be sure. When done, set the roast on a platter for 10-15 minutes to make it easier to carve.

Meanwhile, make the gravy. Pour the applejack and stock into the roasting pan and place it on a burner over medium heat, stirring to loosen the brown bits from the bottom of the pan. Carefully pour this mixture through a strainer into a saucepan, and set aside. Meanwhile, in a skillet, heat the remaining oil and sauté the onions slowly until they are golden brown. (This part can be done earlier and just be reheated when needed.)

Toss the flour over the onions, and then pour in the heated stock and cook until thickened. Add the ginger, if desired, and adjust seasonings as needed. The roast and gravy taste great served with oven-roasted potatoes, hot cooked rice, or pasta. Serves 8-10.

Variations:

Tex-Mex: You can make a great south of the border version of this pork roast by changing the seasonings, and following all other directions for regular Pork Loin with Herbs.

3 T. fresh chopped cilantro
2 t. salt
2 t. chili powder
2 t. ground cumin seed
1 t. paprika
1 t. dried oregano
½ t. freshly ground pepper
dash of hot red pepper sauce
3-4 cloves garlic, minced

For the applejack you can substitute 2 T. tequila, or ½ cup Mexican beer of your choice. Eliminate the ginger. You can garnish each serving with chopped green chilies, or salsa. Serve Tex-Mex pork roast with Spanish rice, or on a bed of shredded lettuce with refried beans.

Fruited: *In this version, we create a sweet and sour dish.*

3 T. fresh parsley, chopped
2 T. fresh mint, chopped, or 2 t. dried
1 T. fresh pineapple sage leaves, or additional mint leaves
1 T. fresh lemon thyme leaves, or 1 t. lemon zest.
1 T. fresh or dried lavender blossoms
1 T. fresh orange zest
salt and pepper to taste
3-4 cloves garlic, minced

For the applejack you might prefer to use ½ cup fresh-squeezed orange juice. Add ¼ cup chive blossom vinegar, if available. If not, add ¼ cup apple cider vinegar. Also, for the gravy, peel, pit, and chop 1 lb. of fresh peaches, or nectarines.

Note: To peel peaches or nectarines, just put the fruit in boiling water for 1 minute, then remove to ice water for a few minutes. Skins will slip off easily.

Poach the fruit in the stock to soften, and set aside until the gravy is being thickened. Add fruit to the gravy. Serve Fruited Pork Roast over hot pasta or rice.

Italian: Yet another variation of this dish is an Italian version, great served with hot cooked pasta and steamed broccoli.

3 T. fresh basil, or 1 T. dried
1 T. dried oregano
1 T. dried parsley
2 t. salt
2 t. dried marjoram
2 t. dried rosemary
2 t. fennel seed
2 t. fresh ground pepper
3-4 cloves garlic, minced

Use ½ c. dry red wine in place of the applejack, and add 1 cup tomato sauce and 2 T. tomato paste to the gravy. Sprinkle servings with freshly grated Parmesan cheese, or serve it on the side.

Asian: In yet another version of the roast, use:

1 T. Chinese five spice powder (see Chapter 4)
2 t. fresh grated ginger
2 t. soy sauce
2-3 cloves garlic, minced

Substituting for the applejack, use ½ cup hoisin sauce, available in some supermarkets and Asian groceries. Thicken the gravy with cornstarch instead of flour. Garnish with chopped green onion. Serve over hot cooked rice.

Asian 2: *I know, I know, enough already! Well, I promise this is the last version. Take it as proof that by changing the seasonings you can make endless variations on most dishes.*

1 T. sesame oil (rub into roast)
1 T. soy sauce
1 T. pink peppercorns, crushed slightly
1 T. coriander, crushed slightly
2 t. freshly grated ginger
3-4 cloves garlic, minced

For the applejack, substitute ½ cup dry sherry and add 2 T. hoisin sauce. Use cornstarch to thicken the gravy instead of the flour. Garnish with toasted sesame seeds and chopped green onions. Serve over hot cooked rice.

Stuffed Pork Chops

4 (1-inch thick) rib pork chops
1 T. olive oil
salt and pepper to taste

Stuffing:
1 medium onion, diced
2 cloves garlic, minced
1 T. fresh rosemary, chopped, or 1 t. dried
2 c. bread cubes, toasted lightly
½ c. chicken broth or a little more if needed
pinch nutmeg

Start by making a pocket in the chops. Using a very sharp knife, cut into the chops horizontally, splitting the meat to the bone, but leaving it slightly uncut at the top and bottom of the chops. Salt and pepper chops lightly and set aside.

In medium bowl, combine all stuffing ingredients and stir to blend, or use your hands to lightly knead the ingredients together. Stuff ¼ of this mixture into each chop, and secure with toothpicks if necessary. Heat oil in skillet and pan fry chops, turning to brown evenly. Turn the heat down and cover pan, turning chops if needed. Cook until juices run clear.

Note: You can substitute sage for the rosemary for a different flavor.

Another nice flavor is 2 T. cilantro, 1 t. cumin, and a dash of chili powder. Makes 4 servings.

Taco Casserole

1 lb. lean ground beef or turkey
1 large onion, chopped
1 green pepper, chopped
1 sweet red pepper, chopped
1 c. chunky salsa
1 c. taco sauce
2 t. cilantro
1 T. chili powder
2 t. cumin
2 t. oregano
½ t. cinnamon
1 bag tortilla chips
8 oz. shredded cheddar cheese
8 oz. shredded Monterey Jack cheese
1 (4 oz.) can green chilies, drained and sliced
½ c. sliced black olives
1 c. sour cream or Greek yogurt

In non-stick skillet cook beef until no pink is visible. Remove from pan and drain off excess grease. Return the pan to the heat, and sauté onions and peppers until onions are translucent. Return the beef to the pan, and add the salsa and taco sauce. Stir in seasonings, and place mixture in an ovenproof dish. (A flat pan works better than one that is narrow with high sides.)

Sprinkle the cheeses over the top, then the chilies and olives, and place in a preheated 350-degree oven for 20-30 minutes, or until the casserole is heated through. To serve, place a handful of the tortilla chips on each plate, and spoon some of the casserole over the chips. Dollop with sour cream or yogurt, if desired. For a lower calorie version, the casserole can be spooned into corn or flour tortillas, and folded into a burrito rather than using the fried tortilla chips. Makes 4-6 servings.

Pizza Burgers

1½ lbs. lean ground beef, turkey, or chicken
1 medium onion, diced
2 T. tomato paste, optional
¼ c. breadcrumbs
2 T. Pizza Seasoning (see Chapter 4)
1 clove garlic, minced
1 t. salt

Toppings:
Mozzarella cheese
pepperoni
grilled onions
sweet peppers, chopped
black olives
tomato slices
romaine lettuce
pizza or spaghetti sauce
sautéed mushrooms

Combine burger ingredients and form into 6-8 burgers. Grill, pan fry, or broil to desired doneness. Place on buns, and finish with assorted toppings. Serves 6-8.

Herb Stuffed Veal Breast

1 (7-8) lb. veal breast
olive oil
salt and pepper to taste
3-4 cloves minced garlic

Stuffing:
6-8 cups day old bread, cubed
oil
1 large onion, diced
2 large carrots, peeled and diced
2 ribs celery, diced
2 c. chicken or veal stock
½ c. fresh chopped parsley
1 T. fresh thyme
1 T. fresh savory
2 t. fresh marjoram
1 t. fresh rosemary
1 cup chicken or veal stock
½ c. white wine

Prep veal breast by rubbing with oil. Season with salt and pepper inside and out. Place about half the garlic in the cavity, and press the remaining garlic into the breast after it has been stuffed. Place the veal breast in a lightly oiled baking dish.

To prepare the stuffing, place the bread in a large bowl. Heat some oil in a skillet and sauté the onion, carrots, and celery until tender. Add the vegetables to the bread, and pour in the stock.

Note: Warming the stock a little will make it easier to incorporate into the bread.

Depending on the type of bread you use, you may have to use a little more stock.

Stir the herbs into the stuffing, and stuff this mixture into the cavity of the veal breast. The stuffing should stick out somewhat. Press remaining garlic into the surface of the breast. Pour the stock and wine into the bottom of the baking dish. Add the stuffed veal breast, and cover with a lid or foil. Bake in a 350-degree oven for about 3 hours. The veal will be very tender. Remove foil or lid, and bake veal breast uncovered at 450 degrees for about 20 more minutes to crisp up the stuffing a little. Pan juices can be strained and served on the side if you like. Serve with rice or boiled new potatoes. Serves 6-8.

Mexican Meatballs

Meatballs:
1 lb. lean ground beef (or ground chicken or turkey)
1 c. breadcrumbs, or more if mixture is too soft
½ c. chunky salsa
½ c. taco sauce
1 medium onion, minced
3-5 green chilies, seeded and chopped **or** use canned chilies
2 eggs
½ c. fresh chopped cilantro
1 t. salt
1 t. pepper
1 t. cumin
1 t. dried oregano
1 t. chili powder

Sauce:
1 c. salsa
1 c. tomato sauce
½ c. fresh chopped cilantro
2 t. cumin
8 oz. shredded cheddar cheese

Combine all meatball ingredients and form into 12 meatballs. Place on lightly oiled baking sheet and bake in a 350-degree oven for about 40 minutes, turning occasionally. Place meatballs under the broiler for 5-10 minutes, turning once or twice to brown, if desired. Meanwhile, heat together the sauce ingredients. Place meatballs on a serving platter, and top with sauce. Serve the cheese on the side. These can be eaten with pasta, but I really like them with Spanish rice. Serves 4.

Spicy Beef Ribs

12 meaty beef rib bones, separated
½ c. cider vinegar
½ c. honey
2 T. soy sauce
2 T. Dijon mustard
1 T. chili powder
1 T. paprika
1 t. coriander
1 t. cayenne pepper
1 t. garlic powder
1 t. onion powder
juice of 1 lime or lemon

Combine ribs and vinegar, and marinade the ribs in a covered dish in the refrigerator overnight. In a separate bowl, combine the rest of the sauce ingredients and refrigerate overnight. The next day, drain the vinegar off the ribs and add it to the honey sauce. Pour this sauce over the ribs, and let stand 1 hour. Transfer the ribs to a broiler-safe dish or pan. Boil the sauce. Heat broiler, and broil the ribs about 4 inches from the heat source, turning to cook evenly. Brush with sauce each time you turn the ribs. Or, you can cook the ribs over a grill. Broiling will take 10 minutes total for medium rare, and 15 minutes total for medium. Serves 4-6.

Korean Beef Stir Fry

1½ lbs. boneless steak, trimmed of excess fat and cut into thin strips (bottom round or sirloin will both work well)
4 cloves garlic, minced
¼ c. sesame oil
2 T. light soy sauce
2 t. freshly grated ginger
1 t. hot red pepper sauce
2 T. oil
1 large onion, chopped
2 celery ribs, sliced
½ c. sliced water chestnuts
½ lb. fresh bean sprouts
½ lb. fresh pea pods, washed and trimmed
1 red sweet pepper, seeded and cut into julienne strips
1 green sweet pepper, seeded and cut into julienne strips
1 15 oz. can baby corn on the cob, drained
½ c. beef stock
1 T. cornstarch
3 T. sugar
2 T. rice vinegar
2 T. toasted sesame seed
3 green onions washed, trimmed and cut into julienne strips
Hot cooked rice or Asian noodles

Note: This recipe can also use chicken, pork, or turkey.

Combine the beef strips with the garlic, sesame oil, soy sauce, ginger and hot pepper sauce. Marinade in the refrigerator for at least 3 hours. Heat salad oil in wok or large skillet, and stir fry the onions until lightly browned. Add celery and stir fry 4 more minutes, then add the water chestnuts, bean sprouts, and pea pods and stir fry 2 more minutes. Toss in the peppers and baby corn, and stir-fry 1 minute. Remove vegetables from pan. Return pan to heat and add extra oil if needed. Stir-fry beef until just cooked through, about 7 minutes. Combine the beef stock with the cornstarch to dissolve. Add to wok along with the sugar and vinegar. Cook, stirring constantly, until sauce is thick and bubbly. If sauce is too thick you can add some of the liquid, which generally accumulates in the vegetables when they sit. Return vegetables to pan and toss to combine. Add extra soy sauce, if needed. Place in serving dish and sprinkle with the sesame seed and green onions. Serve with the rice or noodles. Serves 6-8.

Sauerbraten

This recipe comes from my sister, Cindy Morgner of Central Lake, Michigan. She has made adjustments over the years, and I can attest to her success.

Marinade:
1 c. red wine vinegar
½ c. cider vinegar
½ c. Burgundy wine
1 large onion, sliced
2 carrots, peeled and sliced
top from 1 bunch celery
few sprigs of fresh parsley or 1 T. dried
1 bay leaf
4 whole cloves
3 whole allspice
½ t. whole peppercorns
1 t. salt
4-6 lb. lean boneless chuck roast
additional flour for dredging
⅓ c. oil
2 c. warm water
¼ c. flour
1 T. sugar
1 c. crushed gingersnaps
water

Combine marinade ingredients in a large glass or ceramic bowl. Add meat and cover. Refrigerate 3-5 days. Turn meat at least once a day. Remove meat from marinade and pat dry. Dredge in flour. Heat oil in Dutch oven and brown meat in pan. Add warm water and simmer, covered, for 1-2 hours or until fork tender. Start testing meat for doneness after the first hour.

Remove meat to platter and keep warm while sauce is being prepared.

For sauce, strain the pan juices and discard solids. Skim off any fat. Return the juices to the Dutch oven and keep hot. In small bowl combine the ¼ c. flour, sugar, and gingersnaps. Stir in cold water until smooth paste is formed. Whisk this paste into the hot marinade and simmer, stirring until thickened. If it's not thick enough, make a little more paste with flour and water. Serve meat sliced thin, with sauce on the side, and hot cooked noodles, potato dumplings, or spaetzle. Serves 8-12.

Curried Steak

1½ lb. round or flank steak, cut into thin slices about
4-inches long
2 T. oil
1 large onion, cut into chunks
3 cloves garlic, minced
1 large tomato, seeded and diced
1 lb. green beans, trimmed and cut into 1-inch pieces
1 large yellow or red sweet pepper, seeded and cut into
chunks
1 large sweet potato, cooked and cut into chunks
1 T. honey
1-2 T. curry powder (see Chapter 4)
1 t. salt
1-2 c. beef stock
2 T. cornstarch

Heat oil in skillet, and add the meat. Stir-fry until meat
loses its pink color. Set meat aside. Adding extra oil if
needed, stir fry the onion until just brown. Add the
garlic, tomato, and beans and cook until tomato softens
a little, about 5 minutes. Stir in the pepper and sweet
potato. Cook 2 more minutes. Return beef to pan. Add
the honey, curry powder, and salt. Reserving ¼ cup,
heat beef stock in the pan until it begins to boil.
Combine the remaining stock with cornstarch and stir
until smooth. Pour this mixture into the pan and cook
1 minute more to thicken. Serve over hot cooked
couscous, basmati rice, or use any white or brown rice
that suits you. Serves 6-8.

Hearty Oxtail and Herb Stew

4-5 lbs. oxtails, trimmed of excess fat
2 T. oil
4-6 c. beef stock
2 c. red wine
2 large onions, sliced thin
1 lb. carrots, peeled and cut into chunks
2 medium turnips, peeled and diced
3 lbs. new red potatoes, washed
2 (14.5 oz.) cans whole tomatoes, un-drained
2 T. fresh parsley, chopped or 2 t. dried
2 t. dried oregano
2 t. dried marjoram
1 t. dried rosemary
1 t. dried savory
1 t. dried thyme
1 t. fresh ground pepper
3 T. butter or oil
½ c. flour
additional fresh parsley for garnish if desired

In a large ovenproof pot or Dutch oven, heat the oil and brown the oxtails until evenly cooked on all sides. Add 4 cups of the stock, and the wine, onions, carrots and turnips. Cover pot, and place in a preheated 350-degree oven. Cook for 2-3 hours, or until oxtails are almost tender. Add the potatoes and tomatoes, and return to the oven for 45 minutes more. Remove from oven, add the seasonings, and stir to blend. Let the pot simmer on the stove while you make the roux.

To make the roux, combine the butter and flour and mix until smooth. Add a little (a cup or so) of the hot stock, and whisk to prevent lumps. Add more stock until you've added 2 cups in all. Whisk as you add the stock to prevent lumping. Add the roux to the stew and stir. The sauce will thicken in about 1 minute, but cook for about 5 minutes to improve the texture. Stir as needed to prevent sticking, adding extra stock if needed or desired. Serve the oxtail stew plain or over hot cooked pasta or rice. Garnish with parsley. Serves 6-8.

Cassoulet

This hearty French stew has a hundred variations. This is the way I make it, adjusting according to what's on hand

2 lbs. dry navy or baby lima beans (but use what you like)
water for cooking the beans
3 qts. chicken stock
1 lb. smoked sausage, cut into 2-inch pieces
½ lb. thick sliced bacon, cut into small cubes
4 large onions, cut into chunks
2 lbs. carrots, peeled and cut into chunks
4 garlic cloves, minced
1 lb. lamb stew meat, cut into chunks
1 (4-5 lb.) duck, skinned and cut into eighths
3 (14.5oz.) cans tomatoes, un-drained and chopped
5 ribs celery, sliced
½ c. fresh parsley
2 T. fresh lovage leaves, or celery leaves
1 T. fresh thyme, or 1 t. dried
1 T. fresh savory, or 1 t. dried
1 T. fresh tarragon, or 1 t. dried
½ t. dried sage
6-8 cups homemade or good quality croutons

Soak the beans in water overnight. Rinse and drain them in the morning. Place the beans in a large pot, and add fresh water to cover by a couple of inches. Cook until the beans are tender. Drain and discard the cooking liquid. Return the beans to the pot. Add 2 quarts of the stock (reserve one quart) and the smoked sausage. Simmer 30-45 minutes more.

Meanwhile, in large skillet, cook the bacon until crisp. Drain off most of the fat. Add the onions, carrots, and garlic and cook in the bacon fat until onions start to brown. Transfer vegetable-bacon mixture to a bowl. In same pan, adding more bacon fat or oil if necessary, brown the lamb cubes, stirring to brown evenly. Set aside. Brown the duck pieces in the same fashion. In a large casserole dish, add the ingredients, half of at a time, to make 2 layers of each. (The order is not really that important.) Add the stock and beans, the tomatoes, and the celery.

Heat the reserved one quart of stock and pour it into the skillet. Cook over medium heat, stirring to remove all the brown bits from the bottom of the pan. Strain this liquid, and add it to the casserole dish. Place the cassoulet in a 350-degree oven for 2 hours. Remove the cassoulet from the oven and add the seasonings, stirring to blend well. Top with the croutons and return to the oven, uncovered, and cook until the croutons start to brown, about15 minutes. Serves 8-10 generously.

Sausages

The nicest thing about homemade sausage is the control you have over the ingredients. Yet sausage making is an area of cooking that most home cooks rarely try. The hard part is getting the meat mixture into the casings. But you don't have to use casings at all. In the following recipes, you use bulk sausage, forming it into patties or cigar shapes. Of course, if you want to use casings, or if you have a sausage stuffer, great. But most of us simply won't bother to make homemade sausage if special equipment is required Just a reminder about safety. Since you are cutting the food into such small pieces, the risk for contamination increases. To prepare safely, keep ingredients cold, work quickly, cook completely and handle foods as little as possible.

Lamb Sausage

½ c. cracker crumbs
3 T. chicken stock
2 T. soy sauce
1 lb. lean ground lamb
¼ c. minced red onion
3 T. fresh chopped mint or 1 T. dried
2 T. fresh chopped parsley
2 T. fresh chopped thyme or 2 t. dried
1 t. fresh rosemary or ⅓ t. dried
¼ t. pepper
1 egg

Combine all ingredients. Chill several hours to blend flavors. Form into patties and fry or bake. Makes 4 servings.

Breakfast Sausage

2½ lbs. ground pork or turkey (leave on a little fat)
1 T. dried sage
2 t. salt
2 t. pepper
1 t. dried marjoram
½ t. dried thyme
¼ t. allspice
¼ t. nutmeg
¼ t. dry mustard
⅛ t. cloves
pinch of cayenne pepper
⅓ c. warm water

Mix herbs and spices with water and let stand 10 minutes. Add the water and spice mixture to the meat and blend thoroughly. Form into patties, and chill or cook immediately. Patties can be fried or baked. This sausage can also be frozen for later use. Makes almost 3 pounds.

Chorizo

This Spanish sausage is quite popular. Commercially prepared chorizo is sometimes quite hot. This recipe is pretty mild, but you can increase the heat if you prefer.

2 lbs. lean ground pork
2 T. paprika
2 T. chili powder
2 t. oregano
1 t. cumin
1 t. garlic powder
1 t. pepper
½ t. ground cinnamon
½ t. ground cloves
½ t. ground coriander
½ t. fresh ground ginger
2 T. red wine vinegar
2 T. balsamic vinegar
¼ c. red wine

Combine all ingredients in a large bowl. Mix very well. Chill several hours until flavors blend and sausage firms up. Form into patties or into cigar-shaped tubes. Fry, bake or broil. Makes 2¼ pounds.

Italian Sausage

3 lbs. ground pork
½ c. fresh chopped parsley
2 T. salt
1 T. fennel seed
1 T. dried oregano
1 T. dried minced garlic
2 t. black pepper
2 t. red pepper flakes (omit for mild sausage)
2 t. thyme
2 bay leaves, crumbled
½ t. allspice
¼ t. nutmeg
¼ c. red wine

Mix all ingredients together in a large bowl. Mix well and chill several hours before using. Can be used bulk, or formed into patties or links. Makes 3¼ pounds.

Poultry
Herbed Chicken and Dumplings

1 T. oil
1 (3 lb.) broiler-fryer, cut into serving pieces
salt and pepper
flour for dredging
1 medium onion, chopped
2 carrots, peeled and sliced
3-4 medium potatoes, cut into chunks
2 c. chicken stock
1 c. buttermilk baking mix
⅓ c. milk
2 t. Fine Herbes or Poultry Seasoning (see Chapter 4)

Heat oil in skillet. Season chicken pieces with salt and pepper and dredge in flour. Brown chicken pieces in skillet and remove from pan. Sauté onions in skillet until browned. Add carrots, potatoes, chicken stock and chicken to skillet. Bring to a simmer and cover. Allow to simmer about 20 minutes. Sprinkle chicken with the herbs.

Combine the baking mix and milk. Spoon into pan in 8 mounds. Cover pan and simmer until dumplings are cooked, about 20 minutes. Remove lid and cook 5 more minutes. Serves 4.

Variations
Italian: Use 1 T. Italian Seasoning (see Chapter 4). Add 2 T. tomato paste to sauce, if desired.

Indian: Use 1-2 t. curry powder. Add ½ cup yogurt to sauce.

Mexican: Use 1-2 T. taco seasoning. Add 2-3 chopped green chilies to sauce.

Chicken Marsala

6 boneless, skinless chicken breast halves
2-3 T. oil
1 medium onion, chopped
8 oz. sliced mushrooms salt and pepper to taste flour
½-1 c. Marsala wine (not cooking wine, it's too salty)
1 T. fresh chopped tarragon
1 T. fresh chopped parsley

Pound chicken breasts until thin (about ¼-½ inch thick). Season with salt and pepper. Set aside. In skillet, heat oil and cook onion until well browned. Add the mushrooms and cook 3-5 minutes longer. Set aside. Heat additional oil in skillet, if necessary. Dredge the chicken in flour and sauté in skillet until lightly browned. Add wine and onion mixture, and cook until sauce is thickened and bubbly. Add herbs, and cook 1-2 minutes more to blend flavors. Serve over hot cooked rice or pasta. Serves 6.

Asian Chicken and Shrimp

2 large whole or 4 halves boneless, skinless chicken
breasts
¾-1 lb. medium shrimp, shelled and deveined, tails
left on
1 T. soy sauce
1 T. sesame oil
1 T. freshly grated ginger
1 t. coriander seed, crushed
⅛ t. cayenne pepper
1 T. cornstarch
2 T. oil
1 large sweet onion, cut into chunks
1-2 summer or yellow squash, or zucchini cut into
slices
1 rib celery, sliced
½ lb. fresh pea pods, trimmed
1 sweet red or yellow pepper, cut into julienne strips
½-1 c. chicken stock
Hot cooked rice

Cut the chicken into thin strips and place in medium
bowl. Add the soy sauce, sesame oil, ginger, coriander
and cayenne pepper. Refrigerate for at least 2 hours to
blend flavors.

Heat oil in wok. Toss the chicken mixture with the
cornstarch. Add the chicken to the wok and stir-fry
until no pink is visible. Add the shrimp, and stir-fry 3-
5 minutes more, until the shrimp has turned pink.
Remove chicken and shrimp from wok. Using more oil
if needed, add the onions to the wok and stir-fry until
onion starts to brown on edges. Add squash and celery
and stir-fry 3 minutes more. Add the pea pods and
pepper and stir-fry 2 more minutes. Add stock to wok,

and add the chicken and shrimp. As sauce comes to a boil it will thicken from the cornstarch on the chicken. For thicker sauce, dissolve a teaspoon or two of extra cornstarch in a little water and add it to the wok. Serve over hot rice or over Chinese noodles. Serves 6.

Chicken with Tomato Dressing

2 T. fresh basil, or 2 t. dried
1 T. fresh lemon juice
1 T. fresh lime juice
1 T. fresh chopped parsley
1 (14.5 oz.) can whole tomatoes, undrained
1 clove garlic, minced
⅛ t. cayenne pepper
¼ c. balsamic vinegar
2 t. honey salt to taste
4 boneless, skinless chicken breast halves
1 T. oil
1-2 t. fresh thyme leaves

In blender combine the basil, juices, parsley, and tomato liquid, reserving tomatoes. Blend until smooth. Add the tomatoes, garlic, pepper, vinegar, and honey. Blend until some tomato chunks still remain. Pour this sauce into a pan, and boil until it is reduced by half. Meanwhile, salt the chicken breasts. Heat oil in a skillet and sauté the chicken until it is cooked. Pour sauce over the chicken, simmer about 3-5 minutes more, and add the thyme. Serve over hot cooked pasta, rice, or baked or boiled potatoes. Serves 4.

Herb Roasted Chicken

1 whole broiler/fryer (3-4 lbs.)
salt and pepper
2-4 cloves fresh garlic, chopped
assorted fresh sprigs of rosemary, thyme, lovage,
tarragon, mint, or parsley.

> *Note: If you prefer, you can combine a couple of these, but avoid rosemary and tarragon together as both are strong and could overpower the chicken.*

paprika, optional

Wash chicken and pat dry. Trim off wing tips, if desired, and use with giblets to make stock. Pull the skin away from the chicken and slide the herbs under the skin. The herbs only need to be here and there, not all over the chicken, or the flavor will be too strong. Lay the skin back into place. Salt and pepper the chicken inside and out, if desired, and put the garlic in the cavity. For additional color and flavor, sprinkle the chicken with a little paprika.

Place the chicken on a rack in a roasting pan, and bake in a preheated 350-degree oven for about 1 hour 15 minutes, or until the juices run clear when leg is pierced (the white meat tends to cook faster, so don't use it as a gauge). You can also use a meat thermometer. To use the thermometer, place in the chicken in the thickest part of the meat, avoiding bone. Remove when thermometer reaches poultry level, and serve. Serves 4-6.

Pacific Rim Chicken

Marinade:
⅓ c. chicken stock
¼ c. pineapple juice
2 T. fresh chopped basil, lemon basil if available
1 T. cornstarch
soy sauce to taste
1 t. coriander
½ t. turmeric
¼ t. cayenne pepper
1 lb. boneless, skinless chicken, cut into strips
2 T. peanut oil
1 medium onion, chopped
1 rib celery, chopped
1 carrot, peeled and sliced thin
½ lb. pea pods, trimmed and washed
1 sweet red pepper, cut into julienne strips
1 sweet green or yellow pepper, cut into thin strips
¼ c. peanuts
2 t. sesame oil
2 T. fresh chopped cilantro

Combine ingredients for the marinade. Mix stock, pineapple juice, basil, cornstarch, soy sauce, coriander, turmeric and cayenne pepper. Pour over chicken and set aside, or cover and refrigerate for up to 12 hours.

Heat oil in large skillet or wok. Stir-fry the onion until wilted and tender. Toss in celery and carrot, and stir-fry until carrots are tender-crisp, about 4 minutes. Add pea pods, peppers, and peanuts. Stir-fry 1 minute, and remove vegetables from pan.

Reheat the pan, adding more oil if needed. Drain chicken, reserving marinade. Add chicken to skillet and stir-fry until it is cooked through. To check for doneness, pierce a piece of chicken and check for any signs of pink. Juices that are colorless mean that the chicken is cooked.

Add the sauce to the pan, and stir-fry until sauce is thickened. Add the vegetables to the pan and toss well for 1 minute. Add the sesame oil and cilantro. Toss to distribute evenly, and serve. This goes well over hot cooked rice or Chinese noodles. Makes 4-6 servings.

Four Seasons Chicken Salad

By swapping out a few ingredients you can make a chicken salad for any time of the year.

Spring

Vinaigrette:
⅓ c. apricot nectar
3 T. olive oil
2 T. red wine vinegar
1 T. balsamic vinegar
1 T. fresh parsley or 1 t. dried
1 T. fresh chopped cilantro
1 t. Dijon mustard
1 t. sesame oil
salt and pepper to taste

4 boneless, skinless chicken breast halves
12 asparagus spears
4-6 cups mixed baby greens.
(This mix could include lettuces, spinach, dandelion, lambsquarters and sorrel)
3 T. chopped green onion or chives
8 whole strawberries
½ lb. pea pods, washed and trimmed
3 oz. enoki mushrooms, washed and trimmed
3-4 T. Pine nuts or sunflower seeds

Combine ingredients for vinaigrette in a blender, or just with a whisk. Pour a little of the dressing over the chicken breasts and place them in the refrigerator for 1 hour. Meanwhile, chill the remaining dressing. Wash and trim asparagus spears and blanch in boiling water for 5 minutes. Remove spears and immediately plunge them in a bowl of ice water. Remove and drain when the asparagus is cold. Set aside.

Wash and dry greens, and tear into bite-sized pieces. Wash strawberries. Cook pea pods in boiling water for 2 minutes and remove. Plunge pea pods in a bowl of ice water to chill. Remove from the ice water and drain.

Broil or grill the chicken, turning to cook evenly. Brush with any marinade remaining in the chicken dish. When the chicken is cooked, cut it into strips.

Discard any marinade not used on the chicken. Do not recombine the leftover marinade with the vinaigrette dressing, because of the danger of possible bacteria content in raw, uncooked chicken.

To assemble the salads, divide the greens among 4 salad plates. Place 3 asparagus spears on each plate and cover with the chicken slices, one breast half per serving. Sprinkle with the chopped green onions, and place 2 strawberries on each plate at one end. Divide the pea pods per plate, arranging them in spikes between the chicken slices, so they will stand up. Place a few enoki mushrooms at the center of the chicken, slightly fanned, and sprinkled with pine nuts. Serve with the remaining vinaigrette on the side. Serves 4.

Summer

Vinaigrette:
⅓ c. tomato juice
3 T. olive oil
2 T. red wine vinegar
1 T. balsamic vinegar
2 T. chopped fresh basil
1 t. Dijon mustard
1 t. sesame oil
salt and pepper to taste

4 boneless, skinless chicken breast halves
12 green beans
4-6 c. mixed salad greens
3 T. chopped green onions or chives
1 c. diced fresh peaches, nectarines, or plums
or 1 cup cherry tomatoes)
1 c. sweet pepper, any color, cut into strips
3 oz. enoki mushrooms, washed and trimmed
3-4 T. toasted almonds

Autumn

Vinaigrette:
½ c. pumpkin purée or apple cider
3 T. olive oil
3 T. cider vinegar
1 T. fresh thyme, or 1 t. dried
1 t. Dijon mustard
1 t. sesame oil
salt and pepper to taste

4 boneless, skinless chicken breast quarters
2 small zucchini washed, trimmed, and cut into thin spears
4-6 c. mixed salad greens
3 T. chopped green onion or chives
1 c. diced apples or pears
½ c. carrots, cut into julienne strips
3-4 T. walnuts or toasted hulled pumpkin seeds

Winter

Vinaigrette:
½ c. orange juice
3 T. olive oil
2 T. red wine vinegar
1 T. balsamic vinegar
2 T. fresh mint or 2 t. dried
1 t. Dijon mustard
1 t. sesame oil
salt and pepper to taste

4 boneless, skinless chicken breast quarters
12 green beans or 12 asparagus spears
4-6 c. mixed salad greens
3 T. chopped sweet onion
1 c. assorted cubed citrus fruits
½ c. julienne strips of carrots
½ c. julienne strips of zucchini
3-4 T. shelled pistachios

Easy Cacciatore

6 boneless, skinless chicken breast halves
salt and pepper to taste
flour
2-3 T. oil
1 large onion, chopped
3 garlic cloves, minced
12 oz. fresh mushrooms, sliced
1 sweet pepper, chopped
2 (14.5 oz.) cans tomato sauce
½ c. red wine, optional
2 T. Italian Seasoning (see Chapter 4)
cooked pasta
fresh grated Parmesan cheese
fresh chopped basil, oregano, or rosemary, if desired

Pound chicken breasts to flatten slightly. Season with salt and pepper and dredge in flour. Heat oil in skillet and sauté onions until wilted and tender. Add garlic, mushrooms, pepper and sauté 5 minutes more. Transfer vegetables to a bowl. Sauté chicken in same skillet, adding extra oil if needed. Add the tomato sauce to the pan, and the wine, if desired. Heat to simmering. Stir in seasonings and reserved vegetable mixture. Simmer 10-15 minutes, to blend flavors. Serve over cooked pasta, with Parmesan cheese on the side. Garnish with the fresh herbs, as desired. Serves 6.

Curried Chicken

1 whole broiler/fryer cut into serving pieces (about 3-4lbs.)
½ c. plain yogurt
3 cloves garlic
2 T. fresh cilantro
1 t. curry powder, or to taste
salt and pepper to taste
flour
2 T. oil
2 medium onions, cut in chunks

Dipping sauce:
½-¾ c. plain yogurt
⅓ c. cucumber peeled, seeded, and chopped
¼ c. fresh cilantro, minced
juice of one lime, about 1 tablespoon
salt to taste

Combine the yogurt, garlic, cilantro, curry, cumin, and salt and pepper in a blender. Mix until smooth. Dredge the chicken pieces in flour, and then pour the yogurt mixture over the chicken. Cover and refrigerate for at least 4 hours.

Place marinated chicken pieces in a roasting pan, and bake at 350 degrees for about an hour or until juices run clear when the chicken is pierced. While the chicken is baking, heat the oil in a skillet and sauté the onion until tender and brown. Add the onions to the chicken during the last half hour of baking. Also combine the dipping sauce ingredients in a small bowl. Cover and chill until ready to use. Serve chicken with the dipping sauce on the side. Serves 4-6.

Pesto Chicken

4 boneless, skinless chicken breast halves
flour
3 T. olive oil
1 c. basil leaves, loosely packed
salt to taste
3 cloves garlic
½ c. freshly grated Parmesan cheese
3-4 T. pine nuts or sunflower seeds
fresh cooked pasta, if desired

Pound chicken breasts to uniform thickness, about ½-inch thick. Dredge chicken in flour and set aside. In blender or food processor combine the oil, basil, salt, and garlic. Blend until smooth. Pour over chicken, turning to coat all sides. Marinade in the fridge for a couple of hours or overnight.

Place chicken in a broiler pan and broil, turning to brown evenly, until cooked. Juices will run clear when chicken is pierced. Remove chicken from broiler, sprinkle with the Parmesan cheese, and return to broiler for about 2 minutes more, or until the cheese is lightly browned. Sprinkle with pine nuts before serving. Serve with fresh cooked pasta, if desired. Makes 4 servings.

Rosemary Chicken with Oranges

1 broiler/fryer, cut into serving pieces *or* 6 chicken
breasts
salt and pepper to taste
flour
2 T. oil
1 large onion, sliced
2-3 large carrots, peeled and cut into chunks
2 c. orange juice, fresh squeezed, if possible
1 T. fresh rosemary or 1 t. dried
1 T. fresh parsley or 1 t. dried
1 t. orange peel
1 medium orange, sliced thin
pinch of freshly ground nutmeg

Skin chicken if desired. Salt and pepper the chicken
and dredge in flour. Heat oil in skillet and brown
chicken pieces, turning as needed. Place chicken in a
baking dish.

In skillet, brown the onion and spoon over the chicken.
Add carrots. Heat the orange juice, and pour over the
chicken. Bake in a 350-degree oven for 45 minutes.

Meanwhile chop the herbs. Sprinkle the herbs over the
chicken, and add the orange peel and nutmeg. Arrange
the orange slices on the chicken. Return the chicken to
the oven for 15 minutes more, and serve. Goes well with
hot cooked rice or pasta. Serves 4-6.

Spicy Pineapple Chicken

1 whole broiler/flyer, cut into serving pieces
1 (20 oz.) can chunk pineapple in its own juice
1 T. soy sauce, or to taste
1 t. freshly grated ginger
½ t. cinnamon
½ t. red pepper flakes
2 T. red or white wine vinegar
2 T. oil
1 large onion, chopped
1 sweet red pepper, seeded and diced
1 t. cornstarch

Drain the pineapple juice into a small bowl and reserve the chunks. To pineapple juice add the soy sauce, ginger, cinnamon, pepper and vinegar. Marinade chicken, covered, in the fridge for at least 2 hours or overnight in the pineapple juice mixture.

In medium skillet, heat the oil and cook the onion until tender. Place the chicken in a baking dish. Add all the marinade. Spoon in the onions, red pepper, and reserved pineapple chunks. Bake in a 350-degree oven for 1 hour. With a slotted spoon, remove chicken, vegetables and pineapple from the pan, and keep warm on a serving platter.

Dissolve the cornstarch in 1 T. water and pour cornstarch into pan with the drippings. Stir to loosen any brown bits on the bottom of the pan. Using a rubber spatula, scrape all pan drippings into a small saucepan, and heat until thick and bubbly. If there is not enough juice, add ½ cup of chicken stock, water, or white wine to the pan. Serve sauce over chicken. Goes well over hot cooked rice. Serves 4-6.

Chicken with Cucumbers

4 boneless, skinless chicken breast halves
salt and pepper to taste
1 seedless cucumber, sliced thin
2-3 green onions, trimmed and chopped
¾ c. sour cream (regular or reduced fat, or yogurt, but do not use fat-free yogurt in this recipe)
2 T. balsamic vinegar
2 t. sugar
2 T. fresh-snipped dill
1 T. fresh chopped mint leaves
1 c. fresh or frozen green peas
2-3 large baking potatoes, baked and cooled slightly
additional mint sprigs for garnish.

Season chicken with salt and pepper. Broil or grill until cooked. While chicken is cooking, combine cucumbers with onions, sour cream, vinegar, sugar, and herbs in a medium bowl. Stir in peas. Set aside. Cut potatoes into chunks and divide among 4 plates. Slice cooked chicken breasts into strips, and place a breast half on each plate. Divide cucumber mixture evenly over the 4 plates. Garnish with the additional mint sprigs. Serves 4.

Savory Chicken and Mushrooms

4 chicken breast halves, skinned if desired
or chicken legs, or a combination of the two
salt and pepper to taste
garlic powder and paprika to taste
flour
2 T. oil
1 large onion, diced
2 ribs celery, diced
2 medium carrots, peeled and diced
1 c. chicken stock, or part white wine and stock
12 oz. sliced mushrooms
1-2 T. fresh savory, leaves stripped off stems
hot cooked pasta or rice

Salt and pepper chicken breasts. Dust the breasts with garlic powder and paprika. Dredge chicken pieces in flour. Heat oil in skillet and brown the chicken, turning the pieces to brown evenly. Transfer chicken pieces to a baking dish, and cook in a preheated 350-degree oven for 45 minutes.

While the chicken is baking, return the skillet to the heat and add the onion, celery, and carrot. Add a little more oil, if needed. Sauté the vegetables until browned. Add the chicken stock, and scrape the pan to loosen any of the brown bits on the bottom. Simmer a few minutes, then strain the sauce. Return the sauce to the skillet. Add the sliced mushrooms and simmer until heated through. Hold sauce until ready to use. Return cooked chicken to the skillet, and add the savory. Heat until sauce starts to bubble and thicken, about 5 minutes. Serve over pasta or rice. Serves 4.

Saté Chicken

4 boneless, skinless chicken breast halves
½ c. cream of coconut
¼ c. lime juice
2 T. oil
1 T. soy sauce
3 cloves garlic, minced
1 t. coriander
¼ t. hot pepper sauce
pita bread
cucumber slices

Dipping Sauce:
½ c. peanut butter
¼ c. chicken stock or water
2 T. soy sauce
1 T. honey
1 T. white wine vinegar
2 t. balsamic vinegar
2 cloves garlic, minced
⅛ t. cloves
⅛ t. red pepper flakes

Cut chicken into thin strips. Combine next seven ingredients, and pour over chicken strips. Cover and refrigerate overnight. Skewer and grill or broil chicken until cooked. Combine dipping sauce ingredients to serve on the side. Remove chicken from skewers, and put in pita bread. Add a few cucumber slices, and a dollop of sauce, if desired. Use extra sauce for dipping. Makes 4 servings.

Rock Cornish Hens with Herbs

Marinade:
1 c. apple cider
¼ c. balsamic vinegar
½ c. mixed fresh herbs including:
basil, parsley, mint, lavender, savory or thyme
1 T. tamari or soy sauce
2 t. dried minced garlic
½ t. red pepper flakes
several strips of lemon peel

4 Rock Cornish hens, cut in halves
1 T. cornstarch
¼ c. water
2 T. honey

Place all marinade ingredients in a bowl and combine. Place hens in a shallow pan, and pour the marinade over hens. Place in the fridge, covered, for at least 6 hours or overnight.

Preheat oven to 400 degrees. Remove hens from marinade and place in baking dish. Bake the hens for about 35 minutes, or until juices run clear when birds are pierced with a fork. While birds are cooking, strain the marinade, and bring to a boil in a small saucepan. Dissolve cornstarch in water, and stir into the marinade along with the honey. Baste hens with marinade during the last 10 minutes of cooking, if desired. Serves 4.

Ethiopian Chicken

1 chicken, (3-4 lbs.) cut into serving-sized pieces
1 T. paprika
1 t. cayenne pepper
1 t. cumin
1 t. garlic powder
1 t. salt
1 t. fresh grated ginger
½ t. ground allspice
¼ t. cinnamon
½ c. flour
3 T. oil
2 large onions, sliced thin
1 c. tomato sauce
1 c. chicken stock

Rinse chicken. Combine spices and flour in a bag. Add the chicken pieces, a few at a time, and shake to coat. Set chicken aside.

Heat oil in skillet. Sauté onion until well browned. Set onion aside, and brown chicken pieces, turning to brown evenly. When chicken is browned, return the onions to the skillet, and add the tomato sauce and chicken stock. Place lid on skillet, and turn down heat. Simmer chicken until tender, about 35 minutes. Add water if sauce gets too thick. Serve with a cooked grain such as millet, rice, or quinoa. Cooked lentils could also be served, and cooked greens, such as collards or kale. Serves 4.

Chicken with Chutney

Chutney:
2 medium pears, peeled, seeded, and chopped
1 large ripe tomato, peeled and chopped **or** 3-4 canned tomatoes, chopped
1 large mango, peeled, seeded, and chopped
2 dried pineapple slices, diced **or** 3 slices canned pineapple, diced
⅓ c. golden raisins
¼ c. chopped onion
¼ c. brown sugar
¼ c. brandy
¼ c. balsamic vinegar
2 T. fresh mint leaves or 2 t. dried
1 T. lime juice
3 cloves garlic, minced
salt to taste
1 t. fresh grated ginger
½ t. fresh grated nutmeg
¼ t. cloves
¼ t. red pepper flakes

4 boneless, skinless chicken breast halves
cornstarch
1 T. oil
¼ c. chicken stock or water
Hot cooked brown or basmati rice*

In medium saucepan, combine all the chutney ingredients. Simmer, uncovered, for 20-30 minutes, until chutney starts to thicken. As the chutney thickens, stir from time to time so it won't burn.

Meanwhile, cut the chicken into chunks and shake pieces, about 6 at a time, in a bag with the cornstarch. Heat oil in a skillet and stir fry chicken pieces until done. Chicken is done when juices run clear when the chicken is pierced.

Pour the chutney over the chicken and stir together. If chutney is thinner than you would like, use a little of the cornstarch still in the bag, mix it with the stock or water, and add to the chicken. Allow to cook an additional minute or two. Serve over rice. This is a nice change from sweet and sour chicken. Serves 4.

Note: Basmati rice is available in some groceries and gourmet food stores, and in Indian markets.

Company Duck

2 (4-5 lb.) ducks, split into halves, excess fat and/or skin removed, if desired

Marinade:
½ c. peach brandy or plain brandy
½ c. honey
½ c. brown sugar
½ c. tamari sauce
¼ c. balsamic vinegar
¼ c. fresh cilantro
¼ c. fresh parsley
2 ripe peaches, peeled, pitted, and diced fine
2 T. pink peppercorns, slightly crushed
2 T. fresh grated ginger
3 cloves garlic, minced
juice of ½ an orange
2 t. fresh orange zest
2 t. cumin
2 t. tarragon

Hot cooked wild rice or rice pilaf

Combine marinade ingredients and pour over duck halves. Marinate duck, covered, in refrigerator for 24 hours.

Place duck halves on a rack in a baking pan, and bake in a 450-degree oven for 10 minutes. Turn the heat down to 350, and bake until ducks are done. While they are cooking, baste often with the marinade. The skin is supposed to get dark and crispy. If the ducks are getting too brown, turn down the heat to 325 degrees.

The duck should take nearly an hour total to be done. Any unused marinade should be discarded as it may contain bacteria from the raw duck. Ducks may be served with rice, or even couscous or pasta. Serves 4.

Mulled Duck

This recipe came to me in a hotel room on North Carolina, after consuming too much iced cappuccino near bedtime. I'm not sure if there is a lesson in that, but this has turned out to be a favorite way of mine to cook duck.

2 (4-5 lb.) ducks salt and pepper
2 T. olive oil
1 large onion, quartered
2 cloves garlic
1 c. chopped celery
2 large carrots, peeled and chunked
2 c. apple cider
2 c. white wine or apple brandy
1 stick cinnamon
3-4 whole cloves
1 t. whole allspice
1 t. whole peppercorns
1-inch piece fresh ginger root
2 bay leaves
½ c. water
3 T. cornstarch
Hot cooked spinach noodles or wild rice

Cut ducks into quarters, and remove all skin and fat.* Washed skinned duck pieces and pat dry. In large Dutch oven or skillet, heat the oil. Season the duck pieces with salt and pepper and sauté until browned. Remove duck. Add the vegetables and garlic, and sauté until browned. Return duck to the Dutch oven. Add cider, wine, and seasonings. Bring to a simmer. Cover and simmer for 1-1½ hours, or until duck is very tender.

Remove duck from pan and keep warm. Strain vegetables and juices through a fine strainer into a medium size saucepan. Use a wooden spoon to press on the solids in the strainer, to get all the juices into the saucepan. Then discard solids. The sauce should be a little thin.

Simmer sauce to reduce to 3 cups. While sauce is heating, combine the cornstarch and water until smooth. Add this mixture to the sauce in a thin stream. Whisk to prevent lumping. Stop often to check the thickness of the sauce. When it gets to desired thickness, stop adding cornstarch. Simmer the sauce 1 minute longer. Adjust the seasonings at this time. Serve duck pieces on top of pasta or rice. Pour about half of the sauce over the duck, and serve the rest on the side. Serves 4-6.

* *Save fat and skin to render for the fat and cracklings.*

English Poached Goose

Goose is another fowl, like duck, that gets overlooked. This method is an untraditional, but tasty way to serve it. This recipe also lowers the fat content to nearly nothing-without drying out the bird.

1 (12-14lb.) goose, skinned*
3-4 lbs. pearl onions, peeled and left whole
or cooking onions, peeled and quartered
1 lb. granny smith apples (peeled, cored, and quartered)
1 lb. pitted prunes
2 lbs. carrots, peeled and cut into chunks
3-4 lbs. potatoes, peeled if desired, and cut into quarters
1 medium head of cabbage, cored and cut into big chunks
2 lbs. parsnips, peeled and left whole
2-3 qts. chicken stock
3 bay leaves
2 T. dried thyme
2 T. dried savory
1 T. dried marjoram
2 t. dried dill weed
2 t. salt, or to taste
3 T. oil
¼ c. flour
1 c. dairy sour cream or Greek yogurt

Wash and dry goose. Place about 1 pound of the onions in the goose, along with the fruit. Place goose in a deep roasting pan or stockpot. If goose will not fit, cut off the legs and try again. Place remaining onions and the vegetables around, and on top of the goose, depending on the shape of the pan you are using. Heat the stock to boiling, and pour over the goose until it is covered, or nearly so. As the vegetables cook down, there will be more liquid.

Add the brandy and bay leaves, and simmer, covered, for 2-3 hours, until the goose is getting tender. Add the remaining seasonings, and cook 20 minutes more.

Before serving, in a medium saucepan, blend together the flour and oil. Heat until bubbling. Remove about 2 cups of the liquid from the roasting pan, and strain it. Pour this liquid into the flour mixture, whisking to prevent lumps. Cook over high heat, stirring for about 5 minutes, to fully thicken. Add more liquid if thinner sauce is desired. Add ¼ cup of the hot stock to the sour cream, whisking to prevent lumps. Add more sauce to the sour cream, until it is warm. Pour this mixture into the saucepan with the rest of the sauce, and keep warm, but do not boil.

To serve, remove goose to a platter, and let stand 15 minutes. Use a slotted spoon to remove onions and fruit from cavity, as well as the vegetables in the pot. Reserve the leftover liquid for another use.**

Serve the vegetables on a large platter. Cut the goose into serving size pieces, and the breast meat into slices, and place on another platter. Serve the sauce on the side. This goes very well with a crusty white bread, or perhaps pumpernickel or rye. Serves 10-12.

* You can render the skin for goose fat.

**I strain it and pour it hot over cooked noodles for a great soup. You can also strain and freeze it for use even several months later.

Tarragon Chicken

4 boneless, skinless chicken breast halves
2-3 T. olive oil
salt and fresh ground pepper to taste
½ c. chopped shallots
2 cloves garlic, minced
1 medium carrot, peeled and diced
1-2 T. flour, depending on how thick you like your sauces
½ lb. fresh green beans, trimmed and cut into 1-inch pieces
1 c. chicken stock
½ c. white wine
½ c. sour cream or yogurt
2 T. fresh tarragon, snipped, or 2 t. dried
1 c. shredded mozzarella

Pound chicken to about ½-inch thickness. Season chicken with salt and pepper. Heat oil in large skillet and sauté chicken, turning to brown evenly until cooked. Remove chicken and keep warm.

In skillet, sauté shallots, garlic, and carrot until tender. Be careful not to burn the garlic or it will become bitter. Add the green beans and cook 3-5 minutes. Add the flour. Stir in the chicken stock slowly, whisking to prevent lumps. Stir in the wine and cook for 3-5 minutes, until sauce is thickened.

Add a little of the hot stock to the sour cream, and stir to combine. Then add this mixture to the skillet. Stir in the tarragon and cook 1 more minute. Place the chicken on a broiler-safe pan, pour the sauce and vegetables over the chicken then sprinkle with the cheese. Broil for about 5 minutes or until cheese has melted and browned a little. Serves 4.

Seafood
Gumbo

¼ c. oil
¼ c. flour
3 ribs celery, diced
1 large onion, chopped
1 green pepper, seeded and chopped
1 sweet red or yellow pepper, seeded and chopped
4 cloves garlic, minced
½ lb. okra, trimmed and sliced
1 T. oil
2 qts. chicken stock
1 T. Worcestershire sauce
hot pepper sauce to taste
2 T. tomato paste
1 large tomato, chopped
salt to taste
1 cup cubed smoked ham
1 bay leaf
2 T. Cajun or Creole Seasoning (see Chapter 4)
1 c. cubed cooked chicken
1 lb. fresh lump crabmeat
2 lbs. raw shrimp, peeled and deveined
1-2 dozen mussels in the shell, scrubbed-discard any with open shells
¼ c. fresh chopped parsley

Heat oil and flour together in Dutch oven, stirring until well browned. Add the celery, onion, peppers and garlic, and continue cooking, stirring occasionally, for 15-20 minutes.

Meanwhile, in a small skillet, heat remaining oil and cook the okra until softened. Add the next nine ingredients, and cook, simmering, for 2 hours. Add the

219

chicken, crabmeat, and shrimp and cook 10 more minutes. Add the mussels and parsley and cook 5 more minutes, or until mussels are opened. Before serving, for the safety of you and your guests, discard any mussels whose shells have not opened. Serve in bowls over hot rice. Serves 8.

Mussels Steamed with Herbs

2 lbs. fresh mussels, de-bearded and shells scrubbed
Discard any mussels with open shells.
2 c. water or vegetable stock
1 c. white wine
3-4 sprigs parsley, or 2 t. dried
1-2 sprigs fresh basil, or 2 t. dried
2 T. fresh-snipped celery or lovage leaves, or 2 t. dried
1 T. fresh thyme leaves, or 1 t. dried
1 t. peppercorns
2-3 cloves garlic
melted butter
crusty bread

Place cleaned mussels on steamer rack. Place remaining ingredients-except the butter and bread-in the bottom of the steamer, and bring to a boil. Steam mussels until they open, about 5-10 minutes. Discard any mussels that did not open.

Keep mussels warm. Meanwhile, strain the cooking liquid into a large skillet. Cook on high until liquid is reduced to about ¾ cup. Stir in melted butter and pour this sauce over the mussels. Serve with the bread. Makes 3-4 servings.

Seafood Kabobs with Herbs

2 lbs. salmon, shark, or swordfish fillets cut into 1-inch cubes
½ c. dry white wine
¼ c. lemon balm leaves
¼ c. fresh parsley leaves
¼ c. pineapple sage leaves (or mint leaves)
salt and fresh ground pepper
juice of 1 lime
several thin strips of lime peel
2 cloves garlic, minced
¼ c. olive oil
2 small onions, quartered
2 sweet peppers, red, yellow or green seeded and cut into 1-inch chunks
1 small yellow summer squash, sliced 1-inch thick
1 small zucchini, sliced 1-inch thick
1 pint cherry tomatoes
12 oz. medium mushrooms, washed and stems trimmed

In a medium bowl, place the fish. In a blender combine the wine, herbs, salt and pepper, and lime juice. Blend until smooth, and pour over the fish. Add the lime strips, garlic, and olive oil to the fish, and toss to coat evenly. Place in fridge and marinade 30-60 minutes. Meanwhile, soak wooden skewers in water, and prepare grill if necessary.

Skewer the fish and the vegetables. Brush kabobs with marinade, and place over the hot coals, turning to cook evenly.

Note: If set 6-8 inches above hot coals, the kebobs will be cooked in 10-15 minutes. Adjust your cooking time based on the distance from the coals, and the heat of the fire.

You can also broil the kebobs in the oven broiler for about 12 minutes, or until fish is cooked through. To test for doneness, choose a kabob not directly over the coals. Cut into the center of the kabob. The fish should be opaque. Brush kabobs with the marinade after 5 minutes of cooking, and discard any remaining liquid. Kabobs will serve 6-8.

Marinated Shrimp

This wonderful recipe comes to me from my friend Marisa Warrix, who always seems to have a new recipe on hand.

Marinade:
1 stick butter, melted, or ½ c. olive oil
2 cloves garlic, minced
juice of 1 fresh lemon, or about 1½ oz.
½ c. fresh chopped parsley
1 t. ground coriander

1-2 lbs. raw shrimp, peeled and deveined

Combine marinade ingredients. Add the shrimp. Cover and refrigerate for a couple of hours.

Skewer shrimp, and grill until done, turning to cook evenly. You can also broil the shrimp. Brush with the marinade as needed. Discard any leftover marinade. Serves 4-8.

Creole Jambalaya

1 large sweet red pepper
1½ lbs. smoked sausage, sliced
2 large onions, chopped
3 ribs celery, diced
1 green pepper, seeded and chopped
3 cloves garlic, chopped
2 T. olive oil
2 boneless, skinless chicken breast halves, cubed
3½ c. chicken stock
1½ c. rice, uncooked, white or brown
1 (14.5 oz.) can whole tomatoes, undrained and chopped
2 T. Creole, or Creole Seafood Seasoning, (see Chapter 4)
1 lb. shrimp, peeled and deveined
1 lb. green beans (trimmed and washed cut into 1-inch pieces)
1 c. frozen baby peas
salt to taste
1½-2lbs. mussels, scrubbed (Any open shells discarded)
1 T. fresh thyme leaves
1 t. fresh rosemary leaves
1 t. saffron threads or ¼ t. turmeric

Roast the red pepper by placing it directly on the flame of a burner, or on the heating element of an electric range. Turn the pepper until all sides are black. Remove the roasted pepper from the heat, and wrap in a kitchen towel. Allow pepper to cool. Remove pepper from the towel. Using a paper towel, rub off the blackened skin of the pepper. Seed the pepper, and cut it into small cubes. Set aside.

Heat oil in a large Dutch oven or deep skillet, and cook the sausage, onion, celery, green pepper, and garlic until the vegetables are tender and lightly browned. Add the chicken, stock, rice, and tomatoes. Simmer, covered, until the rice is about cooked, 15 minutes for white rice, and about 40 minutes for brown. Add the Creole seasoning, shrimp, and beans. Cook, covered, 10 minutes. Add the peas, salt, if desired, mussels, herbs, and red pepper, simmering 5 minutes more, or until the mussels are opened. Discard any unopened shells. Spoon Jambalaya onto a large serving platter, or into individual bowls. Serves 8.

Grilled Swordfish

4 (1-inch thick) swordfish steaks
2 T. olive oil
salt and fresh ground pepper to taste
1 fresh lemon, sliced thin
Assorted sprigs of fresh herbs, including at least some
of the following: basil, chives, dill, fennel, garlic,
chives, lemon balm, lovage, parsley, savory, thyme.

Brush fish with oil. Season with salt and pepper. Place lemon slices on top of the fish. Let fish stand while heating the grill. Use a grilling rack made for fish. Oil the rack lightly, and place a layer of mixed fresh herbs over it. Place the swordfish on the bed of herbs. Replace any lemon slices that have fallen off. Place more herbs on top of the fish, and secure the rack top. Grill as usual. The herbs will prevent the fish from sticking, and add great flavor to the grilled meat. This method works for any seafood that you can grill. I've even grilled chicken breasts this way and was quite pleased. Serves 4.

Tuna and Pasta Pesto

1 (5 oz.) can tuna, drained
1 c. fresh basil leaves
½ c. grated Parmesan cheese
¼ c. olive oil
2 T. pine nuts or hulled sunflower seeds
2 cloves garlic salt to taste
8 oz. angel hair pasta, cooked and drained

Combine all ingredients-except pasta-in a blender or food processor. Blend until smooth. Toss over fresh cooked hot pasta. Serves 4.

Angel Hair Pasta
with Herbed Clam Sauce

2 T. olive oil
3 green onions, trimmed and chopped
3-4 T. flour
1 (10 oz.) can whole baby clams, undrained
12 oz. clam juice
½ c. half and half or evaporated milk
2 T. fresh chopped parsley
1 T. fresh chopped dill
1 t. fresh thyme leaves
½ t. garlic powder
fresh ground pepper
8 oz. angel hair pasta

Heat oil in skillet. Add onions and cook 3-4 minutes. Add flour and toss to coat. Stir in clams and clam juice, and heat until simmering. Turn down heat and add milk and seasonings, cooking until thickened and bubbly. While sauce is cooking, prepare the pasta according to package directions. Serve clam sauce over hot pasta. Serves 3-4.

Crab Cakes with Basil Sauce

I couldn't decide whether to put this recipe with the Appetizers, or in Main Dishes. I find this hearty enough to be a meal with a salad on the side, but also a good first course.

2 eggs
2 T. sour cream or yogurt
2 t. dried thyme
1 t. dried oregano
1 t. fresh lemon or lime juice
½ t. cayenne pepper
½ t. dry mustard
salt to taste
¼ c. fresh chopped parsley
¼ c. fresh chopped chives or green onions
⅓-½ c. breadcrumbs
1 lb. lump crabmeat
2 T. olive oil

Basil Sauce:
½ c. packed basil leaves
½ c. sour cream or Greek yogurt
2 T. mayonnaise
1 t. celery seed
1 t. dill seed
1 t. Worcestershire sauce
½ t. salt
1 garlic clove, minced
⅛ t. cayenne pepper
pinch of lemon zest
lemon wedges

Mix all crab cake ingredients together-except the oil. Add enough breadcrumbs for the cakes to stick together. Divide this mixture into 8 portions, and form into patties. They are going to be a little crumbly, so do the best you can. Cover tightly and refrigerate the patties 1-2 hours to firm.

Transfer cakes to a greased baking sheet, and brush them with the oil. Bake in a preheated 450-degree oven until crab cakes brown lightly. This takes about 15-18 minutes, and the cakes should be turned over during the baking to brown both sides.

While crab cakes are cooking, combine sauce ingredients in a blender until smooth. Serve sauce on the side, with the lemon wedges. Serves 4.

Vegetarian
Vegetarian Tacos

1 T. oil
2 c. cooked beans (pinto, kidney, black, etc...)
1 c. cooked white or brown rice
½ c. fresh chopped cilantro
2 t. chili powder
2 t. cumin
2 t. oregano
1 t. salt
1 t. paprika
1 t. garlic powder
½ t. cayenne pepper
12-15 taco shells, warmed briefly to soften

Toppings:
2 large chopped tomatoes
2 chopped sweet red or green peppers
1 large sweet onion, chopped
½ c. sliced black olives
2 c. chopped lettuce
2 c. finely shredded cheddar cheese
1 c. sour cream or Greek yogurt

Heat oil in skillet. Mash beans a little, and add to the skillet along with the rice. Add seasonings, and stir until bean mixture is heated through and browned. To serve, put bean mixture and assorted toppings into serving bowls, and set them up next to the taco shells so guests can make their own. Serves 4-6.

Vegetarian Burritos

Same as the Vegetarian Taco recipe, but use soft tortilla and fill them with bean mixture and toppings. Fold in each side of a burrito about one-quarter to one-third toward the center, and then hold from the bottom side and roll up. Serves 4-6.

Lentil Chili

1 lb. dried lentils
water for cooking lentils
3 T. olive oil
2 large onions, chopped
4 cloves garlic, minced
2 (28 oz.) cans tomatoes, undrained and chopped
2 T. chili powder
1 T. cumin
2 t. oregano
2 t. salt, or to taste
1 t. cinnamon

Rinse lentils, and place in medium saucepan. Cover lentils with cold water and bring to a boil. Turn the heat down to simmer and cook until the lentils are tender, about 30 minutes, depending on the type and age of the lentils. Drain lentils. Heat oil in a large saucepan. Add the onions and garlic, and cook until the onions are tender. Add the lentils and the remaining ingredients and simmer gently, covered, for 40 minutes. Stir occasionally. Serves 4-6.

Vegetarian Chili

3 T. oil
2 large onions, chopped
1 c. chopped sweet pepper
2 c. chopped celery
3 cloves garlic, minced
1½ c. tomato juice
2 (28 oz.) cans tomatoes, cut up
2 (15 oz.) cans kidney beans, rinsed and drained
1 (15 oz.) can garbanzo beans, rinsed and drained
2 medium apples, peeled and chopped
¼ c. red wine vinegar
2 T. chili powder
2 T. fresh chopped parsley or 2 t. dried
2 T. fresh chopped cilantro, optional
1 T. dried basil
2 t. cumin
2 t. oregano
2 t. salt
1 t. allspice
1 t. hot pepper sauce
½ t. cloves
½ t. cinnamon
1 bay leaf
1 c. peanuts, chopped coarsely
2 c. shredded cheese, optional

Heat oil in a large saucepan. Sauté onions, pepper, celery, and garlic until tender but not browned. Add the tomato juice, and the undrained tomatoes, kidney and garbanzo beans, apples, and vinegar. Bring this mixture to a boil, then turn the heat down to simmer, covered, for 1 hour. Add the seasonings and simmer, uncovered, 40 more minutes. Remove the bay leaf. To serve, ladle the chili into bowls, and sprinkle with the nuts and cheese. Serves 8-10.

Mushroom Quiche with Herbs

1 prepared 9-inch deep-dish pie crust, unbaked
12 oz. mushrooms, washed, trimmed, and sliced
1 T. oil
½ c. chopped shallots
1½ c. shredded Swiss cheese
2 T. flour
1 c. ricotta cheese
1 c. milk
5 eggs
2 T. fresh chopped parsley
1 T. snipped chive
1 T. snipped fresh dill
1 t. savory leaves
1 t. thyme leaves
¼ t. salt
¼ t. pepper

Heat oil in a skillet, and sauté mushrooms until cooked. Add shallots and cook 3 minutes. In a small bowl, toss together the flour and Swiss cheese. Place cheese mixture in the bottom of pie crust. Add mushroom mixture. Place remaining ingredients in a blender and combine until smooth. Pour this mixture into the pie shell, and bake in a preheated 400-degree oven for 20 minutes. Turn the heat down to 325, and bake about 35-40 minutes longer. To test for doneness, insert a knife off center. If the knife blade comes out clean, the quiche is done. Serves 6.

Spicy Beans and Rice

4 c. cooked beans, use one variety or a combination
2 c. water or vegetable broth
1 large sweet onion, chopped
2 c. diced celery
1 green pepper, seeded and chopped
1 red or yellow sweet pepper, seeded and chopped
1 large carrot, peeled and diced
2 T. red wine vinegar
2 t. dried oregano
2 t. chili powder
2 t. dried thyme
2 t. paprika
½ t. cayenne pepper
salt to taste
1 c. chopped cilantro
½ c. chopped parsley
5-6 c. cooked brown rice

In a Dutch oven or large saucepan, combine beans with broth, vegetables and vinegar. Simmer, covered, until mixture thickens, about 45 minutes. Add seasonings-except cilantro and parsley-and simmer, uncovered, for 15 minutes. Stir in the cilantro, parsley, and rice. Stir to combine. Cook, stirring occasionally, until heated through. Adjust seasonings. Serves 6-8.

Spicy Lentils and Spoonbread

½ lb. lentils
2 c. milk
Salt to taste
⅔ c. cornmeal
4 T. butter
4 eggs
2 large onions, chopped
3 cloves garlic, minced
¼ c. chopped cilantro
2 T. chopped parsley
2 T. chili powder
2 t. cumin
1 t. savory
½ t. salt
⅛ t. cloves
1 c. tomato sauce
3 or 4 (fresh or canned) tomatoes, chopped

Rinse lentils. Place in a saucepan, cover with cold water, and bring to a boil. Simmer for about 20 minutes, or until the lentils are tender. Some types of lentils, such as red lentils, cook more quickly. Some may take longer. When the lentils are tender, drain.

While lentils are cooking, start preparing spoonbread. In a saucepan, heat the milk with the salt. When the milk starts to boil, stir in the cornmeal, stirring constantly to prevent both lumps and burning. The mixture will thicken quickly. When it thickens, remove from heat. Stir in the butter and eggs, beating until mixture is smooth and well blended. Set aside. To prepare vegetables, heat oil in skillet. Sauté onions and garlic until soft. Add seasonings, tomato sauce, and tomatoes. Simmer for 5 minutes. Stir in the drained lentils, and cook 5 minutes more. Lightly oil a 2 qt. saucepan and pour in the lentil mixture. Pour the spoonbread batter over the lentils, and bake in a 350-degree oven for 35-40 minutes, or until lightly browned on the top. Serves 6.

Curried Vegetables with Rice Noodles

2 T. oil
1 large onion, cut in chunks
3 cloves garlic, minced
1 T. curry powder, or to taste
2 t. cumin
¼ t. cinnamon
⅛ t. cloves
1 c. water or vegetable stock
3 large carrots, peeled and cut into chunks
1 large potato, cut into chunks, peeled if desired
1 large sweet potato, cubed, peeled if desired
2 red sweet peppers, seeded and cubed
12 oz. mushrooms (trimmed, cleaned, and quartered)
1 lb. fresh tomatoes, seeded and cut into chunks *or* 1 (14 oz.) can whole tomatoes, cut up
½ c. raisins
8-12 oz. rice noodles, prepared according to package directions
½ c. cashews

Heat oil in a large skillet or Dutch oven. Sauté the onion until lightly browned. Add the garlic, seasonings, water, vegetables, mushrooms, and raisins. Cover and simmer for about 20-25 minutes, until vegetables are tender, and flavors are blended. Spoon vegetables over the cooked noodles on a large serving plate, and sprinkle with the cashews. Serves 4-5.

No Pigs in These Blankets

1 large head cabbage
1 medium onion, chopped
2 T. oil
2 small apples, peeled, cored, and cut into cubes
1 c. t.v.p. (textured vegetable protein, available in health food stores)
1 c. tomato juice
2 c. cooked brown rice
½ c. raisins
2 t. fresh chopped parsley
2 t. dried oregano
2 t. dried thyme
1 t. celery seed
½ t. dill seed
½ t. dill weed
½ t. salt
¼ t. nutmeg

Sauce:
2 c. tomato sauce
1 t. garlic powder
1 t. dried thyme
½ t. fresh ground pepper

12 oz. shredded cheddar or Colby cheese

First remove 12 large leaves from the cabbage. Cut out the thick base of the leaves to make rolling easier. Set the cabbage leaves aside, and use the rest of the cabbage in another dish.

Note: To remove cabbage leaves easily, freeze the cored head overnight, then thaw it out and carefully peel off the leaves.

Another method is to put the whole head of cabbage, cored, into a large pot of boiling water for 15 minutes. Remove the cabbage from the pot and plunge into a bowl of ice water. When cabbage is cool enough to handle, peel off leaves. If after a few leaves, it becomes difficult, return the cabbage to the boiling water and repeat the earlier process.

In a skillet, heat the oil and cook the onions until tender. Stir in the apples, and cook 5 minutes more. Pour this mixture into a medium sized bowl. Add the t.v.p. and tomato juice, and stir to combine. Let stand 5 minutes, so the t.v.p. can soak up the juice. Stir in the rest of the ingredients-except the sauce ingredients and the cheese-and mix well.

Spoon this mixture into the cabbage leaves. You will use about ¼ cup of filling per leaf. Place the filling at the bottom of a leaf. Fold the sides in, and then start rolling up the leaf. Secure each leaf with a toothpick and place in a casserole dish. Repeat with the remaining ingredients. In a medium bowl, combine sauce ingredients and pour over cabbage rolls. Cover the casserole with a tight fitting lid or foil and bake in a 350-degree oven for 40 minutes. Remove the lid or foil, sprinkle with cheese, and return to the oven to melt the cheese, about 10-15 more minutes. Serves 4.

Stuffed Peppers

I would be remiss if I did a recipe for stuffed cabbage, and neglected stuffed peppers. I love peppers, and grow a lot of them in my garden. By August, I'm looking for any interesting new way to use them.

2 T. butter or oil
1 large onion, chopped
1 rib celery, diced
3-4 cloves garlic, minced
1½ c. rice (brown or white)
3-4 ripe plum tomatoes, cored and diced
2 c. water or vegetable stock
4 oz. mushrooms, diced
⅓ c. fresh chopped basil leaves
⅓ c. fresh chopped parsley
2 T. fresh chopped savory
1 t. cumin
salt and pepper to taste
6 large sweet bell peppers green, red, or yellow
2 c. tomato sauce
2 T. fresh chopped oregano
½ t. red pepper flakes, or to taste

Heat butter or oil in a large skillet, and sauté onion until lightly browned. Add celery, garlic, and rice. Sauté 3 minutes more. Stir in tomatoes, water and mushrooms and reduce heat. Cover skillet, and simmer until liquid is absorbed, about 15 minutes. Meanwhile, cut the tops off the peppers. Save the tops. Clean out the seeds and white membrane. When the rice is cooked, stir in the basil, parsley, savory, cumin, salt and pepper. Spoon rice mixture into the peppers, and set the stuffed peppers in a casserole dish.

Combine tomato sauce with oregano and the red pepper flakes. Pour about 2 T. of the sauce over the top of each pepper, and top with the reserved pepper top. Pour the remaining sauce in the base of the dish, and cover the casserole with a lid or with foil. Bake in a 350-degree oven for about 45 minutes. Uncover, and let the peppers cook I5 minutes longer. Serves 6.

Black-eyed Pea Casserole

1 lb. dry black-eyed peas
2 T. oil
2 large onions, chopped
1 28 oz. can tomatoes, chopped but undrained
⅔ c. tomato juice
2 t. salt
2 t. savory
2 t. thyme
2 t. marjoram
2 t. oregano
1 t. rosemary
½ t. hot pepper sauce
8 oz. grated Monterey Jack cheese
2 T. fresh grated Parmesan cheese

Rinse and pick over the peas. Put peas in a large container, cover with cold water and soak overnight. The next day, drain and rinse the peas and put them in a large kettle. Cover with fresh cold water, and cook until tender, about 1½ hours. Drain the peas and return them to the kettle. While the peas are cooking, heat the oil in a skillet and sauté the onions until lightly browned. Add the remaining ingredients-except the cheeses-to the drained peas. Add the onions. Stir to mix well, and pour into a 3 qt. casserole dish. Bake in a 350-degree oven until the mixture has thickened and heated through, about 40 minutes. Remove from the oven and sprinkle the cheeses over the top. Return to the oven and cook 10 more minutes. Serves 6-8.

Multi Grain Pizza

Dough:
½ c. cracked wheat
water
1 c. whole-wheat flour
2 T. wheat germ
1 package quick-rising yeast
1 t. salt
1 T. olive oil
1 t. honey
¾ c. water
about 1 c. bread flour
2 t. fresh rosemary leaves, or scant teaspoon dried

Topping:
olive oil
3 cloves garlic, minced
12 oz. mushrooms (cleaned, trimmed, and sliced)
2 large fresh tomatoes, cored and sliced thin
½ c. fresh chopped basil
1 (10 oz.) package frozen chopped spinach
thawed and squeezed dry
1 cup ricotta cheese
1 large sweet red pepper, seeded and chopped
1-2 t. Pizza Seasoning, (see Chapter 4)
1 c. mozzarella cheese
2 T. grated Parmesan cheese

Cover the cracked wheat with boiling water, and soak 5
minutes. Drain and put the wheat in a medium bowl.
Add the whole-wheat flour, wheat germ, yeast, and salt.
Heat together the water, oil, and honey until very warm.
Pour this into the bowl with the flour mixture, and stir
until well mixed.

Begin adding bread flour until the dough starts to come away from the sides of the bowl. Knead the dough on a floured surface until smooth and elastic, adding flour as needed. Place the dough in a lightly oiled bowl, turning to grease the top. Cover the dough with a towel. Let it rise for about 30 minutes. Punch dough down.

On lightly floured surface, roll the dough out to fit a jellyroll pan. Grease a jellyroll pan, and sprinkle with the rosemary. Transfer the dough carefully, pressing to stretch the dough to the edges of the pan, and up the sides a ½ inch.

Brush the dough lightly with the olive oil. Sprinkle the garlic over the dough, and then the mushrooms. Arrange the tomato slices in three rows lengthwise, with 1 row on either edge and one down the middle. Mix the basil, spinach, and ricotta cheese together and spread it in the rows between the tomatoes. Scatter the red pepper over the whole pizza, and then sprinkle with the Pizza Seasoning, adding more to suit your taste. Sprinkle with the cheeses, and bake in a preheated 450-degree oven for 15-20 minutes, or until toppings are bubbling and the crust is set. Serves 8.

Italian Pinto Bean Casserole

1 lb. dried pinto beans, picked over and rinsed
1 medium eggplant
salt
2 large onions, chopped
3 cloves garlic, minced
2 T. oil
4-5 c. vegetable broth or water (if using water, you can substitute 2 cups with tomato juice)
1 28 oz. can tomatoes, chopped and undrained
1 green pepper, seeded and chopped
1 red sweet pepper, seeded and chopped
2 zucchini, trimmed and cut into chunks
½ c. sun dried tomatoes (not in oil), crumbled slightly
2 T. Italian Seasoning, (see Chapter 4)
½ c. fresh basil leaves, coarsely chopped

Soak beans overnight in water, or cover beans with water in a large pot, and boil for 1 minute. Then turn off the heat and let the beans stand for 1 hour. (This is called quick soaking). Whatever method you choose, drain the beans when done. Place the beans in a large kettle with fresh cold water, and bring them to a boil. Turn the heat to low, and simmer until beans are tender, about 1 hour. Drain beans, and set aside.

While the beans are cooking, prepare the eggplant. Peel the eggplant, and cut into cubes. Place the cubes in a bowl, and salt them thoroughly. (Salting might not be necessary for young and fresh eggplant.)

Anyway, back to the eggplant in the bowl of salt. After a few minutes, it will start to sweat brown fluid. Let this process continue for 30 minutes or so. Then drain and rinse the eggplant cubes, squeezing out all the water until they are dry. Set aside. In the large kettle in which you cooked the beans, heat the oil. Add the onions and garlic, and sauté until the onions are tender. Add all the ingredients-except the seasonings-and the basil. Simmer for 1 hour. Add the seasonings, and cook 15 minutes more. Add the basil, and stir to mix well. Serves 6-8.

Eggplant Parmesan

2 large eggplant or 4 medium
salt
flour
oil
4-6 c. tomato sauce
2 T. Italian Seasoning, (see Chapter 4)
1 (15 oz.) carton ricotta cheese
12 oz. mozzarella cheese, shredded
½ c. grated Parmesan cheese

Start by preparing the eggplant. Peel and slice the eggplant about 1-inch thick. Place the slices in a bowl, salting them well. Allow the eggplant to stand and sweat at room temperature for about 30 minutes, then drain the eggplant, rinse well, and pat dry.

Pour a small amount of oil into a jellyroll pan. Dredge the eggplant slices in flour, and place them in the jelly roll pan. Place the jellyroll pan in a preheated 375-degree oven, and bake until the eggplant begins to brown on the bottom. Turn the slices, and continue baking until both sides are brown and the eggplant is tender.

Note: You can also heat oil in a skillet, and pan fry eggplant, but I find the baking method seems to use less oil. Drain the eggplant.

Combine the sauce and seasoning, and place about ½ cup in the bottom of a baking dish. Add 1 layer of eggplant slices, using about half the slices, and cover with the ricotta cheese, and 1 cup of the sauce. Add the remaining eggplant, and cover with the mozzarella cheese. Pour on enough sauce to cover the mozzarella, and to suit your taste. Sprinkle with the Parmesan cheese, and bake in a 325-degree oven until eggplant is bubbly and browning around the edges, about 35-45 minutes. Makes 6-8 servings.

Veggie Burgers

2 c. cooked pinto beans (or beans of your choice)
1½ c. cooked brown rice
1 c. chopped onion
1 carrot, grated
1 sweet green or red pepper, seeded and minced
1 rib celery, minced
2 cloves garlic, minced
2 eggs
¼ c. breadcrumbs
1 T. fresh chopped parsley, or 1 t. dried
1 T. fresh chopped basil, or 1 t. dried
1 T. fresh savory leaves, or 1 t. dried
½ t. salt
½ t. pepper
Extra bread crumbs for coating burgers
oil for flying

Mash beans until nearly smooth. Stir in the remaining ingredients, and place in fridge, covered, several hours or overnight. Form bean mixture into patties, and coat in crumbs. Fry patties in hot oil until well browned and cooked in the middle. The patties can be topped with cheese, if desired.

Note: Unlike meat burgers, these vegetable burgers do not shrink at all, so be careful not to make them too big.

You can also make these into meatballs and fry as for the burgers, serving them as appetizers, or as a main dish with sauce. Makes about 8-10 burgers.

Veggie Burgers 2

1 c. t.v.p. (textured vegetable protein flakes, found in health food stores) *
1 c. water
1 c. tomato juice
½ c. breadcrumbs
½ c. flour
1 egg
1 small onion, minced
2 cloves garlic, minced
1 T. Italian Seasoning (see Chapter 4)
salt and pepper to taste
extra bread crumbs for coating burgers
oil for frying

In a bowl, combine the t.v.p. with the water and tomato juice, and let stand for 30 minutes or more. You can also cover the bowl, and place it in the fridge for several hours, or overnight.

Drain the liquid from the t.v.p., and reserve. Combine the solids with remaining ingredients, and let stand for 30 minutes. If burgers are too dry, add a little of the reserved liquid.

Form the mix into patties, and bread the patties with the breadcrumbs. Fry patties in hot oil until well browned and cooked through. (Like the other veggie burgers, these will not shrink at all, so be careful not to make them bigger than desired. These also can be made into meatballs, fried as burgers, and served as an appetizer, or as a main dish, with sauce.) Makes 6-8 burgers.

T.V.P. is what remains after the soy oil is pressed from soy beans. T.V.P. is very low in fat, and an inexpensive protein source.

Chapter 9
Vegetables, Pasta
& Other Side Dishes

Broiled Tomatoes with Herbs
Corn with Basil
Green Bean with Oil
Herbed Grilled Eggplant
Minted Peas
Mexican Corn
Zesty Zucchini
Ginger Glazed Carrots
Curried Mixed Vegetables
Curried Vegetables 2
Spiced Beets
Boiled Herbed Potatoes
Whole Roasted Potatoes
Herbed Roasted Potatoes
Nacho Sprouts
Stuffed Herb Tomatoes
Stuffed Tomatoes
Vegetables with Red Lentils
Greek Peppers
Creamed Spinach with Dill
Vegetable Chili
Asparagus with Chives
Curried Spuds
Potato Pancakes
Zucchini Pancakes
Zucchini/Tomato Bake
Veggie-Rice Casserole
Eggplant & Bulgur
Rice Dressing
Zucchini Dressing

Dilled Twice-Baked Potatoes
Sweet Potatoes with Herb Butter
Minted Pasta
Pasta with Pesto
Corn and Lima Beans
Herb and Cheese Strata
Spiced Pears
Carrot Custard
Spiced Spaghetti Squash
Curried Eggplant
Curried Rice
Herbed Couscous
Caponata
Rice with Saffron
Herbed Pasta
Party Pasta
Gingered Broccoli and Cauliflower
Spicy Acorn Squash
Herbed Risotto

Broiled Tomatoes with Herbs

Homegrown beefsteak tomatoes, cut into thick slices
fresh chopped basil, oregano, marjoram, and parsley
fresh minced garlic or garlic powder
salt
fresh ground pepper
thin slices of mozzarella cheese

Arrange tomato slices on a broiler-safe dish. Sprinkle with garlic, either a combination of the herbs listed, or Italian Seasoning or Pizza Seasoning, (see Chapter 4). Salt and pepper tomato slices to taste. Place tomatoes under the broiler for 5 minutes. Remove from the oven, and place a slice of cheese on each tomato. Return under the broiler and cook for 5 minutes more, or until the cheese is melted and bubbly. Allow 2-3 slices per serving as a side dish.

Note: You can substitute eggplant slices if you like. Prep the slices by salting and rinsing slices, then proceeding as with tomatoes.

Corn with Basil

4-8 ears fresh sweet corn
2-3 T. olive oil
salt
fresh ground pepper
½ c. fresh chopped basil

Soak the unhusked corn in a large container of cold water for at least 1 hour. Remove corn from water. Pull back husks from corn, but do not remove. Pull off as many of the silks as you can. Brush the corn with oil, then season with the salt, pepper, and basil. Pull the husk back over the ears, and secure husk by tying with water-soaked twine, if needed. Place ears of corn on or very near hot coals, and grill for about 20 minutes, or until ears are heated through. Serves 4-8.

Green Beans with Dill

1 lb. fresh green beans, washed and trimmed salt to taste
2 T. fresh-snipped dill, or 2 t. dried
1 T. butter or olive oil

Boil or steam beans until tender. Drain beans, and salt if desired. Place beans back in saucepan. Add dill and butter or oil. Heat until the dill's fragrance is released, and the butter has melted. Serves 4.

Herbed Grilled Eggplant

1 large, or 2 medium eggplant, peeled and sliced into
1-inch thick slices
salt
¼ c. olive oil
Pizza Seasoning (see Chapter 4)
3 cloves garlic, minced
¼ c. Parmesan cheese, optional
marinara sauce of your choice

Place eggplant slices in a large bowl and salt them. Let them stand for 30 minutes, then rinse slices thoroughly. Drain well and pat dry. Brush the eggplant slices with the oil, and sprinkle with the Pizza Seasoning and garlic, according to taste. Broil, or preferably, grill the eggplant, turning often, until it is browned, but tender. Sprinkle with the Parmesan cheese near the end of the cooking, if desired. Heat your favorite marinara, pizza, or spaghetti sauce to serve with the eggplant. Serves 6-8.

Minted Peas

1 lb. shelled peas
or sugar snap peas or pea pods, washed and trimmed
2 T. butter
salt to taste
3 T. fresh chopped mint (use a combination of mints, if available), or 1 T. dried mint
1 T. snipped fresh chives, or green onions

Steam or boil peas until just tender. Drain and add remaining ingredients. Heat through and serve. Serves 4.

Mexican Corn

2-3 c. fresh corn, cut off the cob, or frozen
1 sweet red pepper, seeded and diced
2 t. cumin
1 t. chili powder
1 t. dried oregano
½ t. ground coriander
salt to taste
¼ t. red pepper flakes
½ c. fresh chopped cilantro

In a small amount of water in a skillet, heat corn. Add all ingredients, except cilantro, and simmer until water is gone. Stir in the cilantro, and cook until it is wilted, about 2 minutes. Serves 4.

Zesty Zucchini

1-1½ lbs. small zucchini, washed, trimmed, and cubed
1 T. olive oil
1-2 T. Italian Seasoning or Pizza Seasoning, (see Chapter 4)
1-2 c. tomato sauce
¼ t. red pepper flakes, optional
salt and pepper to taste
Parmesan cheese

Heat oil in a skillet and sauté zucchini until tender. Add remaining ingredients, except Parmesan cheese, and heat until bubbly. Serve with Parmesan cheese on the side. Serves 4-6.

Ginger Glazed Carrots

1 lb. carrots, peeled and sliced
salt to taste
2 T. butter
¼ c. brown sugar
1 T. freshly grated ginger, or to taste

Boil or steam the carrots until just tender. Drain and add remaining ingredients. Heat over moderately high heat, stirring to prevent scorching. Heat until the carrots are very hot and glistening. Serves 4.

Curried Mixed Vegetables

2 T. olive oil
1 large onion, cut in chunks
2 cloves garlic, minced
2 medium carrots, peeled and cut into chunks
2 ribs celery, trimmed and cut into chunks
2 c. chopped cabbage
2 small zucchini, trimmed and cut into chunks
1 green pepper, seeded and cut into chunks
1 sweet yellow pepper, seeded and cut into chunks
salt to taste
1 T. curry powder, or more to taste
¼ t. cloves

Heat oil in skillet. Add onion and sauté until tender. Add the garlic, carrots, celery, and cabbage. Stir-fry until vegetables are tender. Add remaining ingredients and cook, covered, over low heat until vegetables are tender, about 10-15 minutes. Add more curry powder if you like. Serves 6-8.

Curried Vegetables 2

2 T. olive oil
1 large onion, chopped
3 cloves garlic, minced
4 carrots, peeled and cut into matchsticks
3 zucchini, trimmed and cut into matchsticks
1 bunch broccoli, trimmed and cut into chunks
1 small cauliflower, trimmed and cut into chunks
1 sweet potato, peeled and cubed
2 c. chicken or vegetable stock
salt to taste
1 T. curry powder
⅓ c. flour
1 c. milk or coconut milk

Heat oil in Dutch oven or large saucepan. Add onion and cook until tender. Add remaining vegetables and stock. Heat to simmering, and add salt and curry powder to taste. Simmer until vegetables are tender, about 10-15 minutes. In a small jar with a lid, combine the milk and flour. Shake the jar until no lumps are visible. Pour this into the vegetable mixture, and bring to a boil. Cook, stirring, until sauce is thickened and bubbly. Serve vegetables plain, or over rice. Serves 6-8.

Spiced Beets

2 lbs. young fresh beets
salt to taste
2 T. butter
1 t. fresh grated ginger
1 t. celery seed
1 t. dried parsley
1 t. orange peel
¼ t. red pepper flakes
⅛ t. ground cloves
⅛ t. ground nutmeg
2 T. orange juice concentrate
½ c. sour cream or Greek yogurt

To prepare beets, trim off stems, leaving about 1 inch intact to reduce bleeding. Wash beets well, and leave roots intact. Boil or steam beets until tender, about 20-45 minutes, depending on the size of the beets. Drain beets, and cool in ice water until you can handle them. Trim off stems and roots, and slip off skins. Slice beets about ½-inch thick.

Place beets in a saucepan and add all ingredients-except the sour cream. Cover and cook over low heat until beets are heated through. Stir in sour cream or yogurt, and serve. Serves 6-8.

Boiled Herbed Potatoes

1-1½ lbs. redskin or other potatoes, scrubbed and cut
into chunks
1 T. olive oil
1 T. butter
2 T. fresh chopped parsley
1 T. snipped fresh chives
1 t. fresh chopped mint
1 t. fresh thyme
1 t. rosemary leaves
1 t. paprika

Boil or steam potatoes until tender. Drain. Return
potatoes to pot, and add remaining ingredients, heating
through gently. Serves 3-4.

Whole Roasted Potatoes

4 medium baking potatoes
2 T. olive oil
salt to taste
1 T. Italian Seasoning, or any herb blend that appeals
to you, (see Chapter 4)
¼ c. fresh grated Parmesan cheese

Scrub the potatoes. Make thin deep cuts into the
potatoes, so the potato will bend like a fan, not slicing
them all the way through. Place the potatoes in a baking
dish, cut side up, and fanned. Drizzle oil over the
potatoes, then sprinkle evenly with the herbs. Bake
potatoes in a 400-degree oven for about 1 hour.
Remove, sprinkle with Parmesan cheese, and return to
the oven for 15-20 minutes more. Serves 4.

Herbed Roasted Potatoes

Make a bunch of these for dinner, because they go like crazy. You can serve these potatoes as a side dish, or with a dip as a finger food. You can also use ketchup as a dipping sauce.

4 lbs. potatoes, scrubbed, and cut into chunks
¼ c. olive oil (amount can be halved)
1 T. parsley flakes
2 t. salt
2 t. onion powder
2 t. garlic powder
2 t. paprika
2 t. oregano
2 t. thyme
1 t. chili powder
1 t. rosemary leaves
¼ t. cayenne pepper

In a large bowl, combine the potatoes with the oil. Toss to coat well. In a small bowl, mix seasonings thoroughly. Toss the seasonings in with the potatoes, and stir to coat evenly. Arrange the potatoes on a baking sheet in a single layer, and bake in a preheated 400-degree oven until golden brown and crisp, about 45 minutes. Stir occasionally for even cooking. Serves 6-8.

Nacho Sprouts

Even your kids will eat Brussels sprouts this way.

1 pt. Brussels sprouts, washed and stems trimmed
1 T. oil
1 t. cumin
1 t. chili powder
1 t. oregano
¼ t. red pepper flakes
1 c. shredded taco cheese or cheddar cheese
2 c. tortilla chips
1 c. salsa

Boil or steam the sprouts until just tender. Drain. Heat oil in a skillet, and add sprouts. Sauté 3-4 minutes, until sprouts just start to brown. Add seasonings, and cook 2 minutes more. Sprinkle cheese over sprouts and cover the pan, turning heat to low. While cheese is melting, place ½ cup of tortilla chips on each of 4 plates. Divide the sprouts on the 4 plates. Garnish with ¼ cup of salsa on each plate. Makes 4 servings.

Stuffed Herbed Tomatoes

2 medium tomatoes, halved and scooped out
2 c. cubed day-old bread, toasted until lightly browned
2 T. olive oil
1 small onion, minced
½ c. tomato juice or chicken stock
2 cloves garlic, minced
¼ c. fresh chopped cilantro
2 T. fresh chopped chives
2 t. thyme
2 t. chopped basil (purple-leaved basil, if available)
Parmesan cheese

Combine the bread with the oil, onion, juice, garlic and seasonings. Mix well, and let stand 30 minutes, or until bread cubes have softened. Divide this mixture evenly into the four tomato halves. Sprinkle with Parmesan cheese, and place tomatoes in a baking dish. Bake in a 400-degree oven for 10-15 minutes. If you want a browner top, place the tomatoes under a broiler for 1 minute, or in a toaster oven to brown.
Serves 4.

Note: This recipe works well with zucchini, or other summer squash as well.

Stuffed Tomatoes 2

2 medium tomatoes, halved and seeded
1 c. cooked brown rice or quinoa
(white rice is O.K., but not preferred in this dish)
2 T. butter
½ c. minced onion
¼ c. hulled sunflower seeds
2 T. fresh chopped chervil or parsley
1 T. fresh or dried lavender blossoms
2 t. fresh chopped mint
1 t. salt
fresh ground pepper to taste

Set tomatoes in shallow baking dish. Combine remaining ingredients in a bowl, and mix well. Pack this mixture into the tomatoes evenly. Bake in a preheated 400-degree oven until heated through. For a browner top, place the tomatoes under the broiler for 1 minute, or in a toaster oven to brown. Serves 4.

Vegetables with Red Lentils

Red lentils are found in specialty food stores and some grocery stores. They're actually not red, but more of a salmon color. Red lentils cook much faster than other lentils. They will be falling-apart tender in 10-15 minutes of cooking. This makes them a fast and easy meal, so you can enjoy legumes more often.

1 large onion, chopped
2 medium carrots, peeled and sliced
2 ribs celery, trimmed and sliced
1 medium zucchini, trimmed and cubed
2 c. water
1 c. raw red lentils, rinsed
1 c. tomato sauce
2 T. fresh chopped purple basil
1 T. fresh chopped parsley
1 T. fresh chopped mint
1 T. chili powder
1 t. garlic powder, or 2 cloves garlic, minced
1 t. sugar
1 t. cumin
¼ t. cayenne pepper

Heat oil in a saucepan, and cook the onion until tender. Add remaining vegetables and cook, stirring, for 5 minutes. Add water, bring to a simmer, and cook, uncovered, until the vegetables are almost tender, about 10 minutes. Add lentils and cook until lentils are tender and starting to fall apart. They will thicken the water and create a sauce as they cook.

Add remaining ingredients and simmer 5 minutes more, adjusting seasonings if needed. Red lentils go well with chicken or lamb. They also become a main dish over rice, or in a pita. Serves 3-4.

Greek Peppers

2 green sweet peppers, seeded and cut into strips
1 sweet red pepper, seeded and cut into strips
1 yellow sweet pepper, seeded and cut into strips
1 hot wax pepper, seeded and sliced into rings
juice of 1 lemon
2 T. olive oil
2 T. fresh chopped oregano, or 2 t. dried
1 T. fresh chopped basil
1 t. rosemary leaves
1 t. salt
½ c. olives, brine-cured, pitted, and sliced
½ c. crumbled feta cheese

Place pepper slices in a medium bowl, and toss with the lemon juice. Let stand 20 minutes. Heat oil in a skillet, and sauté peppers for 3-5 minutes, until just heated through, but still crisp. Add remaining ingredients-except the feta cheese--and stir fry until heated through. Spoon onto a serving plate, and top with feta cheese. Serves 4.

Creamed Spinach with Dill

1-2 lbs. fresh spinach, New Zealand spinach, or lamb's quarters **or** 2 (10 oz.) packages frozen chopped spinach, thawed and drained
2 c. milk
⅓ c. flour
salt and pepper to taste
2 T. fresh-snipped dill, or 2 t. dried
1 T. fresh chopped mint, or 1 t. dried
2 T. butter, or to taste

Clean the spinach in several changes of water to remove all sand. Boil spinach until tender, then drain and chop. Return to saucepan. Add 1 cup of the milk. Shake remaining milk in a jar with the flour until smooth. Add this to the spinach. Add the rest of the ingredients, and heat over medium heat, stirring to prevent sticking, until mixture starts to bubble and thicken. Cook 1 minute longer, adjusting seasonings if needed. Serves 4-6.

Vegetable Chili

2 T. oil
1 large onion, chopped
1 sweet pepper, seeded and chopped
3 small zucchini, trimmed and diced
1 small eggplant, peeled and diced, salted and rinsed
after 30 minutes
1 lb. mushrooms (trimmed, washed, and chopped)
2 (14 oz.) cans tomatoes, chopped and undrained
4 garlic cloves, minced
½ c. fresh chopped cilantro
¼ c. fresh chopped basil
¼ c. fresh chopped parsley
1 T. chili powder
2 t. cumin
2 t. paprika
2 t. cocoa
1 t. cinnamon
½ t. fresh grated ginger
¼ t. cayenne pepper
⅛ t. ground cloves
salt to taste

Heat oil in saucepan. Add onion and sauté until onion is browned. Add pepper, zucchini, eggplant and mushrooms. Sauté until vegetables start to wilt. Add tomatoes with their liquid, and simmer for 30 minutes, or until vegetables are very tender, and most of the liquid has evaporated. When most of the liquid has cooked down, add the remaining ingredients and simmer 20 minutes more, to blend flavors. This dish goes well with cornbread or can be served over rice. Serves 4-6.

Asparagus with Chives

1 lb. fresh asparagus
2 T. butter
salt and pepper to taste
3-4 T. fresh-snipped chives
chive blossoms for garnish, if available

Wash and trim tough ends from the asparagus. Tie the asparagus together to prevent the tips from breaking during cooking. Steam or boil the asparagus until tender, yet still crisp. In a small pan or microwave, melt the butter and combine with remaining ingredients-except chive blossoms. Pour the butter mixture over cooked asparagus on a serving plate. Garnish with chive blossoms. Serves 4.

Curried Spuds

3 T. butter
2 t. curry powder
½ t. salt
1 medium onion, chopped
3-4 large potatoes, scrubbed and cubed
1 (14 oz.) can tomatoes, chopped and undrained

In a medium skillet, melt the butter. Add curry powder and salt. Cook, stirring, until spices have darkened slightly. Add onions and potatoes and cook, stirring, until potatoes start to brown. Add tomatoes, and cover the skillet. Reduce heat, and simmer until potatoes are tender, and liquid is gone.

Note: If the liquid evaporates too quickly, you can add a little water during cooking.

Serves 4-6.

Potato Pancakes

3-4 medium potatoes
1 small onion
1 egg
¼ c. flour
2 T. fresh chopped parsley
1 T. snipped chives
1 T. chopped savory
½ t. dried oregano
½ t. salt
oil for frying

Grate the potatoes and onions. Add remaining ingredients-except oil-and mix thoroughly. Heat ½ inch of oil in a skillet. Spoon batter up by the tablespoonful, and fry in oil. Flatten pancakes slightly, and turn to brown both sides. Remove when the pancakes are crispy on both sides, yet tender in the middle. Serve pancakes plain, or with catsup, sour cream, or applesauce. Serves 6.

Zucchini Pancakes

3 c. shredded zucchini, about 2-3 small
2 eggs
1 medium onion, grated
1 medium carrot, peeled and shredded
½ c. flour
1 t. salt, or to taste
fresh ground pepper to taste
¼ c. fresh chopped parsley
2 t. dried basil
2 t. dried thyme
1 t. dried marjoram
½ t. dried sage
pinch of nutmeg
oil for frying

Combine all ingredients, and let stand 15 minutes. If batter is too thin, add more flour. Heat the oil in a skillet. Place batter by heaping teaspoons in the pan, and flatten pancakes slightly. Turn to brown evenly on both sides. Remove when the outside is crispy, but the inside is still moist. Serves 6-8.

Zucchini/Tomato Bake

Inspired by a recipe from my friend, Alice McKnight, I've included the basics, and have made a few changes I know she would like.

4-5 medium zucchini, trimmed and sliced
3 lbs. fresh homegrown tomatoes, sliced
2 large sweet onions, sliced thin
salt and pepper to taste
2 T. butter
2 T. Italian Seasoning (see Chapter 4)
½ c. breadcrumbs
1 c. shredded cheddar cheese

In an ovenproof dish layer slices of zucchini, tomatoes, and onion. Salt and pepper to suit your taste. Melt the butter, and drizzle it over the top of the vegetables. Sprinkle on the seasoning, breadcrumbs, and cheese. Bake in a preheated 350-degree oven for about 45 minutes, or until the vegetables are tender and the top is browned.

A fair amount of liquid will accumulate in the bottom of the pan. I spoon this "sauce" over the vegetables, rice or pasta. Serves 8.

Veggie-Rice Casserole

3 c. cooked rice (white or brown), made from 1 cup raw rice
2 T. oil
1 c. chopped onion
2 cloves garlic, minced
2 carrots, peeled and cut into matchstick pieces
2 medium zucchini, trimmed and cut into cubes
12 oz. sliced mushrooms
salt and pepper to taste
2 t. celery seed
1 t. dried lovage leaves, or 1 T. chopped lovage or celery leaves
1 t. dill weed
1 t. dill seed
½ t. caraway seed
¼ t. turmeric
⅛ t. saffron threads, crumbled
1 c. shredded cheddar cheese
½ c. breadcrumbs

While rice is cooking, heat oil in a skillet and sauté onion until tender. Add garlic and vegetables and sauté until veggies are tender, about 5 minutes. Add seasonings and set aside. When rice is cooked, transfer it to a large bowl, and add the vegetable mixture. Stir to mix well, and pour rice mixture into a lightly oiled casserole dish. Sprinkle cheese and crumbs on top of the casserole, and bake in a preheated 350-degree oven until heated through and lightly browned on the top. (About 35 minutes if you cook the rice. Bake a little bit longer if the rice was pre-cooked and refrigerated.) Serves 6.

Eggplant and Bulgur

⅔ c. bulgur wheat
⅔ c. water
½ t. salt
1 T. butter
1 large eggplant, peeled, cut into 8 slices
½ c. flour
1 t. dried thyme
½ t. dried rosemary
oil for frying
1 large sweet onion, sliced thin
2 large tomatoes, sliced
2 T. fresh chopped cilantro
2 T. fresh chopped parsley
1 T. fresh chopped basil
8 oz. sliced mushrooms
2 T. butter
1 T. flour
⅔ c. milk
salt and pepper to taste

Combine bulgur, water, and salt in a small saucepan, and heat to boiling. Remove from heat. Cover and let stand 30 minutes. Add butter. When butter is melted, fluff cooked bulgur with a fork. Combine the ½ cup of flour with the thyme and rosemary. Rinse eggplant slices in water, and dredge in the flour. Fry eggplant in hot oil until slices are browned and tender. Place the bulgur in a 2-quart casserole dish. Place the eggplant slices over the bulgur. Layer the onion slices, and the tomato. Sprinkle the cilantro, parsley, and basil over the top. Season with salt and pepper, if desired.

Sauté the mushrooms in the remaining butter. Add the flour and stir to blend. Add the milk and stir until sauce is thickened. Pour sauce over the tomatoes. Bake casserole at 350 degrees for 35-45 minutes, or until bubbly and browning at the edges.

I like this as a main dish sometimes, but as a side dish it goes well with chicken, beef, or pork. Serves 4-6 as a main dish, or 8 as a side dish.

Rice Dressing

3 c. cooked rice, white or brown
1 c. grated cheddar cheese
3 eggs, beaten
1 lb. fresh spinach, New Zealand spinach, or lamb's quarters trimmed, washed, and cooked until tender
¼ c. chopped parsley
2 T. chopped green onion
1 T. fresh thyme
2 t. fresh rosemary
1 t. cumin
1 t. paprika
salt and pepper to taste
2 T. butter, melted

Combine all ingredients in a lightly oiled casserole dish. Cover, and bake in a preheated 350-degree oven for 35-40 minutes, or until heated through. Serves 4-6.

Zucchini Dressing

2 T. oil
2 T. butter
4 small zucchini, trimmed and cut into cubes
1 c. chopped onion
2 ribs celery, trimmed and cubed
8 oz. sliced mushrooms
6-8 c. bread cubes
¼ c. fresh chopped parsley
2 T. fresh chopped savory or 2 t. dried
1 t. dried sage
1 t. dried thyme
salt and pepper to taste
2 c. chicken stock
1 c. evaporated milk
2 T. chopped chives or green onions

In a skillet, heat the oil and butter and sauté vegetables until the onion is tender. Place the vegetables in a large bowl, and add the bread, seasonings, and stock. Stir until well blended. Drizzle the milk to distribute it evenly over the mixture. Stir to mix well. If the dressing seems a little dry, add more chicken stock. Place dressing in a casserole dish and bake, covered, in a preheated 350-degree oven for 25 minutes. Uncover, and bake 15 minutes longer. Sprinkle the casserole top with chives before serving. Serves 6-8.

Dilled Twice-Baked Potatoes

4 medium baking potatoes, scrubbed
½ c. sour cream or Greek yogurt
1 green onion, trimmed and minced
2 T. fresh minced dill
1 T. butter or margarine
1 t. salt
1 t. dried parsley
¼ t. fresh ground black pepper or to taste
1 c. shredded cheddar cheese
paprika

Bake potatoes in a 425-degree oven until fork tender, about 45-55 minutes. Remove from oven and allow to cool enough to handle. Cut potatoes in half, lengthwise, and scoop out the middle, being careful not to break the potatoes. In a medium bowl combine the potato flesh with all the ingredients except the cheese and paprika. Mash with large spoon until well blended.

Fold in the cheese and spoon or pipe this mixture back into the potato skins, dividing evenly. Sprinkle with the paprika and bake in a 375-degree oven for 25-30 minutes, or until heated through and browning on the top.

After filling, the potatoes can be refrigerated for 2-3 days before reheating, or you can wrap and freeze them at this stage for up to 2 months. If potatoes have been frozen or refrigerated, allow extra time for reheating. Serves 4.

Sweet Potatoes with Herb Butter

4 medium sweet potatoes, scrubbed
3 T. butter
2 T. honey
2 T. fresh-snipped chives
1 T. fresh thyme leaves
2 t. fresh savory leaves
2 t. fresh rosemary leaves
1 t. grated fresh ginger
salt and fresh ground pepper to taste

Cook potatoes until tender, either steamed, baked, grilled, or microwaved. Combine the other ingredients into an herbed butter. Cut cooked potatoes in half lengthwise, and place them in a broiler safe dish. Brush with the herb butter. Place the potatoes under the broiler for 5 minutes, or until brown and sizzling on top. Makes 6 to 8 servings.

Minted Pasta

8 oz. uncooked pasta (shells work well)
2 T. olive oil
2 green onions, trimmed and chopped
2 c. fresh or frozen green peas
3 T. fresh chopped mint leaves (use an assortment of mints, if available)
salt and pepper to taste

Cook pasta according to package directions. While pasta is cooking, heat oil in a skillet and sauté green onions. Add peas, mint leaves, and salt and pepper to taste. Drain cooked pasta. Toss pasta with the pea mixture. Serves 4.

Pasta with Pesto

Pesto sauce:
1 c. basil leaves
¼ c. olive oil
3-4 cloves garlic
salt to taste
¼ c. pine nuts **or** walnuts **or** hulled sunflower seeds
½-¾ c. shredded Parmesan cheese
8-12 oz. uncooked pasta

Place all sauce ingredients in a blender or food processor, and blend until smooth. Cook pasta according to package directions. Drain hot pasta, place in a large bowl, toss with pesto sauce and serve. Serves 4-6.

Corn and Lima Beans

2 c. corn kernels
1 c. fresh or frozen lima beans
1 T. thyme
1 T. fresh chopped basil
1 T. chopped chives
1 t. celery seed
1 t. salt
1 T. butter

Heat together corn and beans. Drain, add remaining ingredients, and heat until butter is melted and all is heated through. Serves 4.

Herb and Cheese Strata

This recipe was inspired by a brunch I attended several years ago. I've adjusted the herbs to suit my taste. On the advice of my cousin Jim, I've added garlic, which Jim loves with any egg dish.

Note: In this strata the bread will eventually absorb the liquid of the strata ingredients. Because the casserole needs a lengthy time to set up, consider assembling the strata the night before, or early in the day for an evening meal.

1 large onion, chopped
2 T. olive oil
2 ribs celery, diced
1 (1 lb.) loaf Italian or French bread cut into 1-inch thick slices
1 lb. Muenster cheese, shredded
½ lb. sharp cheddar cheese
¼ c. fresh chopped basil leaves
2 T. fresh chopped parsley leaves
1 t. dried minced garlic, or garlic powder
1 t. fresh chopped sage
1 t. fresh thyme leaves
3 c. evaporated milk
1 c. sour cream
8 eggs
salt to taste paprika
fresh-snipped chives

Sauté the onion in oil until tender. Add celery and sauté until celery is softened. Set aside. Toast the bread. In a large baking dish, place ⅓ of the bread slices. Place ⅓ of the onion mixture on top, and follow with ⅓ of each of the cheeses. Repeat layers two more times, finishing with cheeses on top. Combine the remaining ingredients-except the paprika and chives in a blender, and blend well. Pour this mixture over the strata, and cover and chill.

Before baking, sprinkle the casserole top with paprika and chives. Bake, uncovered, in a preheated 350-degree oven for 50 minutes, or until strata is bubbly and the edges are golden. Makes 8 servings.

Spiced Pears

2 T. butter
4 medium-sized pears (peeled, cored, and cut in halves)
½ c. apple cider or apple juice
1 t. orange zest
1 t. cinnamon
¼ t. cardamom
⅛ t. cloves
⅛ t. cayenne pepper
salt to taste
½ c. whipping cream
fresh-snipped rosemary

Heat butter in a skillet and add pears, cooking until they are tender. Add remaining ingredients-except cream and rosemary-and cook 5 minutes longer, or until sauce is reduced by half. Remove pears and set aside. Stir cream into sauce, and transfer to a gravy boat or other server. Place pear halves in a serving dish, and sprinkle with snipped rosemary. This dish goes well with pork or duck. Serves 4.

Carrot Custard

6 medium carrots, peeled and sliced
1½ c. evaporated milk
5 eggs
2 T. fresh chopped dill or 2 t. dried
2 t. fresh grated ginger
salt and pepper to taste
1 lb. pea pods, washed and ends trimmed
1 T. butter
1 T. fresh chopped mint leaves
1 t. fresh lemon juice

Cook carrots in simmering water until very tender. Drain. Place carrots in food processor and add the milk, eggs, dill, ginger, salt and pepper. Pulse several times until carrots are smooth. Place mixture in an oiled 4 or 5-cup casserole.

Place the dish in a roasting pan in a 350-degree oven. Pour boiling water in the roasting pan until it comes up the side of the casserole dish by 1-2 inches. Bake for 50-55 minutes or until knife inserted in center comes out clean. Remove from the oven and set aside.

In a skillet, heat the butter and sauté the pea pods until just tender, about 4 minutes. Stir in the mint and lemon juice, and remove from the heat. Spoon carrot custard onto plates and serve with the pea pods. Serves 6-8.

Spiced Spaghetti Squash

1 large spaghetti squash
½ c. hulled pumpkin seeds
2 T. butter
2 t. cumin
2 t. ground coriander
1 t. chili powder
1 t. dried oregano
1 t. cinnamon
1 t. fresh grated ginger
1 t. salt
½ t. fresh grated nutmeg
½ t. fresh ground pepper
¼ t. cayenne pepper

Place squash in a large pot of boiling water and cook until fork tender, about 40 minutes. (Time will vary from squash to squash.) While the squash is cooking, toast the pumpkin seeds. Place the seeds in a small skillet, and toast over medium heat. Toss gently until the seeds jump in the pan and puff. Remove from heat, and set aside.

When squash is cooked, remove to a plate and let cool 15 minutes. Slice squash lengthwise and cool until it is easily handled. Scoop out and discard the seeds. Remove the long stringy squash pulp, shredding it into strands with a fork. Discard the hollowed-out skin.

Heat butter in a large skillet, and add the spaghetti squash. Sauté until squash in very hot and starting to brown. Toss in remaining ingredients, and heat for another few minutes. Adjust seasonings. Serves 4-6.

Curried Eggplant

1 medium eggplant, peeled and cut into cubes
2 T. oil
2 large onions, chopped
5 cloves garlic, minced
1 t. grated fresh ginger
1 T. cumin
1 T. curry powder
2 c. tomato sauce
½ c. chopped cilantro

Place eggplant cubes in a bowl and salt well, stirring to coat. Let stand 30 minutes, then rinse well and drain cubes. Set aside. In a large saucepan or Dutch oven, heat the oil and sauté onions until onions start to brown. Stir in all remaining ingredients; except the cilantro, and bring to a simmer. Simmer, covered, until eggplant is very tender, about 40 minutes. Remove cover, add cilantro, and cook 5 minutes more. In my humble opinion, this dish goes well will grilled fish, meats, and especially lamb. Serves 6-8.

Curried Rice

2 c. long grain white rice (jasmine rice, if available)
1 T. butter
½ c. chopped green onion
1 large carrot, peeled and diced
1-2 t. curry powder
3 c. water, chicken or vegetable stock
salt to taste

Place all ingredients in a saucepan, and bring to a boil. Turn heat down to low, cover, and cook until liquid is absorbed and rice is tender.

Note: This takes 12-15 minutes with white rice, and longer if you use brown or wild rice. If you decide to use brown or wild rice, increase cooking time to 40 and 50 minutes, respectively. Also, increase liquid to 3 cups. Serves 6.

Herbed Couscous

1½ c. chicken broth or water
2 T. fresh chopped cilantro
1 T. fresh chopped chives, or 1 t. dried
1 c. couscous
1 T. butter
salt and pepper to taste

Bring broth or water to a boil. Stir in the remaining ingredients-except salt and pepper. Remove from heat, cover pot, and let stand 5 minutes. Fluff couscous with a fork, and add salt and pepper if needed. Serves 4.

Caponata

This wonderful eggplant dish comes in many variations. While it is often served as a first course or party food, I like it with baked fish or chicken. Its rich flavor adds zest to simple foods. Caponata is also good when piled on toasted pita wedges!

2 small eggplants, unpeeled and cut into ½-inch pieces, about 5-6 cups
1 large onion, chopped
½ c. olive oil, or a little more
4 celery ribs, sliced
2 sweet peppers, seeded and chopped
1 heaping tablespoon chopped garlic
3 tomatoes, chopped
1 c. sliced black olives
3-4 T. red wine vinegar
2 t. dried basil
2 t. dried oregano
salt and pepper to taste.

Soak eggplant in salted water for at least 15 minutes. Rinse, drain and pat dry. Set aside. Meanwhile in skillet cook onion in 2 tablespoons of the oil until tender. Add the celery and cook until the celery is tender-crisp. Place mixture in a mixing bowl and set aside. Heat 2 tablespoons more of the oil and cook the peppers until tender. Add garlic and cook 1 minute longer. Add the tomatoes and cook 1 minute longer. Add this mixture to onion mixture and return skillet to the heat. Add remaining oil to skillet and cook eggplant until golden brown and tender. You may have to do this in 2 batches. Add remaining ingredients to bowl while eggplant is cooking. When eggplant is done add it to the bowl and mix well. Season to taste. Serve with crusty breads cold, hot or at room temperature. Serves 10-12.

Rice with Saffron

1-1½ c. long grain white rice (Jasmine rice is preferred. Look for this rice in Asian markets and some grocery stores)
1 T. olive oil
1 T. butter
2-2½ c. water or chicken stock
salt to taste (less or none if using stock)
¼ t. crumbled saffron threads
1-2 c. fresh or frozen green peas

In a medium saucepan, heat the oil and butter and add the rice. Heat until rice is just starting to brown. Add water or stock, salt if desired, and bring to a simmer. Sprinkle saffron over the top of the rice, and cover. Cook on low heat. Rice will be ready in about 15-20 minutes. About 5 minutes before the rice is ready, when there is still adequate liquid, add the peas. Replace the cover, and cook until rice and peas are done, about five more minutes. Transfer hot rice to a serving bowl, and stir to combine the rice and peas. Makes 6 servings.

Herbed Pasta

2 c. flour, plus extra for rolling
1 T. olive oil
4eggs
¼ c. packed fresh basil, parsley or cilantro leaves
½ t. salt

Mound flour on a work surface, and make a well in the center. Combine remaining ingredients in a blender, and blend until smooth. Pour this mixture into the flour well, and mix together gently with a fork.

Knead the dough, adding flour if needed, until a firm dough is formed. Cover dough in plastic wrap, and let it rest on the work surface or board for 15 minutes.

Note: Although the dough can be hand-rolled, a pasta rolling machine is suggested.

To roll pasta in a machine:

1. Work with about a quarter of the dough at a time, keeping the rest well wrapped to avoid drying out.

2. Place the roller at the thickest setting for the dough, and roll the dough through the machine. After the dough comes out, fold it into thirds, and roll it through again two more times.

3. Start rolling the dough on thinner and thinner settings, until you reach the next-to-last setting (1/16 inch thick).

4. Now, run the dough through the cutting blades to desired width-or use at this width for herb lasagna noodles.

5. Repeat with remaining dough quarters. Pasta can be dried on a rack for later use, or cooked right away. For long-term storage, pasta-even dried pasta-must be frozen.

Cooking time will be about 3 minutes. Don't overcook the pasta. Toss homemade pasta with melted butter, or perhaps an herb butter. Or, toss with your favorite pasta sauce. (Be creative! For example, I enjoy parsley pasta in chicken soup.) Makes 4 servings.

Whole Herb Pasta

For special occasions, try this lovely dish. Fresh herb sprigs are rolled between two layers of fresh pasta. They show through, and make a real hit at parties.

2 c. flour, plus extra for rolling
4eggs
1 T. olive oil
½ t. salt
½ c. water
small sprigs and leaves from assorted fresh herbs, such as: parsley, dill, fennel, green and purple basil, thyme, tarragon, or cilantro.

Mound flour on a work surface, and make a well in the middle. Combine eggs, oil, and salt in a bowl and whisk to blend well. Set aside 2 Tablespoons of this mixture. Pour rest of mixture into the flour well, and use a fork to blend with the flour.

Begin kneading the dough, adding flour if needed. Cover dough in plastic wrap, and let dough rest for 15 minutes. Work with a quarter of the dough at a time, keeping the rest well wrapped to avoid drying out. Begin rolling out in pasta rolling machine, staring at thickest setting. After rolling the dough through once, fold it into thirds, and roll through again 2 more times. Then, start rolling out the dough in increasingly thinner settings, until the second-to-the-thinnest setting is reached.

Combine the remaining 2 tablespoons of egg mixture with a ½ cup of water, and blend well. Place dough on the work surface. Brush egg mixture on bottom half of dough. Place herbs on bottom half of dough, not closer than ½-inch from the edge.

Brush edges of top half of dough with additional egg mixture. Fold dough in half, carefully lining up the sides and edges. Press dough together from the middle on out toward the edges, to insure a good seal. Press the edges firmly together, and run the dough through the pasta rolling machine again, being careful to use additional flour as necessary to prevent sticking.

Repeat with remaining dough. Dough can be cut crosswise into 3-inch pieces, and boiled 3 minutes or so. Serve herbed pasta with a butter sauce, or use these fancy noodles for the top layer in a pan of vegetable lasagna.

Another really fun way to use this pasta is to make ravioli with it. Cut the dough into squares, and spoon in some filling, adding another layer of dough on top. These ravioli will cook in about 4 minutes. Be careful not to overcook. Serves 4.

Ginger Broccoli and Cauliflower

1 bunch broccoli, washed, trimmed, and cut into bite-sized pieces
1 medium head cauliflower, washed, trimmed, and cut into bite-sized pieces
1 T. butter
1 T. fresh grated ginger
2 cloves garlic, minced
½ t. ground coriander seed
salt and pepper to taste
1 c. chicken stock
2 t. cornstarch

Steam or boil broccoli and cauliflower until tender-crisp. While the vegetables are steaming, heat the butter in a small saucepan. Add the ginger, garlic, and coriander and heat, stirring, until the spices brown slightly. (Take care not to let the garlic burn as it will become bitter.)

Add salt and pepper to taste, and stir in half of the chicken stock. As the stock simmers, dissolve cornstarch into the remaining stock, and add this to the saucepan. Heat until the butter sauce is bubbly and thickened. When broccoli and cauliflower are ready, drain and place in a serving bowl. Top vegetables with the sauce, and toss to coat. Serves 6.

Spicy Acorn Squash

My dear friend Martha got me started grilling winter squash. She would roll up a butternut or acorn squash in foil, and place it a little to the side of the hot coals. By the time the rest of the meal ended up on the grill, the squash were cooked tender. She would split the squash open, spoon out the seeds, and put some butter and salt in the cavity. We would all just spoon out what we wanted. One of my favorite dinners happened one warm July evening, when we ate squash and grilled pizza by the light of a very uncooperative oil lamp. This is a baked version of what Martha created.

3 acorn squash, cut in half, seeds removed
3 T. butter
salt and pepper to taste
¼ c. fresh chopped parsley
2 T. honey
1 t. cinnamon
1 t. cardamom
½ t. ground ginger
¼ t. ground allspice

Place squash cut side up on a baking dish. Divide all ingredients between the six halves. Wrap each half securely in heavy-duty foil. Place squash cut side up around the edges of hot coals. Or, leave squash on the baking sheet, and bake in a 350-degree oven. Bake squash until tender, about 45 minutes. Remove foil, and place the squash halves on a serving platter, being careful not to tip them over. Serves 6.

Herbed Risotto

3 c. chicken stock
2 c. water
1 large onion, chopped
2 T. olive oil
¾ c. medium-grain rice
1 clove garlic, minced
½ c. fresh chopped basil
1 T. fresh chopped parsley
½ t. fresh thyme
salt to taste
fresh ground pepper to taste

In a medium saucepan, heat together the stock and water and keep warm. In another saucepan sauté the onion in the oil until starting to brown. Add the rice and garlic, and sauté 3-5 minutes longer. Stir in 1 cup of the hot liquid as the rice cooks. As the liquid is absorbed, add more liquid, a cup at a time. Keep stirring to prevent scorching. When about ¾ of the liquid has been added, stir the other ingredients into the rice. Continue adding liquid until the rice is tender and creamy. (You may not need all the liquid.) Serves 4.

Chapter 10
Breads

Judi's Herb Braids
Herbed Pita
Swedish Limpa
French Tarragon Bread
Martha Merrick's Nisu
Sweet Potato Biscuits with Herbs
Sage Rolls
Thyme Muffins
Herb and Cornmeal Muffins
Mint and Pineapple Scones
Scarborough Fair Biscuits
Chive and Cheddar Biscuits
Herbed Whole Wheat Bread
Mexican Cheddar Cheese Bread
Chili Corn Muffins
Rosemary Oatmeal Bread
Herbed Pepperoni Bread
Herb and Cheese Bread
Spicy Zucchini Bread
Herbed Focaccia
Fennel Breadsticks
Seedy Muffins

Judi's Herb Braids

This bread has evolved over several years of testing and tasting. It is frequently requested for casual and formal dinners alike. I make it in two versions, white and multi-grain. Both are foolproof, and a breeze to handle.

Versions

White:
5½-6½ c. bread flour
2 packages quick rising yeast
¼ c. toasted dried shallots or onions
2 T. dried marjoram
2 T. dried parsley
1 T. dried oregano
1 T. dried minced garlic
1 T. honey
2 t. dried thyme
2 t. salt
¼ c. olive oil
2¼ c. hot water

In a mixing bowl, combine 2 cups of flour with the yeast, herbs, seasonings, honey and salt. Stir to combine. Heat the oil and water together until very warm, to a temperature of about 120 degrees. Pour the water/oil mixture into the flour, and beat with an electric mixer for 4 minutes. Add flour, ½ cup at a time, until dough thickens. Stir thickened dough by hand, until dough starts to leave the sides of the bowl.

Turn the dough onto a lightly floured surface and knead, adding flour as necessary, until a soft, smooth dough is formed. Place this dough in a lightly oiled bowl, turning to coat the top. Cover with a towel and place in

304

a warm place to rise. The dough will double in about 25 minutes.

Punch dough down and divide into 2 equal portions. Cover with the towel, and let the dough rest 10 minutes. Place one piece of the dough on a lightly floured surface, and divide this into 3 equal pieces. Roll each piece into an 18-inch rope. Place the three ropes side by side. Starting in the middle of the length, braid the ropes together. When one side of the ropes is braided together, hold the braided portion of the dough securely. Flip this side away from you on the work surface. The unbraided portion of the ropes of dough will now be facing you. Finish braiding the other side of the dough. Pinch both ends well to prevent the braid from coming apart. Place the braid on one side on a greased baking sheet, and cover with a towel.

Repeat the braiding process with the other half of the dough. Place the second braid on the baking sheet. Allow braids to rise until doubled in bulk, about 20 minutes. Bake in a preheated 375-degree oven for 25-30 minutes, or until loaves are golden brown and sound hollow when tapped lightly.

Multi-Grain:

Replace 2 cups of the white flour in the White recipe with whole-wheat flour. Also, add ¼ c. wheat germ, ¼ c. oat bran, 2 T. cracked wheat, 2 T. sesame seed and 2 T. hulled sunflower seeds. Add all these ingredients with the herbs in the beginning. You will use less flour in the entire recipe because of these additional ingredients, so begin with the 2 cups of whole wheat flour, to include the entire amount in the dough.
Note: *You can use 2 packages of regular yeast in this*

recipe. To adapt to regular yeast, use warm rather than hot water, and allow about twice the rising time for the dough.

Herbed Pita

about 5 c. bread flour
1 package active dry yeast
2 t. dried basil
2 t. dried parsley
2 t. sugar
1 t. dried rosemary
1 t. dried mint
1 t. salt
2 c. warm water
¼ c. olive oil

In a mixing bowl, combine 2 cups of flour and the remaining ingredients. Mix until well blended. Using an electric mixer, beat the dough for 4 minutes. Then, using a wooden spoon, begin to add more flour, stirring and adding the flour until dough comes away from the sides of the bowl. Turn the dough onto a floured surface and knead, adding more flour if needed, until the dough is firm and smooth. Leave the dough on the board, and cover with plastic wrap and a towel. Let the dough rise for about 30 minutes.

Punch the dough down, and divide into 12 equal pieces. Roll each piece into as smooth a ball as possible. (Seams may cause the bread to rise improperly, so this step is important.) Place the balls of dough on the floured surface, leaving some room in between, and cover with a towel only. Let them rise for 30-40 minutes. Preheat the oven to 500 degrees.

Roll the dough balls into 6-8 inch circles. Place 3 circles at a time directly onto the oven rack, and bake until they puff and become golden brown, about 3-5 minutes. Remove pitas to a rack to cool, and proceed to bake the remaining circles. Makes 12 pitas.

Note: You can make a whole-wheat version of this pita by adding 1 ½ cups whole-wheat flour in place of the same amount of white flour.

Swedish Limpa

6 ½ c. bread flour
2 c. rye flour
⅓ c. brown sugar
1 T. salt
1 T. caraway seed
2 t. grated orange peel
2 packages quick rising yeast
¼ c. olive oil
2 c. hot water
⅔ c. hot orange juice

Set aside 1½ cup white flour. Combine the remaining dry ingredients in large bowl. Add liquid ingredients, and stir to blend. Stir in enough remaining flour until a soft dough forms. Turn this dough onto a floured board and knead, adding flour as necessary, until the dough is smooth and elastic. This will take about 8-10 minutes. Place the dough in a greased bowl, and turn to grease the top. Cover, and let rise in a warm place until doubled in bulk, about 30 minutes.

Punch dough down. Divide dough into 2 equal pieces, and shape each into a ball. Place the balls on a greased baking sheet, and cover. Let loaves rise until doubled, about 20-30 minutes. Preheat oven to 400 degrees. Slash the tops of the loaves just before baking. Bake bread 25-30 minutes, or until the loaves sound hollow when tapped lightly. Makes 2 loaves.

French Tarragon Bread

7-8 c. bread flour
¼ c. sugar
2 T. dried tarragon
1 T. salt
2 packages active dry yeast
2¼ c. warm water

Set aside 1 cup of the flour. Combine the remaining ingredients in a large bowl, and mix until well blended. Stir in extra flour until a soft dough forms, and comes away from the sides of the bowl. Turn the dough onto a lightly floured surface, and knead until a moderately stiff dough forms, which is smooth and elastic. Place the dough in an oiled bowl, turning to coat the top. Cover, and allow the dough to double in bulk, about 50 minutes.

Punch dough down. Place the dough on a floured surface, and cover with the bowl. Allow the dough to rest 10 minutes. Divide dough in half, and roll each half into a 17-18-inch loaf. Place diagonally on a greased baking sheet. Repeat with remaining dough. Cover the loaves and allow them to double in bulk, about 45 minutes. While they rise, place one oven rack in the top third of the oven, and the other rack in the bottom third. Preheat the oven to 400 degrees.

Just before baking, slash the loaves diagonally, and brush with water. Slide the baking sheets onto the oven racks, one on top and one on the bottom. After 15 minutes of baking, switch the two baking sheets. Bake the bread a total of 25-30 minutes. For crispier crust, mist loaves with fresh, cold water 3-4 times in the first 10 minutes of baking. Test loaves for doneness by tapping lightly. Bread should sound hollow. Makes 2 loaves.

Variations

Italian Bread: Add 2 T. Italian Seasoning (see Chapter 4), in place of the tarragon.

Basil and Sage Bread: Add 2 T. dried basil and 2 t. dried sage in place of the tarragon.

Martha Merrick's Nisu

This bread comes to me from the Finn grandmother of my best friend back when we were roommates; we were sometimes blessed with these tender and fragrant loaves. I started making it some years later, and during my father's last months it became one of his favorite breads. As a former baker, his opinion of bread meant a lot to me.

½ c. warm water
2 packages active dry yeast
6-7 c. bread flour
2 c. milk, scalded
2 eggs
½ c. sugar
2 t. -1 T. ground cardamom
6 T. butter
1 t. salt

In a small bowl, combine the warm water and yeast. Allow to stand for 5 minutes. Meanwhile, in a large mixing bowl combine 2 cups of the flour and the remaining ingredients. Add the yeast mixture, and beat with an electric mixer for 3 minutes. Add 1 more cup of flour, and beat 1 minute longer. Stir in the flour by hand, until a soft dough forms and comes away from the sides of the bowl.

Turn the dough onto a floured surface and knead, adding flour when necessary, until a firm, smooth dough is formed, about 5-10 minutes. Place dough in an oiled bowl, turning dough to grease the top. Cover and allow to rise until doubled, about 1 hour. Punch dough down, and allow to rise again, covered.

While the bread is rising, grease either 2 (9x5-inch) loaf pans, or 3 (8x4-inch) loaf pans. Punch dough down again. Depending on the number of pans, divide the dough into either 2 or 3 pieces. Roll or press each section of dough into a rectangle, and roll up jellyroll fashion. Pinch ends to seal well, and place loaves, seam side down, in prepared pans. Cover, and allow to rise once more, about 40 minutes, until doubled in bulk.

Bake in a preheated 375-degree oven for 30-35 minutes, or until loaves test done. To test for doneness in bread, tap loaves lightly. Bread should have a hollow sound. Nisu is an especially good bread for sandwiches and French toast. Makes 2-3 loaves.

Sweet Potato Biscuits with Herbs

2½ c. flour
1 T. baking powder
½ t. salt
1 t. dried thyme
1 t. dried savory
1 t. dried parsley
1 t. dried rosemary
1 egg, beaten
1 large raw sweet potato, peeled and shredded (about 1⅔ c.)
½ c. minced green onions
1 clove garlic, minced
⅓ c. sour cream
¼ c. olive oil, divided

In a medium bowl, stir together the dry ingredients. In a separate bowl, combine the remaining ingredients, reserving 2 T. of the oil. Stir the wet ingredients into the dry ingredients, and mix until dough starts to come together. Turn dough onto a lightly floured surface and knead about 10 times, or until the dough just holds together. Don't over mix or the biscuits will be tough.

Lightly flour a 9-inch baking dish, and press dough evenly into pan. In a quick motion, flip pan over onto the floured surface. Dough will be in a 9-inch square. Cut dough in half. Then cut each half into half crosswise. You will have 4 squares. Cut each square with 2 diagonal slices (an x shape), so that each piece becomes 4 triangle pieces. Place dough triangles on a greased baking sheet, and brush with remaining oil. Bake in a 425-degree oven for 20 minutes. Makes 16 biscuits.

Sage Rolls

¾ c. milk
½ c. sugar
⅓ c. butter
1 t. salt
2 packages active dry yeast
½ c. warm water
4½-5 c. bread flour
½ c. chopped green onion or chives
1 T. dried sage
2 eggs, lightly beaten

Heat milk to almost simmering, being careful not to burn. Stir in sugar, butter, and salt. Cool milk to lukewarm.

Dissolve yeast in warm water. Set aside. Place 2 cups of flour in a large bowl. Add the milk mixture, and beat together. Stir in yeast mixture, sage, and eggs. Beat with an electric mixer for 4 minutes. Gradually stir in enough of the flour to make a soft dough that leaves the sides of the bowl. Turn onto a floured surface and knead until the dough is smooth and elastic, about 8-10 minutes. Place the dough in oiled bowl, turning to grease the top. Cover, and allow dough to rise until doubled in bulk, about 45-55 minutes.

Punch dough down, turn onto a floured surface, and cover with the bowl. Allow the dough to rest 15 minutes. Divide dough into 24-32 pieces, depending on the size you like. Shape dinner rolls as desired. I like to roll pieces into 6-inch ropes, and then tie them into a loose knot. Place the rolls onto greased baking sheets, allowing them room to grow. Cover, and let rise until doubled in bulk, about 45 minutes. Bake rolls in a 350-degree oven until golden brown, 15-18 minutes.

Variations

Italian Rolls: Add 1 T. Italian Seasoning (see Chapter 4) in place of the sage.

Curry Rolls: Add 2 t. curry powder in place of the sage.

Old English Rolls: Add 2 t. thyme and 2 t. parsley in place of the sage.

Dilly Rolls: Add 2 T. dill in place of the sage.

Herb Rolls: Add 1-2 T. Everyday Herb Blend or Fine Herbes (see chapter 4).

Rosemary: Add 1 T. dried rosemary in place of the sage.

Thyme Muffins

2 c. flour
1 T. baking powder
½ t. salt
2 t. thyme
2 t. parsley
⅓ c. sugar
1 stick butter
1 egg
¾ c. milk

In a medium bowl, combine the dry ingredients. Cut in butter until coarse crumbs form. Combine the egg and milk, and pour into dry ingredients. Stir just until combined. Over mixing will make the muffins tough. Divide batter among 12 greased or paper lined muffin cups. Bake in a preheated 375-degree oven for 20-25 minutes. Makes 12 muffins.

Variation: I sometimes add 1 t. rosemary along with the thyme, for a stronger-flavored muffin.

Herb and Cornmeal Muffins

1 c. flour
¾ c. cornmeal
¼ c. sugar
1 T. baking powder
1 t. cream of tartar
1 t. salt
1 t. basil
1 t. parsley
1 t. marjoram
¼ c. butter
¾ c. milk
⅓ c. sour cream
2 eggs beaten

In a medium bowl, combine the dry ingredients and seasonings. Cut in butter until coarse crumbs are formed. In a small bowl, combine the milk, sour cream, and eggs. Fold into dry ingredients and mix until just combined. Divide dough among 12 greased or paper-lined muffin cups. Bake in a preheated 400--degree oven for 20-25 minutes. Makes 12 muffins.

Mint and Pineapple Scones

3 c. flour
½ c. sugar
1 T. baking powder
½ t. salt
3 T. fresh or 1 T. dried mint
¾ c. butter
1 (8 oz.) can juice packed crushed pineapple,
undrained
2 T. milk
½ t. cinnamon
¼ t. nutmeg
2 T. sugar

Combine dry ingredients in a medium bowl and mix well. Cut in butter until coarse crumbs are formed. Stir in pineapple, and turn dough onto a lightly floured surface. Knead only until scones hold together. Dough will be very soft.

Lightly flour an 8 or 9-inch round cake pan. Place half the dough in the pan, and press in evenly. Flip pan over quickly onto an ungreased baking sheet, releasing the dough. (Trust me, after you do this a few times, it does get easier.) Cut the dough into 6, 8, or 12 wedges depending on the size of scone desired. For browner, crispier scones, use a spatula to separate the scones slightly. Or, you can leave them touching for softer scones.

Repeat this process with the remaining dough. I get both circles on the same baking sheet, but it is a tight fit. Use 2 baking sheets, if that makes it easier for you.

In a small bowl, combine the cinnamon, nutmeg and sugar. Brush the tops of the scones with the milk, and sprinkle with the sugar mixture. Bake in a preheated 375-degree oven for 18-20 minutes. Scones should be light brown, and will have puffed up somewhat. Makes 16-24 scones.

Scarborough Fair Biscuits

2 c. flour
4 t. baking powder
1 T. sugar
2 t. parsley
2 t. sage
2 t. rosemary
2 t. thyme
1 t. cream of tartar
1 t. salt
½ c. shortening-part butter
⅔ c. milk

Combine dry ingredients in a medium bowl. Cut in shortening until the mixture resembles coarse crumbs. Stir in milk, reserving 1 T. for brushing the biscuits. Stir until dough starts to come together. Turn dough onto a floured surface, and knead just until dough holds together. It will be soft. Lightly flour an 8-inch baking pan. Press dough into pan evenly. Unmold by quickly turning pan over onto the floured surface.

Cut dough in half, and then cut each half into 6 strips. Place on an ungreased baking sheet, and brush with reserved milk. Bake in a 425-degree oven for 10-15 minutes. Makes 12 biscuits.

Variation: Add ¼ c. Parmesan cheese and 2 t. garlic powder to the other seasonings.

Chive and Cheddar Biscuits

2 c. flour
1 T. baking powder
1 t. salt
3 T. fresh-snipped chives, or 1 T. dried
1 t. dried savory
¼ c. butter
¾ c. milk
1 c. shredded cheddar cheese

Mix dry ingredients in a medium bowl. Cut in butter until coarse crumbs are formed. Stir in milk and cheese. Knead the dough on lightly floured surface until just holding together. Press or roll dough into a square, one-half-inch thick. Cut the square in half: and then cut each half into 6 pieces crosswise. Place on an ungreased baking sheet, and bake in a preheated 425-degree oven for 12-15 minutes. Makes 12 biscuits.

Herbed Whole Wheat Bread

2 packages active dry yeast
½ c. warm water
1 c. water
1 c. milk
¼ c. sugar
¼ c. olive oil
½ c. minced sweet onion
2 T. Everyday Herb Blend, Fines Herbes, or Salad and Vegetable Herb Blend, (see Chapter 4)
2 t. salt
2 eggs, beaten
2 c. whole-wheat flour
½ c. wheat germ
¼ c. cracked wheat
3½-4 ½ c. bread flour

In a small bowl, combine the yeast and warm water. Set aside. Heat together the 1 cup of water, milk, sugar and oil, until very warm, about 120-130 degrees. Pour into a large mixing bowl. Stir in onion, herbs and salt. Stir in yeast mixture, eggs, and whole-wheat flour, and beat with an electric mixer for 3 minutes. Add wheat germ, cracked wheat, and 1 c. bread flour. Beat 2 more minutes. Dough will be sticky.

Start stirring in additional flour until the dough begins to pull away from the sides of the bowl. Turn dough onto a floured surface and knead, adding more flour, until dough is smooth and elastic. This will take about 8-10 minutes. Place dough in an oiled bowl, turning to coat the top. Cover with a towel, and let rise in a warm place until the dough has doubled in bulk, about 1 hour and 15 minutes. Punch dough down, and cover with the bowl on a floured surface. Let rest 15 minutes.

Divide dough in half. Shape dough into balls and place on a baking sheet that has been greased and lightly dusted with cornmeal. Cover, and allow to rise until doubled in bulk, about 50 minutes. Bake loaves in a preheated 375-degree oven for 40-45 minutes, or until the loaves sound hollow when tapped lightly. Makes 2 loaves.

Mexican Cheddar Cheese Bread

1 c. milk
3 T. sugar
1 T. salt
1 T. butter
2 packages active dry yeast
1 c. warm water
1 c. grated cheddar cheese
½ c. fresh chopped cilantro
2 t. cumin
1 t. chili powder
1 t. dried oregano
1 t. paprika
4½ c. bread flour

Scald milk. Stir in sugar, salt and butter. Cool to lukewarm. In a large bowl, combine the yeast and warm water. Add the milk mixture, cheese, flour, and combine well. Batter will be sticky. Cover batter in bowl, and let rise until doubled, about 1 hour. Stir batter down, and beat vigorously. Turn into 2 (9x5-inch) greased loaf pans. Cover, and let rise 1 hour, or until doubled in bulk. Bake in a preheated 375-degree oven for about 1 hour. Makes 2 loaves.

Chili Corn Muffins

⅔ c. cornmeal
1⅓ c. flour
1 T. baking powder
2 t. chili powder
2 t. cumin
1 t. paprika
1 t. dried oregano
1 t. dried parsley
1 t. salt
2 T. oil
½ c. milk
2 eggs, beaten

Combine dry ingredients in a medium bowl. In a separate bowl, combine the oil, milk and eggs. Fold gently into flour mixture, and stir until just blended. Divide batter evenly between 12 greased or paper-lined muffin cups. Bake in a preheated 400-degree oven for 20-25 minutes. Makes 12 muffins.

Rosemary Oatmeal Bread

5-6 c. bread flour
1 package active dry yeast
2 T. dried rosemary
2 t. salt
1¼ c. water
⅓ c. milk
¼ c. molasses
3 T. olive oil
1 egg
1¼ c. oatmeal
¼ c. oat bran

In a large bowl, combine 2 cups flour, yeast, rosemary and salt. In a saucepan, combine the water, milk, molasses and oil. Heat until warm. Add to the flour, and beat 2 minutes. Stir in the egg, oatmeal, and oat bran. Beat 3 minutes more. Start stirring in flour until a soft dough is formed, that pulls away from the sides of the bowl. Turn dough onto a floured surface and knead, adding flour as necessary. Knead until dough is smooth and elastic, about 8-10 minutes. Place dough in an oiled bowl and turn to grease top. Cover, and allow to double in bulk, about 1 hour.

Punch dough down, and divide in two. Shape each half into a ball, and place on a greased baking sheet. Cover, and allow to rise until doubled, about 45 minutes. Bake in a preheated 375-degree oven for 30-35 minutes, or until loaves sound hollow when tapped lightly. Makes 2 loaves.

Herbed Pepperoni Bread

4-5 c. bread flour
1 package quick rising yeast
2 T. Pizza Seasoning, (see Chapter 4)
1 T. sugar
2 t. salt
1½ c. water
¼ c. olive oil
1 egg, divided
1 large onion, minced
3 cloves garlic, minced
1 c. chopped pepperoni
¼ c. Parmesan cheese

In a large bowl, combine 2 cups of flour with the yeast, Pizza Seasoning, sugar and salt. Heat water with oil until very warm. Pour water mixture into the bowl with flour, and beat with an electric mixer for 4 minutes. Add egg yolk and 1 more cup of flour, and stir until blended. Stir in the onion, garlic, and pepperoni. Add extra flour, stirring the dough until it comes away from the sides of the bowl.

Turn dough onto a floured surface, and knead until dough is smooth and elastic, about 8-10 minutes. Place dough in an oiled bowl, turning to coat the top. Cover and let rise until doubled, about 40 minutes.

Punch dough down, and roll into a rectangle. Sprinkle with Parmesan cheese. Roll dough up jellyroll fashion, sealing seams and edges well. Place on a greased baking sheet and cover, allowing to rise until doubled, about 20-30 minutes.

Dilute egg white with a little water, and brush gently on the top of the loaf. With a very sharp knife, make 3 diagonal slashes across the top of the bread. Place in a preheated 400-degree oven and bake for 45-55 minutes, or until loaf sounds hollow when tapped gently. Refrigerate leftovers, due to the meat content of this bread. Makes 1 large loaf.

Note: For a crispier crust, after you put the bread in the oven, throw ½ cup of water into the bottom of the oven, and close the door quickly. The steam will crisp the crust.

Herb and Cheese Bread

1 c. whole-wheat flour
3-3½ c. bread flour
2 T. sugar
2 T. dill
2 t. salt
2 t. caraway seed
2 t. celery seed
1 package active dry yeast
1 stick butter
½ c. milk
½ c. water
2 eggs
1 lb. soft cheese, such as Monterey Jack, Muenster, Swiss etc. shredded
2 T. snipped fresh chives
2 T. fresh chopped chervil, or parsley

In a large bowl, combine the whole-wheat flour, 1 cup of the bread flour, sugar, salt, yeast and seasonings. Heat water, milk, and butter until very warm. Pour into the bowl with the flour, and beat on high speed for 5 minutes. Beat in one of the eggs, and stir in enough flour to make a soft dough. Turn the dough onto a floured surface and knead 5-8 minutes, adding flour, until dough is smooth and elastic. Place dough in an oiled bowl and turn to coat top. Cover and let rise until doubled in bulk, about 45 minutes.

Meanwhile, separate the remaining egg. Combine the yolk with the shredded cheese, chives, and chervil or parsley. Set aside. Punch dough down, and roll into a rectangle about 18x6 inches. Lay the cheese along the middle of the dough, squeezing to compact the cheese as you set it down. Leave a little space at each end of the dough.

Roll the dough lengthwise around the cheese--so that you form a long tube of dough with a filled center. Place the loaf seam-side down on a greased baking sheet. (You can shape the tube to form a circle, heart shape, or oval, if you desire.) Overlap the edges a little, and seal well to contain the filling within.

Cover, and let rise 15 minutes. Brush loaf with the remaining egg white, and bake in a preheated 375-degree oven for 50-60 minutes, or until bread sounds hollow when tapped lightly. Let stand 20 minutes before serving. Makes 1 loaf.

Note: This bread can be made ahead, and reheated by wrapping in foil and heating for 30 minutes. Or, it can be made ahead and frozen, then reheated at 325 degrees for 45 minutes or until hot.

Spicy Zucchini Bread

3 eggs, beaten
1½ c. sugar
¾ c. oil
1 T. vanilla
2 c. shredded zucchini
3 c. flour
1 T. cinnamon
1 t. fresh grated ginger
1 t. grated orange peel
1 t. grated nutmeg
1 t. baking powder
1 t. baking soda
½ t. salt
Pinch of ground cloves
1 c. raisins, optional
1½ c. chopped nuts, optional

Grease two (9x5) loaf pans and preheat oven to 325 degrees. In a medium bowl, beat eggs until light and frothy. Add sugar, and beat 2-3 minutes. Beat in oil and zucchini until well blended. Combine flour and 8 dry ingredients in a separate bowl, then add to the zucchini mixture. Beat until mixed well. Fold in raisins and nuts, if using. Divide batter between the two pans. Bake for 1 to 1¼ hours, or until the bread springs back when pressed lightly. Cool 15 minutes before removing from pan. Makes 2 loaves.

Herbed Focaccia

This Italian flatbread is great as is, or you can layer it with toppings like a pizza.

4-4½ c. flour
1 package quick rising dry yeast
1 T. sugar
1 t. salt
1¾ c. hot water
2 T. olive oil
1 t. dried basil
1 t. dried oregano
1 t. dried parsley
1 t. dried rosemary
2 cloves garlic, minced
½ c. minced shallots

In a medium bowl, combine 2 cups of the flour, yeast, sugar, and salt. Add hot water and stir until a smooth batter forms. Stir in the remaining ingredients, and enough flour to form a soft, sticky dough. Place the dough in a greased bowl, cover with a towel, and allow to rise for about 30 minutes, until the dough is doubled in bulk.

Punch the dough down and place on a work surface. Cover with the bowl, and allow dough to rest 10 minutes. Grease a jellyroll pan. With oiled fingers, press the dough into the pan. Cover and let dough rest 10 more minutes. Bake in a 400-degree oven for 25-30 minutes. Allow bread to cool slightly before serving. Makes 1 loaf.

Fennel Breadsticks

2 c. all-purpose flour
1-2 c. whole-wheat flour
1 package active dry yeast
1 T. brown sugar
2 t. salt
1 T. fennel seed
¼ t. red pepper flakes
1¼ c. warm water
1 egg
1 T. water
sesame seeds

Place all-purpose flour, yeast, sugar, salt, fennel seed, and pepper in a mixing bowl. Add warm water, and beat with an electric mixer for 4-5 minutes, or until the batter gets thick and sticky. Stir in whole-wheat flour a little at a time, until the dough comes away from the sides of the bowl. Turn the dough onto a lightly floured surface and knead, adding more flour as necessary. Knead until a soft, smooth dough is formed. Place the dough in lightly greased bowl, turning to grease the top, and cover. Allow the dough to rise in a warm place until doubled in bulk, about 1 hour.

Punch dough down, and divide dough into four equal pieces. Take each quarter piece, one at a time, and divide into quarters again, and then into thirds, ending up with 48 pieces of dough altogether. Roll the dough pieces into 7-8 inch long strips, and place them on greased baking sheets. Brush with the egg wash, and sprinkle with sesame seeds. Bake in a 400-degree oven for 12-15 minutes, or until golden brown. Makes 48 breadsticks.

Seedy Muffins

1 c. all-purpose flour
½ c. rye flour
¼ c. brown sugar
2 t. caraway seed
2 t. celery seed
1 t. dill seed
1 t. poppy seed
1 T. baking powder
½ t. cream of tartar
½ t. salt
1 egg
1 c. milk
¼ c. olive oil

Combine dry ingredients in a medium-sized bowl and mix well. In a separate bowl, beat the egg. Add milk and oil, and whisk together. Pour all at once into the dry ingredients, and fold until just combined. Divide the batter among 12-greased muffin cups, and bake in a preheated 375-degree oven for 20-25 minutes, or until lightly browned. Makes 12 muffins.

Chapter 10: Breads

Chapter 11
Beverages and Teas

Spicy Cider
Gingered Cider
Tomato Smoothie
Pineapple Mint Smoothie
Minted Lemonade
Fragrant Lemonade
Spicy Cantaloupe Frosted
Minted Berry Berry Cooler
Island Shake
Citrus Tea
Lemon Basil Cooler
Julep Slush
Glogg
Cinnamon Coffee Liquor
Minted Rum
Basil Mary
Aqua Marita
Herb Teas

Spicy Cider

1 gallon apple cider
5 cinnamon sticks
2 T. lavender flowers
2 t. whole cloves
1 t. whole allspice
1 t. fennel seed
2 cups applejack, optional, or additional cider

In a large pan, heat together the cider and seasonings.
Simmer 5 minutes. Strain. Stir in applejack, if desired.
Serve warm or cold. Garnish with additional cinnamon
sticks, if you like.

Gingered Cider

1 qt. apple cider
a 2-inch piece of ginger, sliced
2 T. honey
juice of a fresh lemon
½ c. brandy, optional

Combine all ingredients-except brandy-in a small
saucepan, and simmer 10 minutes. Discard ginger
slices, and add brandy, if desired. Makes 4 servings.

Tomato Smoothie

2 c. tomato juice
½ c. plain yogurt
¼ c. loosely packed basil leaves
2 T. snipped chives
1 T. fresh-snipped dill
juice of 1 lime
salt and pepper to taste
3 ice cubes

Place all ingredients in a blender, and mix until ice is crushed. Makes 2-3 servings.

Variation: This drink can also be made with the addition of ¼-½ cup of vodka.

Pineapple Mint Smoothie

1 (20 oz.) can crushed pineapple (in its own juice)
12 oz. pineapple juice
¼ c. pineapple sage leaves, optional
¼ c. mint leaves
1 scoop vanilla ice cream or ½ c. plain yogurt

Empty pineapple into a shallow pan, and place in the freezer until frozen. Combine herbs and juice in a pitcher, and stir to blend well. In blender bowl place liquid, ice cream, and frozen pineapple. Process mixture, in batches if necessary, until smooth. Serve in tall glasses, and garnish with a mint sprig. Makes 2-3 servings.

Minted Lemonade

2 qts. lemonade
½ c. packed mint leaves

Place 2 cups of lemonade with the mint in a blender, and mix until smooth. Return to remaining lemonade, and chill 1 hour or more. Strain, if desired, before serving. Makes 8 servings.

Fragrant Lemonade

1 c. lemon juice, fresh preferred
5 c. water
1-1½ c. sugar, or to taste
2 T. lavender blossoms
2 T. rose petals
1 orange, sliced thin
lemon slices for garnish

In a medium saucepan, heat together the lemon juice, water and sugar. Boil 1 minute. Remove from heat, and stir in the flower petals and orange slices. Let mixture steep for 10 minutes. Strain and chill, before serving over ice, garnished with lemon slices. Makes 5-6 servings.

Spicy Cantaloupe Frosted

2-3 c. cubed fresh cantaloupe
1 t. fresh grated ginger
1 t. fresh grated nutmeg (pinch of cloves)
1½ c. vanilla ice cream or frozen yogurt
1 c. milk

Combine all ingredients in a blender until smooth. Serve immediately. Makes 2 servings.

Minted Berry Berry Cooler

1 c. fresh or frozen strawberries
1 c. fresh or frozen raspberries
½ c. fresh or frozen blueberries
2 c. milk
¼ c. fresh mint leaves
2 c. strawberry or vanilla ice cream, **or** frozen yogurt

In a blender, combine the berries, milk, and mint. Process until smooth. Add the ice cream, and blend until smooth. Serve immediately. Makes 2-3 servings.

Island Shake

1 large mango, peel and seed removed
3 oranges, peeled and seeded if necessary
2 c. fresh or canned pineapple chunks
1 c. coconut milk or 1 c. milk, almond milk, soy milk
or rice milk
1 t. allspice
½ t. cinnamon
½ t. ginger
½ t. nutmeg
2 c. pineapple sorbet

Place the fruit in a blender, and mix until smooth. Add milk and seasonings, and blend until smooth. Add sorbet, and mix until smooth. If there is too much for your blender at once, remove half the fruit, and blend in batches. Serve immediately. Makes 4 servings.

Citrus Tea

6 c. water
5 tea bags
½ c. fresh mint leaves
½ c. lemon balm leaves
1 t. fresh rosemary leaves
1 (6 oz.) can orange juice concentrate
1 (6 oz.) can frozen lemonade
¼ c. honey, or to taste
ice cubes

Bring water to a boil, and pour over the tea bags and herbs. Allow to steep 10-15 minutes, or until tea is quite strong. Strain tea into a large heatproof pitcher. Stir in the orange juice and lemonade, and honey if needed. Stir well to blend. Allow tea to cool to tepid. Pour tea into tall glasses filled with ice cubes. Makes 8 servings.

Lemon Basil Cooler

5 c. water
1 c. fresh squeezed lemon juice
½ c. lemon basil leaves
¾-1 c. sugar, or to taste

Bring water to the boil, and pour over lemon juice and basil. Allow to steep for 10-15 minutes. Strain and add sugar to taste. Serve in tall glasses over ice. Makes 4-6 servings.

Julep Slush

¼ c. fresh mint leaves
3 c. water
¾ c. sugar, or to taste
1 c. bourbon
mint sprigs for garnish

Place mint leaves in a heatproof container. Boil water and pour it over the leaves. Steep for 15 minutes. Stir in sugar. Purée mixture in a blender to chop the leaves. Cool to room temperature, then combine with the bourbon and freeze. To serve, break out chunks of the slush and purée in a blender. Dilute with a little ginger ale, if desired. Makes 6 drinks.

Glogg

Glogg is a Swedish wine punch, and many excellent versions exist. Glogg is great for a winter or holiday party.

2 bottles red wine (about 7 cups)
1 orange, sliced thin
1 lemon, sliced thin
1 c. prunes, pitted and chopped
½ c. sugar, or to taste
12 cardamom pods, crushed slightly
8 whole allspice
8 whole cloves
1 T. caraway seed
3 cinnamon sticks
4 c. vodka

In a kettle, heat the wine until just warm. Add all ingredient-except the vodka-and warm, but do not boil, for ten minutes. Remove from heat and let stand for 10 minutes. Meanwhile, heat vodka and use a long match to ignite it. Pour vodka into wine mixture. Strain glogg into a heatproof punchbowl, or into individual glasses. Makes 10-12 servings.

Variation: For Yankee Glogg, substitute cranberry juice for the wine.

Cinnamon Coffee Liqueur

1 qt. distilled water
3¾ c. sugar
6 T. instant coffee
1 (4-inch) vanilla bean
3-4 (4-inch) cinnamon sticks
1 qt. vodka

Bring the water to a boil. Remove from heat, and stir in all the ingredients-except the vodka. Stir until well-mixed, and allow mixture to cool to room temperature. Add vodka, and place in a bottle or large jar with a tight-fitting lid. Place liqueur somewhere dark and cool to age. Age at least 1 month before serving. (You can eliminate the cinnamon for plain liqueur.) Makes 2 quarts. *Tastes a lot like Kahlúa.*

Minted Rum

1 T. sugar
juice of 1 lime
2-3 fresh mint sprigs
1 oz. light rum
1 oz. curacao
chilled club soda

Dissolve sugar in the lemon juice. Add the mint leaves, and bruise them with the back of the spoon to release flavor. Add rum and curacao, and stir to blend. Pour into a tall glass over ice, and add enough club soda to fill the glass. Makes 1 drink.

Basil Mary

4-6 oz. tomato juice
1 oz. vodka
juice of ¼ lime
4-5 basil leaves
2 or 3 fresh celery leaves, or ½ t. dried celery leaves
dash of hot red pepper sauce
pinch of celery seed
dash of Worcestershire sauce
dash of salt and pepper

Place all ingredients in a blender, and mix until smooth. Pour over cracked ice. Makes 1 drink

Aqua Marita

Named for a dear friend, this recipe contains no herbs or spices. It's just really good.

1½ oz. Tequila
1½ oz. Blue Curacao
2 oz. frozen Limeade (undiluted)
ice cubes

Place several ice cubes in a blender. Add remaining ingredients and blend until smooth. Serve in margarita glass rimmed with salt and a lime wedge. Makes 1 drink

Herb Teas

In the truest sense of the word-when you infuse herbs in hot water you are not making tea. Tea is a specific plant. It would be no different to put herbs in water and call it herbal coffee. When you are combining herbs with hot water what you are really making is called a tisane. OK, grammar lesson over. When we make tisanes most people, including me, are perfectly OK with calling them teas.

A big difference between making herb "teas" and regular tea is that herb infusions are going to be caffeine free. You can also combine herbs and spices with tea leaves and make flavored teas.

Both fresh and dried herbs can be used. If using fresh herbs, a larger quantity is needed for tea than using dried herbs, because dried herbs are more concentrated. Over time, you can experiment to find your favorite combinations for brewing. I rely very heavily on the mints and their relatives. I grow plenty of them, and their wide assortment of flavor makes each tisane a little different. There is a whole world out there of wonderful flavors and aromas from herbs and spices, just waiting for a pot of steaming hot water to set them free.

The Basics

The amount of herbs and spices that you need to make a good cup of "tea" varies, based on how strong you prefer your tea and what ingredients you are using to make it. Spices such as cinnamon, allspice, and nutmeg are quite strong. They can be used lightly, and still give off plenty of flavor. Leaf and seed herbs are generally less potent, and you'll need to use more to obtain a pleasant flavor. A general rule of thumb is: 3 tablespoons fresh herbs or 1 tablespoon dried herbs per cup of tea desired. You may even need to double that amount with mild-flavored herbs. I know that these recommended measures sound like a lot, but look at a tea bag. There is certainly a tablespoon of tea leaves in there!

To make a pot use: ¾-1 cup fresh leaves, or ¼ cup of dried leaves per 4 cup serving. And always remember that the leaves should be chopped before measuring, and packed pretty tightly. Some people like to boil their herbs in the water to release more flavor, rather than having the water poured over them to steep. Personally, I find that it gives the tea a funny taste. I strongly recommend that you steep your tea, and use fresh herbs, dry herbs, or a combination of fresh and dried, according to what is available to you.

Unless you want loose bits of greenery afloat in your tea, your herbs and spices will need to be contained in some sort of infuser. In this, you have several choices. A tea ball is a handy little device. It is generally made from perforated stainless steel or fine mesh screen. It works well as long as there is a reliable latch to close the tea ball while in use. Tea balls come in a variety of shapes and sizes, from simple spoon-like devices to cleverly wrought charms of houses and teapots.

For your home-brewed herb and spice tea, you can also buy reusable tea bags. These small muslin pouches can be filled and refilled. They are conveniently portable for taking to the office or on trips. Or, you can create your own pouches from food-quality cheesecloth. To do this, cut several squares of cheesecloth the same size, and stack them together. Place the herbs in the middle of the square, and gather the top to seal with a bit of wrapped or knotted string.

Straining the loose tea herbs and spices, as you pour your freshly brewed tea from pot to cup, will also work. Many teapots are available with built-in strainers designed into the spout.

Iced Herbal Tea

I was doing a cooking camp a few years ago and we were talking about cooking with herbs. One of the boys asked if we could make mint tea. I said sure. I brought in a whole bunch of fresh mint the next day. The kids helped me wash and rip up the leaves. We poured boiling water over it and let the mixture steep for about 20 minutes. I sweetened some and left the rest unsweetened. The kids loved the unsweetened one more. I could not believe it. I was so pleased the kids liked it without the sugar.

For a glass or pitcher of tasty homemade iced herbal tea, either cool brewed tea, and then chill before serving or brew a very strong herbal base, by doubling the amount of herbs you steep. This potent base can be used sooner, and will be diluted to a pleasant level when it is poured over ice.

I don't mince herbs with surgical precision when I'm making iced tea. I put a bunch of herb leaves into a stainless steel bowl. I bruise the leaves with the back of a large spoon, and then pour boiling water over the herbs to cover. I let the whole business steep for 10-20 minutes, and then I take a little taste. (Remember, I want it to be strong, because the ice will dilute it.) I strain out the leaves, and pour my tea in a pitcher. I pour in ice to fill the pitcher, and I am ready to enjoy a great glass of tea.

Don't pour hot liquids into a cold glass pitcher that is not intended for hot liquids. It could crack. Better to cool it down first.

Blending Flavors

If you prefer several different herbs mixed together, or if you come up with a special formula all your own, you may wish to mix up a batch. This way, you don't start from scratch each time you want a cup or a pot of tea. If you are using dried herbs and spices, note your proportions, blend a mixture together, and store in a location that is dry, cool and dark.

Fresh herbs can be a little harder. Here is one way that I enjoy fresh herb tea year round. Chop fresh herbs in a food processor, or by hand, until minced. Toss the herbs together to blend completely. Put the herbs on a baking sheet, and place them in the freezer until they are frozen. (Even if they aren't completely frozen, this method will work as long as they have hardened.) Scrape the herbs off the tray, into a large bowl. Working quickly, before they soften, crumble any lumps with your hands. The finer the mixture, the easier it will be to use later. Place this crumbled mixture in a freezer bag or container, and store in the freezer. When you wish to brew tea, just scoop out the amount of fresh herbs you need. The advantage of freezer storage is that some tea herbs, such as lemon balm and pineapple sage, tend to lose flavor when they are dried.

"Tea" Herbs

This is not a complete list, but it's a good start!

Mints: apple, pineapple, lemon, lime, peppermint, spearmint, Corsican mint, orange, chocolate, ginger, or perfume mint.

Also: pineapple sage, ginger, Monarda, rose petals, rosehips, lemon basil, orange peel, lemon verbena, lemon balm, anise, lavender petals, scented geranium leaves, cinnamon basil, citrus peel, fennel, (seeds or leaves) chamomile, angelica, allspice, cardamom, sweet cicely, sage (use sparingly!) anise hyssop, cloves, cinnamon, nutmeg, rosemary (use sparingly!)

Infusions

I would be remiss if I didn't say something about infused water. You just combine fruits and/or veggies with herbs in water and allow the flavors to blend. It is a very refreshing way to dress up water. Infusions are made without heat so the herbal flavor is more subtle, but quite pleasant.

To make an infused water you just cut up fruit or veggies and place them in a jar-add herbs that you like and cover with cold water. Best to put in the fridge for a couple of hours to let the flavors get into the water.

Some of my favorite combos are:

Citrus with mint or basil
Mango with pineapple sage
Berries with mint or basil
Cucumbers with mint, basil or fennel

The combinations are pretty vast. These make a healthy alternative to sodas for sure. When you want to drink them just strain into a glass, add ice, if desired and enjoy!!
Extras for your herbal beverages

1. You can freeze a mint leaf or small edible flower in an ice cube.

2. If you candy small scented geranium leaves, you can drop them into hot cups of tea for some extra sweetness and flavor.

To Candy Leaves:
dried, pasteurized egg whites *
some small leaves
a saucer of extra fine sugar

Wash leaves, and pat dry. Prepare egg whites from dried, pasteurized egg whites, mixing with water according to package instructions. Dip the leaves into the egg white, then press into sugar, turning to coat the leaf evenly. Place leaves on a rack, and dry in a warm and dry place with good air circulation, or use a food dehydrator. Store sugared leaves in an airtight container when brittle. (Inspect them after a few days, to make sure that they are still brittle. Any hidden moisture will make them soft, and eventually spoil them.)

Raw egg whites could contain salmonella, and since these leaves will be uncooked, it would be unsafe to use raw egg white in preparing them.

Words of Caution

If you have pollen allergies be careful when buying herb teas as that may contain flowers-and therefor pollen. There are certain herbs that are to be avoided during pregnancy as well. Please consult with your doctor if you are pregnant.

There are also some herbs, which really should not be consumed but turn up in tea blends anyway. Tansy and comfrey come to mind. To some extent you need to be an informed consumer. Read the labels and know what it is you are drinking.

Chapter 12
Desserts and Sweets

Lavender Shortbread
Pumpkin Spice Cookies
Minted Butter Cookies
Minty Custard
Green Tomato Pie
Minted Orange Ice Cream
Apple Pie Ice Cream
Cinnamon Ice Cream
Mint and Cantaloupe Sorbet
Minted Fresh Melon
Gingerbread
Sweet Potato Bread Pudding
Ginger Cream

Lavender Shortbread

This shortbread recipe originally came from Martha Merrick, the grandmother of a dear friend. I've added the herbs in this version, and in the variations. This is a wonderful special occasion cookie, and a must for the holidays.

1 c. sugar, plus extra for sprinkling
2 c. butter
4 c. flour
3 T. lavender blossoms, dried or fresh

Cream together 1 cup of sugar and the butter. Combine the flour and lavender, and add to the sugar mixture, 1 cup at a time. Grease a 9 x 13 cake pan, and press dough evenly into the pan. Cut dough into small squares, or cut on the diagonal to make diamond-shaped cookies. Sprinkle with the extra sugar, and bake shortbread in a preheated 300-degree oven for 50-55 minutes, or until lightly browned around the edges. Do not over bake. As soon as you remove cookies from the oven, re-cut on earlier marks. Remove from the pan to cool.

Variations

Mint Shortbread: Instead of lavender, substitute 3 T. dried, or ¼ c. fresh mint leaves.

Lemon Shortbread: Instead of lavender, substitute 1 T. each lemon balm, lemon verbena or lemon mint, and lemon zest.

Lemon Pepper Shortbread: Prepare the same as Lemon Shortbread, and add 1 t. freshly ground pepper.

Spice Shortbread: Instead of lavender, substitute 2 t. cinnamon, 1 t. each allspice and nutmeg, ½ t. *each* cloves and mace.

Pumpkin Spice Cookies

½ c. shortening or coconut oil
½ c. sugar
¾ c. light brown sugar
2 eggs
1½ c. puréed pumpkin, canned or homemade
2 t. vanilla
2½ c. flour
1 T. baking powder
2 t. Pumpkin Pie Spice, (see Chapter 4)
1 t. cream of tartar
½ t. salt
1 c. raisins
1 c. toasted hulled pumpkin seeds*

Cream together shortening and sugars. Beat in eggs until light and fluffy. Stir in pumpkin and vanilla. Combine dry ingredients, and stir into shortening mixture. Add raisins and seeds, and stir to blend well. Drop dough by slightly rounded tablespoons onto a greased baking sheet, about 3 inches apart. Bake in a preheated 350-degree oven for 17-20 minutes. Makes 4 dozen.

*Note: To toast pumpkin seeds, place them in a skillet over medium heat, and toss occasionally to prevent burning. As they begin to warm, the seeds will pop like corn, becoming rounder. Toast until all or most of the seeds have popped, about 10-15 minutes. Cool before using.

Minted Butter Cookies

1 c. butter
½ c. sugar
½ c. brown sugar
1 egg
1 t. lemon or mint extract
2¼ c. flour
¼ c. dried mint leaves, peppermint if available
1 t. baking powder
1 t. cream of tartar
¼ t. salt

Cream together butter and sugars until light and fluffy. Beat in the egg thoroughly, and stir in extract. Mix together the dry ingredients, and stir into the butter mixture. Chill dough for 30 minutes. Pipe the dough through a large star tip onto a baking sheet. The raw cookie should be the size and shape of a chocolate kiss. Bake for 7-9 minutes in a preheated 375-degree oven. Makes about 6 dozen cookies.

Variations

Fennel: In place of the mint, use 1 T. crushed fennel seed. Press a pine nut into each cookie before baking.

Lemon Cardamom: Use lemon extract. In place of the mint, use 1 t. lemon zest and 2 t. ground cardamom.

Heritage: Use pecan extract, in place of the lemon or almond. Add 2 t.-1 T. Apple Pie Spice (see Chapter 4) in place of the mint, and sprinkle unbaked cookies with minced pecans.

Rose Butter Cookies: Use lemon or orange extract. In place of the mint, use 2 T. crushed dry rose petals. Make sure that the dry rose petals have not been treated with pesticides!

Minty Custard

⅓ c. mint leaves
1⅓ c. milk
3 eggs
¼ c. sugar
1 t. vanilla
⅛ t. ground nutmeg
1 c. blueberries, fresh or frozen, thawed

Combine mint and milk in a small saucepan, and simmer 5 minutes. Remove from heat and allow to steep for 15 minutes. Strain and discard mint. Set milk aside. In a bowl, beat together eggs, sugar, vanilla and nutmeg. Slowly beat in milk.

Grease 4 (6 oz.) custard cups, and divide the custard between them. Place cups in a baking dish with 2-inch-high sides. Pour in hot water to a depth of 1-inch around the cups. Bake in a 350-degree oven for 20 minutes. Remove from oven and cool.

Chill before serving. Purée blueberries, and pour some on plates. Invert the custard onto plates. Makes 4 servings.

Green Tomato Pie

There are a number of variations of this pie floating around. It is a great way to use tomatoes that are picked green when autumn's first frost is expected.

2 (9-inch) pastry crusts
4 c. quartered green tomatoes
1 c. sugar
½ c. brown sugar
¼ c. flour
2 t. lemon zest
1 t. cinnamon
½ t. fresh ground ginger
½ t. fresh ground nutmeg
½ t. salt
1 c. raisins
3 T. butter
2 T. lemon juice

Note: You can also use 2 t. Apple Pie Spice or Pumpkin Pie Spice for the seasonings, (see Chapter 4).

Drain cut tomatoes in a colander for 35-45 minutes. Combine the sugars with the flour, lemon zest, and seasonings. Sprinkle a quarter of this mixture onto the crust. Add a layer of tomatoes (about a third of the tomatoes), and ⅓ cup of the raisins. Repeat layering until all ingredients are used up, finishing with a layer of sugar. Dot with the butter and sprinkle with the lemon juice.

Place the second crust on top of the pie, and flute the edges. Make several slashes in the top crust, or you can cut in a design. Bake in a preheated 450-degree oven for 15 minutes. Turn oven down to 325, and bake 45-55 minutes longer. Cool several hours before serving. Makes one 9-inch pie.

Minted Orange Ice Cream

½ c. tightly packed fresh mint leaves
2 T. fresh grated orange peel
2 c. milk
2 c. whipping cream
½-1 c. sugar, or to taste
2 T. orange juice concentrate

In a medium saucepan, combine the mint, peel, and milk. Heat until almost boiling, stirring to prevent scorching. Remove from heat and allow to cool to room temperature. Strain this mixture, and combine with the remaining ingredients in an ice cream machine, freezing according to the manufacturer's directions. Makes about 6 cups.

Apple Pie Ice Cream

⅔ c. chunky-style applesauce
2 c. milk
1½ c. whipping cream
½ c. sugar, or to taste
2 t. Apple Pie Spice (see Chapter 4)
1 t. lemon zest

Combine all ingredients in a medium bowl and stir until sugar is dissolved. Freeze in an ice cream maker, according to manufacturer's directions. Makes 5-6 cups.

Cinnamon Ice Cream

2 c. milk
2 c. whipping cream
2 t. cinnamon
⅔ c. sugar, or to taste

Combine all ingredients until sugar is dissolved. Freeze in an ice cream maker, according to the manufacturer's directions. Serve with pumpkin pie or apple strudel. Makes 6 cups.

Mint and Cantaloupe Sorbet

Inspired by a comment from my cousin Kathy, who likes fruit-based drinks like smoothies, try freezing this sorbet in ice cube trays. When frozen, place the cubes in a freezer bag until ready to use. Just drop a few cubes in a blender with milk, other flavorings, and/or fresh fruit. Blend and serve. Kathy also uses yogurt, depending on how thick or tangy she wants it to be, which makes a refreshing and healthy change from regular shakes.

Note: This recipe can also be made with honeydew melon.

½ c. water
2 T. sugar
½ c. mint leaves
1 medium cantaloupe (peeled, seeded, and cut into cubes)

Heat together water, sugar, and mint leaves. Steep for 20 minutes. Strain the liquid, and discard mint leaves. Combine liquid with some of the cantaloupe chunks in a blender or food processor. Purée the mixture and place in a bowl. Purée the remaining cantaloupe until smooth, and add to the puréed mixture. Stir well to combine. Freeze in an ice cream maker according to manufacturer's directions, or freeze in shallow trays. To serve, soften sorbet slightly, and purée in a blender or food processor. Scoop into stemmed glasses, and garnish with a mint sprig. Makes 4 cups.

Minted Fresh Melon

A light summertime dessert, this dish is just wonderful.

¼ c. chopped mint leaves
2 T. sugar
juice of ½ a lime
¼ t. vanilla
½ a small honeydew, seeded
1 small cantaloupe, halved and seeded
1 (3 lb.) piece of watermelon

In a small bowl, combine the mint, sugar, lime juice and vanilla. Set aside. Using a melon baller, scoop out the melons. You should get 2 cups of each melon, or a little more. Place melon balls in a pretty bowl, and toss with the mint mixture. Chill before serving. Makes 6 servings.

Gingerbread

2⅓ c. flour
1 t. baking soda
1 t. baking powder
1 t. cinnamon
½ t. allspice
½ t. salt
½ c. butter
¼ c. sugar
1 egg
¾ c. molasses
1 c. boiling water
2 t. fresh grated ginger

Lemon Glaze:
2 c. powdered sugar
1 T. fresh lemon juice
1 t. lemon zest
milk

In a medium bowl, combine dry ingredients and mix well. Set aside. In a separate bowl, beat together the butter, sugar, egg and molasses. Pour in water and ginger. Stir in flour mixture and mix until batter is smooth. Pour batter into a greased and floured 9-inch round cake pan. Bake in a preheated 350-degree oven for 35 minutes, or until a toothpick inserted in the center comes out clean. Cool 10 minutes before removing cake to rack. Cool cake completely.

Make lemon glaze. Combine sugar, juice, zest, and enough milk so that the glaze will pour. Drizzle glaze over cooled gingerbread cake. Makes 1 cake, which serves 6-8.

Sweet Potato Bread Pudding

2 eggs, separated
1 medium sweet potato, about 1½ c. (cooked, peeled, and mashed)
½ c. packed brown sugar
½ c. applesauce
1 t. cinnamon
1 t. nutmeg
½ t. ginger
2 c. milk
4½ c. bread cubes (good quality white, whole wheat, or even raisin bread)
½ c. chopped walnuts
¾ c. golden raisins
Sauce:
Greek yogurt or sour cream
maple syrup
hulled sunflower seeds

Beat egg whites until stiff peaks form. Set aside. Combine egg yolks, sweet potato, sugar, applesauce, and spices in medium bowl. Mix well. Stir in milk. Add bread cubes, stirring gently to blend. Fold in nuts and raisins. Fold in egg whites. Turn the mixture into a medium casserole dish and bake in a preheated 300--degree oven for 50-60 minutes.

While the pudding is baking, combine the yogurt or sour cream with the maple syrup to suit your taste. Set aside. Serve the pudding warm, with some of the yogurt sauce on the top. Sprinkle with a few sunflower seeds. Serves 6-8.

Ginger Cream

Serve with apple or pumpkin pie, pound cake, or in coffee. Yum.

½ pt. whipping cream
1 T. sugar
1 T. fresh-grated ginger

In a chilled bowl, with chilled beaters, whip the cream until soft peaks form. Stir in sugar and ginger, and beat 2-3 minutes more. Makes one cup.

Chapter 13
Sauces, Condiments, etc.

Herb Dipping Sauce
British Mint Sauce
Cilantro Sauce
Sofrito
Chili Con Queso
Pesto
Dill Gravy
Green Sauce
Onion Relish
Sweet Tomato Chutney
India Sauce
Spicy Mint Sauce
Tomato Relish
Mango Salsa
Mango Chutney
Salsa Verde
Salsa
Tomato Chutney
Favorite Barbecue Sauce
Dill Marinade
Meat Marinade
Marinade for Lamb and Pork
Sweet and Sour Sauce
Croutons
Flavored Butters

Herb Dipping Sauce

This versatile sauce can be used to dress up grilled meat, seafood, or vegetables. It can also be used in tuna or chicken salads, or as a dip for veggies and breads at a party. I like to use this sauce as a spread on sandwiches. Many variations follow the basic recipe. They share the same base ingredients, and the herbs differ according to your menu plan, which herbs you have on hand, or just what you like!

Sauce Base
½ c. mayonnaise
½ c. Greek Yogurt or sour cream
2 T. minced green onion
2 t. fresh lemon or lime juice
salt and pepper to taste
dash hot red pepper sauce

Combine all ingredients, and stir. To this base, you can add any of the variations that follow. Whenever possible, use fresh herbs. It really makes a difference. When any variation is prepared, chill the sauce for several hours or overnight, to blend flavors. Makes 1 cup.

Variations

Dill: 2 T. fresh chopped dill, dash Worcestershire sauce, 1 t. dried minced garlic, or 1 clove fresh garlic, minced. Dill is great with fish and veggies, or nice with cold poached fish, and on salads.

Sorrel: ½ c. fresh chopped sorrel leaves, 1 T. fresh chopped parsley, dash of cayenne pepper. This is good with fish and chicken dishes, or as a topping for a baked potato.

Tarragon: 1-2 T. fresh minced tarragon leaves, 1 clove garlic minced, 1 t. honey. Tarragon enhances the flavor of meats and poultry, and tastes great with grilled foods.

Marjoram: 2-3 T. fresh chopped marjoram, 1 T. chopped parsley. This version is good with meat, especially sausages and burgers

Italian: Use 2 T. Italian Seasoning (see Chapter 4). Add 1 T. fresh chopped basil, 2 cloves minced garlic, and ¼ c. grated Parmesan cheese. Goes great with meats and veggies, and is excellent on sandwiches and on baked potatoes.

Curry: 2 t. curry powder, t. cumin, 3 T. creamy peanut butter. Good with any meat, especially grilled lamb and chicken. Also try this with batter-dipped vegetables.

Pesto: Use ½ c. chopped basil leaves, 3 cloves of minced garlic, ¼ c. grated Parmesan cheese, and 3 T. of either pine nuts, walnuts, or hulled sunflower seeds. Pesto is good with meat and poultry, and makes a good dip for fresh veggies.

Mint: ⅔ c. fresh chopped mint leaves, and a dash of ground coriander. This dip is good with lamb or chicken, and also goes really well with curry dishes.

Mexican: 2 T. fresh chopped cilantro, 1 t. cumin, 1 t. chili powder, 1 t. fresh chopped oregano leaves, 3 minced garlic cloves, or 1½ t. dried minced garlic. This is a good topping for tacos, enchiladas, and tortillas. It also adds a nice touch to a taco salad, or black bean salad.

Herb: 1 T. *each* of fresh parsley, rosemary and thyme leaves. Add 1 t. onion powder. This dip is good with meats and veggies.

Saffron: 1 t. saffron threads, 1 t. turmeric, ½ t. fresh minced thyme. This is excellent with chicken and with rice salads.

British Mint Sauce

¼ c. white wine vinegar
2 T. water
2 t. sugar
⅓ c. dried mint or 1 c. fresh chopped mint salt to taste

Combine vinegar, water, and sugar. Stir until the sugar is dissolved. Add mint and salt to taste. Makes ½ cup.

Cilantro Sauce

½ c. sour cream or Greek yogurt
2 T. minced cilantro
a pinch of cumin

Combine all ingredients, and mix well. Use as a topper for tacos, nachos, baked potatoes, etc. Makes ½ cup.

Sofrito

This recipe comes from my friend Connie Anderson. The sauce is used as a dressing for rice and bean dishes. It keeps in the fridge for a few days, or can be frozen. It can be tossed into hot rice or pasta dishes, or can be added to dishes during cooking to spice up the flavor. You can also sauté sofrito for a few minutes, for a grilled flavor. Experiment to see how you like it best.

¼ c. olive oil
4 green peppers, seeded and chopped
1 medium onion, chopped
½-1 c. chopped cilantro
4 cloves garlic, peeled
1 t. dried oregano
salt and pepper to taste

Combine all ingredients in a blender until smooth. Store in fridge until ready to use. Makes 1½ cups.

Chili Con Queso

1 T. olive oil
1 medium onion, chopped
1 sweet green pepper, seeded and chopped **or** 5-6 green chilies, seeded and chopped
1 sweet red or yellow pepper, seeded and chopped
3 cloves garlic, minced
1 c. tomatoes (peeled, seeded, and chopped) **or** 2-3 medium fresh or canned tomatoes
1 lb. cheddar cheese, cut into cubes or shredded
½ c. fresh chopped cilantro
2 t. cumin
2 t. chili powder
1 t. red pepper flakes, or to taste

In a medium saucepan, heat the oil and sauté the onion until it is tender. Stir in peppers and garlic, and sauté 3 minutes. Add remaining ingredients, including any juice in the tomatoes. Heat, stirring constantly, over medium-low heat. Stir until the cheese has melted.

Note: If the sauce is too thick, add a little milk. This is usually not necessary, because the veggies give off liquid when they cook.

Serve Chili Con Queso with tacos and tortillas, over hot vegetables or potatoes. It can also be used as a dip for raw veggies, or tortilla chips. Also makes a good topper for chili.

Pesto

What can you say about this versatile sauce that hasn't been said already? There are hundreds of versions of pesto around, and you may have a couple of your own. This is my favorite no-frills pesto, but you'll see a few more variations after this one. While the traditional use for pesto sauce is to toss with hot pasta, I baste chicken with basil pesto, or use it as a base for a vinaigrette dressing that always gets rave reviews. Toss a little pesto sauce with hot green beans or zucchini, or top baked or boiled potatoes. You can stir pesto into mashed potatoes, replacing milk and butter.

Don't try to use dry basil in place of fresh. It just isn't the same. To have pesto available all year round, just mix the fresh basil with the olive oil, and freeze this mixture in small containers. It will thaw in the fridge for a couple of hours to overnight, and you will find it tastes fresh when combined with the remaining ingredients.

1 c. tightly packed basil leaves
¼ c. olive oil
3-4 cloves garlic salt to taste
½ c. pine nuts, sunflower kernels, pecans or walnuts
1 c. fresh grated Parmesan cheese

Combine all ingredients-except the cheese-in a blender until smooth. Stir in the cheese. Toss over hot cooked pasta or use as desired. This sauce will keep a few days in the fridge. Makes 1½ cups of sauce, enough for 1 pound of cooked pasta.

Variations

Citrus Pesto: Same as regular pesto, but add 1-2 t. lemon zest and 1 T. fresh lemon juice. Brush sauce on chicken or fish, or toss over hot vegetables, especially peas, beans, carrots, or asparagus.

Sorrel Pesto: Use 1 c. tightly packed sorrel leaves in place of the basil. Add ½ t. hot pepper sauce. Use with chicken or fish. Sorrel Pesto is also good on potatoes, or tossed in a spinach salad with some wine vinegar. Great on grilled vegetables, too!

Parsley Pesto: Use ¾ c. parsley sprigs, and toasted walnuts or pecans in place of the basil and pine nuts.

Cilantro Pesto: Substitute fresh cilantro leaves for the basil. Add a pinch of hot pepper sauce, and 1 t. cumin. Toss with hot legumes, add to chili, or brush on corn on the cob. For a quick appetizer, you can brush some of this sauce over corn or flour tortillas. Cut them into wedges, and place them on a cookie sheet. Bake in a 375-degree oven until toasted, 5-8 minutes. Serve with salsa or chili con queso.

Dill Gravy

This recipe is from Anna Welker, an excellent cook, a terrific gardener, and a dear friend. This gravy is great served with veggies or with chicken or pork

1 T. oil
2 T. flour
½-1 c. fresh chopped dill
2 T. vinegar
1 t. sugar
salt and pepper to taste
about ½ c. water

In small skillet, heat oil and brown the flour. Stir in all ingredients, except water, until dill wilts. Start adding water, over medium high heat, stirring constantly. Add the water slowly, allowing the gravy to come to a boil and thicken. Adjust adding water according to your preference in gravy, or you can add stock in place of the water if you prefer. Serve with meat and potatoes. Makes ½ cup.

Green Sauce

1 c. lightly packed spinach leaves
½ c. lightly packed parsley leaves
¼ c. lightly packed cilantro leaves
2 green onions, trimmed and chopped
½ t. ground pepper
1 c. mayonnaise

In small saucepan, combine the spinach, herbs, onion, and pepper. Cover with a little water and bring to a boil. Boil 30 seconds and remove from heat. Drain and discard liquid from the spinach mixture. Allow to cool for 30 minutes or so. Finely chop the spinach mixture, and combine with the mayo. Cover and chill the sauce for several hours to overnight. Serve with fresh veggies and bread. Makes 1 cup.

Onion Relish

4 large onions, chopped
1 c. tomato juice
¼ c. catsup
¼ c. brown sugar
¼ c. cider vinegar
4 cloves garlic, minced
1 t. salt, or to taste
1 t. red pepper flakes, or to taste
2 T. fresh chopped cilantro
2 T. fresh chopped parsley
1 t. dried oregano
1 t. fresh lemon thyme, or regular thyme

In a saucepan, combine all ingredients-except herbs. Heat to simmering and cook, covered, until the onions are very tender, about 20 minutes. Uncover, and continue simmering until relish thickens a little, about 5 minutes. Stir in cilantro, parsley, oregano, and thyme. Remove from heat and chill well before serving. Serve on the side with meats. Can also be served as an appetizer on crusty bread with cheese or stirred into potatoes. Makes approximately 3 cups.

Sweet Tomato Chutney

2 large onions, chopped
4 cloves garlic, chopped
4 lbs. plum tomatoes (peeled, seeded, and chopped)
1½ c. sugar
2 c. white wine vinegar
1 c. raisins
1 T. ground ginger
2 t. salt
1 t. cumin
½ t. ground allspice
½ t. red pepper flakes, or to taste
¼ t. ground cloves
½ c. fresh chopped cilantro

In a large saucepan, combine the onions, garlic, and tomatoes. Cook over low heat, stirring occasionally, until the onions start to soften, and tomatoes are soft. Add remaining ingredients, except the cilantro, and turn up the heat until the chutney reaches a low boil. Simmer, uncovered, until the chutney begins to thicken, at least one hour, and probably longer. Stir more often as the chutney thickens to prevent scorching. When chutney is thick, remove it from the heat and stir in the cilantro. Cool the chutney to room temperature, and then chill it in the refrigerator. Chutney will keep in the fridge for a couple of weeks, or it can be frozen for a couple of months. Serve with meats, particularly grilled meats, and with cheeses. Makes about 3 cups.

India Sauce

This versatile sauce is great as a sauce for curried dishes, or as a dipping sauce for tempura seafood and veggies.

1 c. mayonnaise
¼ c. tahini (sesame seed paste found in larger supermarkets or ethnic stores)
¼ c. minced mint leaves
1 T. fresh lemon juice
1 T. fresh lime juice
1 t. crushed coriander seed
½ t. dried minced garlic
¼ t. red pepper flakes

Combine all ingredients in a bowl and chill, covered, for several hours. Makes 1 cup.

Spicy Mint Sauce

1-1½ c. mint leaves
¼ c. olive oil
¼ c. fresh lime juice
3-4 cloves garlic
1 T. hot pepper sauce

Combine all ingredients in a blender, and mix until smooth. Marinade chicken, seafood, or lamb with this sauce. Brush the sauce on vegetables when grilling. Makes 1 cup.

Variation: For a cooler dip, add 1 cup of either sour cream or Greek yogurt.

Tomato Relish

3-4 lbs. vine-ripened tomatoes (peeled, seeded, and chopped)
1 large onion, sliced thin
1 sweet red pepper, seeded and chopped
1 sweet green pepper, seeded and chopped
1 sweet yellow pepper, seeded and chopped
2 ribs of celery, diced
1 T. salt
1 c. sugar
1 c. red wine vinegar
1 T. mustard seed
1 t. celery seed
1 t. cinnamon
1 t. parsley flakes
1 t. dried minced garlic
¼ t. allspice
¼ t. red pepper flakes

Combine vegetables with salt in a large bowl, and stir to mix well. Cover and refrigerate overnight. The next day, drain the liquid into a saucepan, and add the remaining ingredients-except the vegetables. Heat the liquid and seasonings together until they come to a boil, and boil hard, uncovered, for 10 minutes. Remove from heat, and cool the sauce completely before combining with the vegetables. Chill several hours before serving. Tomato Relish is great as a side dish with chicken or beef. It is also a nice accompaniment to cheese or sandwich plates. Makes 6 cups.

Mango Salsa

2 large mangoes, (seeded, peeled, and cut into small cubes)
¼ c. sugar
2 T. lime juice
2 T. fresh minced mint leaves
2 T. fresh chopped pineapple sage leaves or extra mint leaves
1 t. red pepper flakes

Combine all ingredients in medium bowl. Cover and chill several hours or overnight. Serve with poultry and seafood. Makes 2 cups of salsa.

Mango Chutney

2 T. olive oil
2 large onions, chopped
5 cloves garlic, chopped
2 large mangoes (seeded, peeled, and cut into chunks)
1 c. raisins
½ c. brown sugar
¼ c. apple cider vinegar
1 t. cinnamon
½ t. ground allspice
½ t. ground cumin
¼ t. red pepper flakes
¼ c. fresh chopped parsley
¼ c. fresh chopped basil leaves

Heat oil in a medium saucepan and add onions. Cook until onions are lightly browned. Stir in garlic, and sauté 3 more minutes. Add remaining ingredients-except parsley and basil. Cook, uncovered, until chutney thickens, about 40 minutes. Stir as chutney thickens to avoid sticking. Add parsley and basil, and cook 5 more minutes. Remove from heat, cool, and chill before serving. This goes well with any meat or poultry, and especially pork, lamb, and duck. Makes 2 cups.

Salsa Verde

1 lb. fresh tomatillos, husked and rinsed
½ c. fresh chopped cilantro
½ c. chopped sweet onion
½ c. chopped sweet red or yellow pepper
3-4 seeded and chopped green chilies
2 T. cider vinegar
1 T. sugar
1 t. cumin
1 t. dried minced garlic
½ t. red pepper flakes
salt to taste

Simmer tomatillos in water until tender, about 15 minutes. Drain well and purée in blender until smooth. Stir in remaining ingredients and chill, covered, several hours or overnight. Serve with tortilla chips, or as a side with Mexican food. Makes 2 cups of salsa.

Salsa

I make plenty of salsa when homegrown tomatoes are abundant, and freeze extra salsa for the rest of the year.

4 lbs. tomatoes (peeled, seeded, and chopped)
While plum tomatoes are the best, any tomato will work. And yellow tomatoes make a wonderful sauce!
1 T. olive oil
1 large onion, chopped
4-5 cloves garlic, minced
1 c. sweet red, yellow, or green pepper, chopped
1-2 t. cumin, or to taste
1 t. chili powder
salt to taste
chopped hot peppers to taste, or hot pepper flakes, or hot sauce
½ c. fresh chopped cilantro

Place oil in a heavy saucepan, and add onion, cooking until onions are translucent. Add tomatoes and garlic and cook until the tomatoes are softened, about 10 minutes. Remove from heat and stir in remaining ingredients-except the cilantro. Cool salsa, then stir in the cilantro. Chill until ready to use. Great with chips, tacos, or as a side dressing for grilled meats, poultry, or seafood. Makes 3-4 cups.

Tomato Chutney

2 lbs. plum tomatoes (peeled, seeded, and chopped)
2 large onions, chopped
3 cloves garlic, minced
½ c. sugar
½ c. cider vinegar
3 green chilies, seeded and sliced into rings
2-3 T. fresh chopped parsley
2 T. fresh cilantro
1-2 T. fresh grated ginger
2 t. salt
1 t. coriander
1 t. cumin
1 t. red pepper flakes
Pinch of cloves

In a heavy saucepan, heat together the tomatoes, onions, garlic, sugar, and vinegar. Cook until tomatoes are very tender and onions are wilted, about 20 minutes. Strain the liquid into a bowl. Combine the solids in the saucepan with the remaining ingredients, and place this mixture in another bowl. Return the liquid to the saucepan, and boil until about ½ cup remains. Pour this sauce over the tomato mixture, and chill for several hours or overnight before serving. Makes about 2 cups.

Favorite Barbecue Sauce

This one takes some work but is really worth the extra effort. It freezes well, if you have any left to freeze after they get a taste!

2 qts. tomato sauce
1 28 oz. can whole tomatoes, undrained
½ c. Pickling Spice (see Chapter 4)
2 sticks cinnamon
2 t. whole allspice
1 t. whole peppercorns
½ t. whole cloves
7 c. vinegar
2 c. sugar
2 c. brown sugar
⅓ c. Worcestershire sauce
¼ c. prepared mustard
¼ c. lime juice
¼ c. lemon juice
3 large onions, minced
6 cloves garlic, minced
2 T. red pepper flakes
2 T. chili powder
1 T. paprika

Heat together the tomato sauce and whole tomatoes, crushing the tomatoes with the back of a cooking spoon. Place pickling spice, cinnamon, allspice, peppercorns, and cloves together in a piece of food-safe cheesecloth and tie securely. Place this bag in the kettle with the tomato sauce, and add all remaining ingredients. Cook over high heat, stirring as sauce thickens, until sauce reaches desired thickness.

Note: Remember, you put in 7 cups of vinegar...this is going to take a while.

The sauce is so thin in the beginning that you won't have to stir it very often. My experience has been that the whole process takes 2-3 hours, but it could take less if you keep stirring, and keep the burner on high. If I have more time than patience, I turn the heat down when the sauce starts to thicken, to avoid scorching. You can also cook the sauce down in a crock-pot. It will take longer - but will be less likely to scorch. The sauce will cook down to about 5 pints, give or take a little. Freeze what you won't use right away.

Dill Marinade

¼ c. white wine
juice of half a lemon or lime
⅓ c. olive oil
2 T. balsamic vinegar
2 T. fresh chopped dill
2 T. Dijon-style mustard
salt and pepper to taste

Combine all ingredients in a blender until smooth. Use with chicken or seafood.

Seafood Marinade

1 c. packed parsley leaves
2 green onions, trimmed and chopped
3 cloves garlic
1 T. lemon thyme or regular thyme
¼ c. olive oil
¼ c. clam juice
¼ c. white wine
1 T. cider vinegar

Place all ingredients in a blender and mix until smooth. Refrigerate several hours before using. Use with seafood. Marinade 1 hour, then grill or broil.

Meat Marinade

½ c. red wine
¼ c. parsley leaves
4 cloves garlic
2 t. thyme leaves
2 t. savory leaves
1 t. basil leaves
1 t. marjoram leaves
1 T. soy sauce
¼ t. red pepper flakes
½ c. olive oil

Combine all ingredients in a blender until smooth. Use with beef, pork or lamb.

Marinade for Lamb or Pork

½ c. red wine
½ c. olive oil
¼ c. balsamic vinegar
2 T. thyme leaves
3 cloves garlic
1 T. soy sauce
2 t. pineapple sage, or 1 t. mint leaves and 1 t. sage
1 t. ground ginger
1 t. rosemary
pepper to taste

Mix all ingredients in blender until smooth. Use with lamb or pork. This marinade works with poultry, too.

Sweet and Sour Sauce

1 c. pineapple juice
½ c. sugar
½ c. vinegar
2 T. catsup
1½ T. cornstarch
1½ T. soy sauce
2 t. grated ginger
1 t. minced garlic
red pepper flakes to taste

Combine all ingredients in saucepan over medium heat. Cook, stirring frequently, until sauce is thickened and bubbly. Makes 2 cups.

Croutons

Homemade croutons can add a nice touch to salads and soups alike. You may find yourself munching a handful now and then. Croutons can be toasted in a skillet or baked in the oven. I prefer the latter method, as it uses less oil, and enables me to make a larger batch at a time.

Basic Herbed Croutons

1 loaf Italian bread (any good quality homemade bread will work)
⅓ c. olive oil (or a little more to suit your taste)
1 T. Everyday Herb Blend, (see Chapter 4) or 1 T. assorted dried herbs
½ t. salt
½ t. garlic powder
¼ t. pepper

Cut bread into cubes, and allow bread to dry out for at least 30 minutes, or up to a couple of hours. Combine the remaining ingredients in a bowl, and let stand while the bread is drying. When bread cubes are dry, toss them in the oil mixture, and spread them out on a baking sheet. Bake in a preheated 350-degree oven for 15 minutes, or until croutons are toasted. Store croutons in an airtight container. Makes about 5 cups.

Variations

Italian Croutons: 1 t. basil and oregano, ½ t. rosemary or 1 T. Italian Seasoning (see Chapter 4). Increase garlic powder to 1 t.

Parmesan Croutons: same as herb or Italian, but sprinkle with ½ c. grated Parmesan cheese halfway through baking.

Tex-Mex: 1 t. each cumin, chili powder, oregano, paprika and garlic powder. Add ½ t. cayenne, or to taste.

Flavored Butters

Herbal or spicy butters can add flavor to any meal. They can be used on breads, crackers, veggies, meats, or fish. Flavored butters can also be molded into shapes for special occasions. They can be made ahead and frozen for several months. There is almost no limit to the variations.

All recipes are for use with one stick (½ cup) butter.

Soften butter slightly to make mixing easier. Roll into logs, balls, or press into molds. Finished butters can be rolled in herbs, spices, or nuts for a decorative appearance. Chill several hours or overnight before using. Keep butter wrapped tightly in waxed paper for freshness. Let stand at room temperature 30 minutes before serving. Flavored butter keeps in the fridge for 1-2 weeks. Makes ½ cup.

Variations

Basil Butter: 2 T. fresh chopped basil, a pinch of fresh oregano, 1 t. lemon juice. Good with meats, poultry, breads, pasta, and vegetables.

Chive Butter: 3 T. snipped chives, ½ t. lemon zest. Good with fish, poultry, carrots, and potatoes.

Chili Butter: 1½ t. chili powder, ½ t. cumin, ½ t. garlic powder. This is good on breads, beans, grilled chicken, or popcorn.

Chocolate Butter: Melt 1 oz. unsweetened chocolate and 2 t. sugar together, and mix with butter. Spread on muffins and croissants.

Chocolate-Cinnamon: Same as chocolate, but add ½ t. cinnamon. Use as you would use chocolate butter.

Curry Butter: 1 t. curry powder, 1 t. fresh lime juice. Use on lamb, poultry, rice, and veggies.

Dill Butter: 2 T. fresh-snipped dill, 1-2 t. fresh lemon juice. Good with chicken, potatoes, seafood, or rice.

Honey-Orange Butter: 2 T. honey, 1 T. orange juice concentrate, 1 t. fresh orange zest, ¼ t. cinnamon, pinch of ground cloves. Good with winter squash and sweet potatoes, or on pumpkin and zucchini bread, and muffins.

Italian Butter: 2 T. fresh chopped basil, 2 t. fresh chopped oregano, ½ t. fresh rosemary, ½ t. garlic powder. Use on meats, poultry, breads.

Lemon Butter: 1 T. fresh lemon juice, 1 t. fresh lemon zest. Use on seafood, chicken, veggies, and cinnamon raisin bread.

Lemon-Mint Butter: 2-3 T. fresh chopped mint leaves, 2 t. fresh lemon juice, 1 t. fresh lemon zest. Same uses as lemon butter, but add peas and lamb to the list.

Lemon-Lime Butter: 1 T. fresh lime juice, 1 t. fresh lemon zest. Use on seafood, or peas, rice, and poultry.

Lemon-Pepper Butter: 1 T. fresh lemon juice, 1 t. fresh lemon zest, 2 t. fresh ground pepper. Good with grilled chicken and fish, grilled veggies, or eggplant.

Lemon-Mustard Butter: 1 T. fresh lemon juice, 1 T. Dijon-style mustard, 1 t. lemon zest, ½ t. coarsely ground pepper. This is great on deli sandwiches, especially roast beef or ham. It is also good with sausage.

Mint Butter: 2-3 T. fresh chopped mint leaves, 1 t. fresh lemon juice, ½ t. lemon zest. This is great with lamb, peas, chicken, or vegetables.

Parsley Butter: 3 T. fresh minced parsley, dash cayenne pepper, 1 t. fresh lemon juice. Good with meats, chicken, and seafood or toss with hot pasta.

Rosemary Butter: 2 T. fresh chopped rosemary leaves, ½ t. lemon zest. Good on pork, lamb, poultry, or potato dishes.

Sage Butter: 1 T. fresh sage leaves, chopped very fine, or 1 t. dried sage, 1 t. **each** lemon juice and lemon zest. This is excellent with chicken or pork dinners.

Savory Butter: 2 T. fresh savory leaves, 1 t. garlic powder, and a dash of red pepper flakes. Use with baked beans, and any vegetable. It is also good with meats or chicken.

Spicy Autumn Butter: 1 T. Apple Pie Seasoning (see Chapter 4), 1 t. orange zest, 1 t. orange juice concentrate. This is wonderful on banana, zucchini, or pumpkin bread. It is also good with muffins, scones, or biscuits.

Spicy Red Butter: 1 t. paprika, 1 t. chili powder, ½ t. cayenne pepper, ½ t. cumin, 1 t. lime juice. Good on meats, poultry, potatoes, cornbread, pasta, or rice.

Spicy Sweet Butter: 1 T. Pumpkin Pie Spice (see Chapter 4), 1 T. honey, ½ t. lemon zest, ½ t. cardamom. This is good with sweet breads, muffins, scones, and biscuits. It is also good on winter squash or sweet potatoes.

Tarragon Butter: 2 T. fresh chopped tarragon, 1 t. lime juice, dash red pepper flakes. Use on poultry, potatoes, breads or crackers.

Thyme Butter: 2 T. fresh thyme leaves, 1 t. lemon juice. Use on chicken and vegetables. It is good with breads and crackers, too.

Chapter 14
Herb Vinegars

Since I first wrote the Charmed Kitchen some of the rules about making herb vinegars have changed. All of the updates and safe methods are included in this chapter.

So what is different?

Jars are to be sterilized before using and lids scalded. To sterilize jars: submerge clean jars in simmering water for 10 minutes, then invert them on paper towels to dry and fill while still warm. Lids should be scalded in water that is almost boiling. If using corks immerse them in boiling water- hold them with tongs and dip in the boiling water several times. Best to buy and use pre-sterilized corks. Plastic lids are great as they won't react to the acidity of the vinegar as some metal lids will.

Herbs should be pretreated. Commercial companies use antibacterial agents we can't get. Treat herbs in a bleach dip. Dip the fresh herbs in a sanitizing bleach solution of 1 teaspoon household bleach per 6 cups (1½ quarts) of water, rinse thoroughly under cold water, and pat dry.

For every pint of vinegar use only a few sprigs of fresh herbs, 3 Tablespoons of dried herbs or 2 tablespoons of seeds. Once herbs vinegars have been steeped and strained you can add another sprig or two of fresh herbs.

Vinegar should be heated to 190 degrees- just below the

boiling point- before being poured into the jars over the herbs.

Herb vinegars should be stored in a cool place while steeping (50-70 degrees). If you don't have a place that cool to store them, then refrigerate.

You don't need any special equipment for vinegar, but keep an eye out for pretty bottles! I've found some great bottles at rummage and estate sales. While you can put the vinegar in any bottle they look nice in decorative bottles. Makes a nice gift, too.

Another nice thing about making herb vinegar is that you can use parts, like blossoms and seed heads, that otherwise might be discarded. Basil leaves make terrific vinegar, and their blossoms impart a strong, clear flavor as well. Since you need to pinch the blooms off the basil plants in order to keep up leaf production, it is a very convenient arrangement. Don't use herbs that are brown, bruised or imperfect.

To make herb vinegars you will need:
- Clean jars or bottles with tight-fitting lids
- Fresh or dried herbs
- Vinegar - 5% acidity
- Food grade cheesecloth
- Coffee filters

Although fresh herbs can be used whole, bruising the leaves, or chopping them a little, will release more of their flavor. For large quantities of greenery, you may find it easier to chop it all in a food processor. Just be prepared to cover the herbs with vinegar as soon as possible after chopping, because some herbs discolor quickly.

Store in a cool, dark place, (50-70 degrees), and allow it

to steep for 3-4 weeks. You can give the jar a little shake from time to time if you like. It isn't really necessary, but it may make you feel better while you wait.

After the vinegar has steeped for the required time, strain the herbs from the vinegar and discard them. I usually strain my vinegars through cheesecloth, although you can use any strainer. After the big pieces of herbs are separated out in the first straining, you'll need to strain the herb vinegar again through a coffee filter. With this procedure, your herbal vinegar will be crystal clear, and will be less likely to develop sediment later on.

After the vinegar is strained, you can pour it into the decorative bottles you have cleaned and sterilized. Or, you can wash out the storage jar that you steeped the vinegar in, sterilize it, and return the vinegar to the jar to store. At this time, you can also place a sprig of fresh herbs into each bottle for decoration.

For the best retention of flavors, store flavored vinegars in the refrigerator or a cool dark place. If properly prepared, flavored vinegars should retain good quality for two to three months in cool room storage and for six to eight months in refrigerated storage. If you notice any signs of mold or fermentation (such as bubbling, cloudiness or sliminess) in your flavored vinegar, throw it away without tasting or using for any purpose.

The type of vinegar you prefer to flavor is up to you. Whatever your preference, it should be labeled as 5% acidity. It is not a good idea to use homemade vinegar, since you do not know the level of acidity. Distilled white vinegar is fine. Or, you can use red wine vinegar, white wine vinegar, or cider vinegar. Different vinegars have different flavors, and not all combinations might taste good to you. Wine and rice vinegars contain protein that provides an excellent medium for bacterial growth, if not stored properly.

I also recommend that you steep your herbs separately, rather than in mixed batches. In this way, you'll know which flavors you prefer. Remember that some herbs are stronger than others, and too much of a hearty herb may overpower your mix. Another reason not to blend at random is color. If you steep all green leaves together, you might be all right. But steeping a variety of colored leaves and blossoms would more likely color your herb vinegar a muddy brown, which would be daunting in appearance on the table. Mix and steep at your own discretion, but I advise you to steep one herb at a time.

Some herbs that make wonderful vinegars are:
- Basil, all varieties (leaves and blossoms)
- Note: Blossoms and leaves from opal basil make a stunning claret-colored vinegar.
- Chives (the blossoms make one of the most beautiful vinegars around)
- Dill (leaves or seeds)
- Fennel (seeds or leaves)
- Garlic Chives (blossoms, leaves)
- Marjoram (leaves)
- Mint (leaves, blossoms)
- Rosemary (leaves)
- Sage (leaves)
- Tarragon (leaves)
- Thyme (leaves, blossoms

Chapter 15
Buying and Storing
Herbs and Spices

Before you start buying either fresh or dried herbs, spend your money wisely.

Remember that even dried herbs lose flavor over time. For dried herbs, proper storage is important for best flavor and longest shelf life. Store dried herbs away from heat, light, and humidity. Light will cause herbs to lose both color and flavor. Since most herbs come in clear glass jars, it is important to store your herbs in a cupboard, or to transfer them to opaque containers to eliminate exposure to light.

Buy your herbs at busy stores. The turnover time is faster, so the herbs that you buy will be fresher. Some companies specialize in herbs and spices, and you can expect a fresher product from these companies, often at a discount price.

Unless you are buying an herb that you know you will use quickly, buy small amounts. Reduced size packages are available for most herbs in stores today. Don't buy more of an herb than you feel you can use in six months to a year. After a year, the flavor of dried herbs deteriorates. In some areas, herbs are available in bulk, and can be purchased in smaller amounts that way.

Purchase herbs in as whole a state as possible. For example, whole leaf herbs will hold their flavor longer than their ground or powdered counterparts. When buying fresh herbs, look for bright-colored and healthy leaves. Avoid buying herbs when the leaves are starting to yellow, for this indicates that the herbs are getting old and losing flavor. With fresh herbs, it is even more important to buy only the amount that you can use quickly. Fresh picked herbs should keep a couple of weeks in the refrigerator, with little care. The problem with store-bought herbs is that you have no way of knowing how old they are when you buy them. Plan on using your store-purchased fresh herbs within a week, or freeze or dry the excess.

When you bring fresh herbs home, store them in a plastic bag that has been ventilated with a hole or two for air circulation. Keep this bag in the refrigerator. Or, place the stems in a glass of water and store the herbs upright in the refrigerator, with a plastic bag loosely placed over them. Don't wash herbs until you are ready to use them. Excessive moisture on their leaves will cause them to rot.

Humidity can also play a role in the flavor loss of stored herbs. Moisture can allow the growth of molds, ruining your herbs flavor and making them unsafe. Dried herbs should always be stored in containers that are airtight. If you buy herbs in little boxes, it is important that you transfer them to an airtight container once they are open. Avoid opening your herb containers over foods that are cooking. Steam rises from hot foods, and will get into the jars. Measure herbs away from food in preparation, then add them to the pot.

Avoid storing your herbs near the stove or oven in your kitchen. Red spices, like paprika, chili powder, or cayenne pepper should always be stored in the refrigerator. They all contain oils, which will become rancid if stored at room temperature for long periods.

Before you begin to use the herbs you already have, check their quality. Open the herbs and smell them. They should smell like the herb that they are. If there is no scent, only a faint scent, or a musty scent, discard those herbs and start over with replacements.
Nor should you store herbs in a cupboard, which has light directly below it. These under-the-counter lights can generate a lot of heat, heating the cupboard above and reducing the quality of your herbs.

So, how long can you expect your dried herbs to last? That is no easy question. Shelf life is affected by several factors. Herbs that are exposed to heat, light, or moisture will lose their flavor quickly. You could notice this loss of flavor in as little as three to six months. Herbs that are crumbled fine or powdered will also lose their flavor faster than herbs stored in whole, or nearly whole, condition.

With all these factors to consider, you can see why any statement about shelf life is hard to answer. The best answer I can give is to try to use herbs within one year of purchase for best flavor. Spices can hold their flavor for about two years, under proper conditions.

Whether you purchase herbs or dry your own, write a date on the container so you will know how long the herb or spice has been stored. I recommend that my students set aside some time to go through their herbs and spices at home, and discard anything that has gone past its prime.

Chapter 15: Buying and Storing Herbs and Spices

Chapter 16
Preservation

Whether you have purchased more fresh herbs than you can use, or whether you are growing your own herb garden, there are times when you may need to preserve herbs for future use. Generally speaking, you can either freeze or dry your herb harvest. Herb vinegars are another form of preservation for herbs. They are covered in Chapter 14.

Not all methods work equally well for all herbs. I've tried to preserve my herbs using all sorts of methods, and I can tell you what has worked for me. Beyond that, you'll probably do some experimenting on your own. You may find that you prefer to dry certain herbs, and freeze others. Again, while I can share my experiences with you, your own preferences are what really matter in the end.

Drying

Drying preserves the herb by removing moisture, thereby preventing the growth of molds and other harmful organisms. You can remove moisture by air drying, oven drying, microwaving, dehydrating in a commercial dehydrator, or even by covering the herb with salt. How you remove moisture is not as important as making sure that you get all the moisture out! Only a small amount of water left in the tissue of the plant will leave it open to mold growth. Dried herbs leaves should be completely brittle. If a hint of pliability remains in the leaves, continue drying by your chosen method to remove remaining water.

Air-Drying

Air-drying is one of the easiest ways to preserve your herbs. You don't need any special equipment, and the results are almost always favorable. A few herbs don't dry well, and some herbs lose their flavor when dried, such as: chervil, cilantro, pineapple sage and lemon balm. Basil leaves will sometimes discolor in humid weather. The large majority of herbs dry just fine, as long as a few guidelines are followed.

When air drying herbs, choose a location that is warm and dry, and out of direct sunlight. Attics, crawlspaces, and even some garages provide a workable drying area, especially during warm weather. Avoid hanging herbs in kitchens (too humid) or on the porch (too sunny). Hanging bunches of herbs may add a certain nostalgic charm to your porch or sunny kitchen, but their function will be purely decorative.

Good air circulation is important to insure thorough and speedy drying. Turning a fan on your drying area will shorten drying time, assist in preserving the flavor, and reduce the chance of mold growth.

To prepare herbs for air-drying, hang a clean and dry bunch of herbs upside down. Leave them until the leaves are very brittle. Small-leaved herbs, such as tarragon, may dry in 4-7 days. Thicker-leaved varieties, like sage, might take 2 weeks. Herbs should always be bundled with rubber bands, rather than twine, firmly around the stems. As the herbs begin to dry, the stems shrink from moisture loss. The rubber bands contract to hold the stems and prevent your herbs from dropping to the floor.

Herbs will also dry in a ventilated paper bag. Cut holes to allow air to circulate, or leave the mouth of the bag loosely closed. Or, cheesecloth can be wrapped loosely around the herbs, which keeps them clean while drying.

Once the herbs are dry, strip off the leaves and store them in an airtight container, away from light and heat. Leave them in as whole a condition as possible to better preserve their flavor.

Seed heads (dill, fennel, lovage, caraway) can also be air dried, but the method is a little different than for leafy herbs. If you were to hang the seed heads, they would ripen and fall out, ending up on the floor. To avoid this, tie a paper bag around the seed heads to catch the seeds as they ripen and fall out. Or, tie some food- safe cheesecloth around the seed heads. Seeds can also be dried on screens, away from humidity and light. Seeds are dry when they turn from a greenish color to more of a brown. This process may take a couple of weeks, depending on the seeds and the environment.

Microwave Drying

You can dry small amounts of most herbs in a microwave oven. Fresh herbs are wrapped in a towel, or put between 2 paper plates, then placed in a microwave oven. This may sound strange, but put a raw potato in the microwave oven with your herbs. Why? Because there is very little volume to herbs, putting them in the microwave alone could damage the oven, similar to the dangers of running it empty. The raw potato sits in the back of the oven, soaking up extra microwaves, and adding mass. The potato comes out nicely baked after a few batches of herbs!

The herbs will take a couple of minutes to dry. If you have a turntable dry the herbs for 2 minutes. If you don't have a turntable cook them on high in the microwave, for 1 minute. Then, give the herbs ¼ turn every 15 seconds for 1 more minute. After 2 minutes total cooking time, remove the herbs and allow them to cool. Test for dryness only after they are cool. You may have to set them back in the microwave for another minute, or even a minute and a half. Ovens vary greatly, but if it's taking longer than 3 minutes, you need to work with smaller batches of herbs at a time. As with other dried herbs, store your microwaved herbs in a cool, dark, and dry storage place.

Dehydrators

Food dehydrators can give some of the best, as well as some of the worst results, when used for herbs. I dry plenty of herbs with a dehydrator, but a dehydrator fan can actually over-dry your herbs, leaving them tasteless. Some processes just will not be rushed, and possibly, herb drying is in this category. When using a dehydrator, please refer to and follow the individual manufacturer's directions. If your dehydrator gives you the choice of temperature settings, choose the lowest, around 85-90 degrees. Watch your herbs carefully, and remove them promptly when dried. If you respect the power of the dehydrator, and carefully follow the instructions, you will be rewarded with dried herbs in a matter of a few hours that retain both their color and flavor.

Salt Drying

With modern alternatives, salt drying has fallen in popularity. But some people still use salt to preserve their herbs in the following way: Layer herbs and salt in a box. Make sure that all the leaves are covered. After a few weeks, the herbs will be dry, and can be removed from the salt and stored until ready to use. When you are ready to use your salt- dried herbs, rinse them under water. They will soften, and can be used as fresh. If you do not rinse your salt-dried herbs thoroughly, the residue salt that clings to the herbs could ruin your recipe.

Oven Drying

Oven drying is harder to regulate than other methods. The exception might be the person who still has a gas oven with an old-fashioned pilot light. These are fast becoming a thing of the past, so I will assume that to use your oven to dry herbs, you would have to turn it on. That's where the trouble starts.

Most ovens are just too warm, even on the lowest settings, to dry herbs. If you have the rare gas oven with a pilot light, you can layer herbs on a baking sheet, and leave them in the oven until they are brittle. Get in the habit of opening your oven anytime you turn it on to avoid torching herbs you may have forgotten. Even if your oven possesses a setting of 120 degrees or less, you should leave the door ajar to allow better air circulation. Another method is to turn on the oven for a few minutes, and then off again, to keep the temperatures low. Frankly, oven drying is a lot of bother when so many other choices exist.

Freezing Herbs

Freezing is a wonderful way to store a lot of different herbs. Some herbs don't hold their flavor well when dried, and are best preserved by freezing.

Avoid freezing garlic, as it tends to get stronger when frozen. Although some references warn against freezing ginger, I keep my ginger root in the freezer until I'm ready to use it, and have always been happy with the flavor. Ginger-laden recipes may change when frozen, perhaps because the ginger has been cooked. (I've never had a bad experience myself)

Herbs that do not respond well to drying can be best stored by being frozen. Among your candidates for frozen storage are: chervil, lemon balm, pineapple sage, and cilantro.

Even herbs that dry well respond well to freezing. Why? Frozen herbs taste closer to fresh as a rule. Herb blends made from fresh herbs store well in the freezer.

You can freeze herbs in several ways. The easiest way is to simply chop clean herbs in a food processor, a blender, or by hand. Place the herbs on a baking sheet and put in the freezer. Once they are frozen transfer to a freezer container or freezer bag. By freezing them first you will avoid your frozen herbs turning into a big green snowball.

I cannot emphasize the freezer container too strenuously. Herbs will give off an odor, even frozen. If you put them in a container that is not vapor proof (made for the freezer), everything in your freezer will soon smell like herbs.

Once your container is filled, label and date the container, and throw it in the freezer. Unlike storing dried herbs, there is no advantage to storing frozen whole herbs in the freezer. So, whenever you need a quantity of an herb, just spoon the chopped herb out of the container.

Some herbs are also frozen encased in water to prevent freezer burn and to hold in flavor. This is done by combining the herbs in a blender or food processor with some liquid, then chopping the herbs to a convenient serving size. This mixture is poured into ice cube trays and frozen. Once frozen, the ice cubes can be emptied into a plastic bag, and stored in the freezer until you need them.

I like to freeze ice cubes that contain herb blends. This is a terrific way to combine the herbs for recipes like chicken soup (parsley, bay leaf, marjoram, tarragon, etc.). For added efficiency, instead of water you can make your "herb cubes" with chicken stock. Or, I take the herbs that I use to make spaghetti sauce, and freeze them in tomato juice. When I toss them in the sauce, the tomato juice won't dilute my sauce as water would. It is important to label what you freeze. All those green things have a way of looking alike by the middle of winter. If you write the name of the herb on the package, you won't have to open all your frozen herb packets to find what you are looking for. Date your packages, because, like their dried counterparts, frozen herbs will not keep forever. Most are best used within a year of freezing. When stored for longer periods of time, many lose their flavor and get a stale taste.

Basil deserves a special mention in this section. I love pesto, as do many of my friends and customers. I get requests for pesto-based dishes all year long. Because I grow a lot of basil, I want to preserve some for this recipe. Since I will combine the basil and oil in the pesto anyway, why shouldn't I combine the two, and then freeze?

To freeze the basil, I combine about 2 cups of basil leaves for every cup of olive oil. Process in a blender or food processor until smooth, and store in small freezer containers, almost to the top. You can also pour the mixture into ice cube trays and freeze. Once frozen just pop out the cubes and place in a freezer container or bag. Olive oil freezes solid so this works really well. When ready to use, defrost basil in the fridge for a couple of hours, then combine with the remaining pesto ingredients.

Cooking Tips

Just a few more things to think about when you cook with herbs.

Dried herbs are more concentrated in flavor than their fresh counterparts. There is basically a 3-to-1 ratio in fresh to dried. Three parts fresh is about the same as 1 part dried. So if a recipe calls for 1 tablespoon of a fresh herb, and you only have the herb in its dried state, you would use 1 teaspoon dried.

Try to add herbs, particularly the fresh herbs, later in the cooking process. They'll taste better this way. Fresh herbs can overcook very quickly, so if they are added early in a long cooking process, some of their fresh taste is lost.

Dried herbs are a little more forgiving, but not completely. If you're using the herbs in a cold or uncooked dish, or in a marinade, add them at the beginning of the process, so the flavors will have time to blend. If you really want to put herbs in your favorite sauce, and then simmer it for 3 hours (because that's the way you've always done it), that's O.K. But perhaps you could throw in a few fresh or dried herbs at the end of the cooking time? It will give the sauce a fresh taste that is a nice change from tradition.

Another benefit of adding herbs at the end of the cooking process is that it is an instant way of adjusting the seasonings to suit your taste. You can add a pinch of an herb or spice to start, and perhaps a pinch more. When you begin to use herbs and spices in new dishes, give yourself several chances to decide about a new flavor. Sometimes you may have used too much, and sometimes not enough, of certain ingredients. Strong herbs, such as rosemary or sage, can add terrific flavor. They can also ruin your dish by overpowering all other flavors.

About The Author

Judi is a local Cleveland lecturer and cooking instructor. She worked for the Extension Service in Cuyahoga County in the horticulture department. She also has received special training in Food Preservation. She currently teaches classes for both adults and children throughout the region and conducts cooking camps for children in the summer months.

While her main interest is herbs she learned to bake from her late father who had been a professional baker.

She is the author of two books on herbs, *The Charmed Garden: An Guide to Herb Gardening* and *The Charmed Kitchen: Cooking with Herbs & Spices*. She is also the author of numerous cookbooks in the Little Red Cookbook Series.

Her website is TheCharmedKitchen.com where you can read her blog, check out where she will be teaching and get more information on her products.

http://TheCharmedKitchen.com

About The Book

The Charmed Kitchen brings you into the world of cooking with herbs and spices. The book includes a lot of recipes for making your own herb and spice blends and plenty of info on pairing herbs and spices with specific foods. **The Charmed Kitchen** makes cooking with herbs and spices a welcoming and easy way to take your food from ordinary to extraordinary.

CPSIA information can be obtained
at www.ICGtesting.com
Printed in the USA
LVOW04s1016071116
511941LV00012B/211/P